ROAD TRIPS IN EUROPE

ROAD TRIPS IN EUROPE

50 ADVENTURES ON THE OPEN ROAD

PREVIOUS PAGE Roads tracing the shoreline of Lago di Garda in Italy

OPPOSITE Medieval Nördlingen, on Germany's Romantic Road

CONTENTS

Introduction	6
Preparing for your road trip	8

THE ROAD TRIPS

On the map	12
Scottish Highlands	14
Causeway Coast	18
Peak District	22
Eryri and the Bannau	26
Atlantic Highway	30
Wild Atlantic Way	34
D-Day Beaches	40
Loire Valley	44
Route des Grandes Alpes	48
Lavender Route	54
French Riviera	58
Costa Norte	62
Castile and Léon	66
Andalusia	70
Route 1	76
The Alentejo	80
The Ardennes	84
Zeeland's Delta Works	88
The Elfstedentocht	92
Romantic Road	96
Black Forest High Road	100
Romanesque Road	104
German Alpine Road	110
High Passes of the Swiss Alps	114
Grand Tour of Switzerland	118
Grossglockner High Alpine Road	122
Baroque Trail	126
The Italian Lakes	132
Stelvio Pass	138
Tuscan Hill Towns	142
Emilia-Romagna	146
Amalfi Coast	150
Baltic Capitals	154
The Great Bieszczady Loop	160
High Tatras	164
Julian Alps	168
Dalmatian Coast	172
Spomenik Circuit	176
Transfăgărășan Highway	180
Central Mountains	184
Albanian Riviera	188
Peloponnese Peninsula	192
Pindus Mountains	198
Anatolia	202
Atlantic Road	206
Norwegian Fjords	210
West Coast Sweden	214
Finnish Lakeland	218
Viking Trail	222
Iceland's Ring Road	226
Index	232
Acknowledgments	238

FEATURES

53
CONNECTING THE CONTINENT

75
HOSPITALITY ON THE ROAD

109
AUTOMOBILE MILESTONES

137
LIFE IN THE FAST LANE

159
TRADING ROUTES

197
THE GRAND TOUR

INTRODUCTION

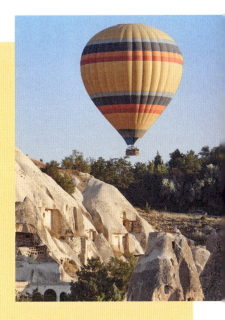

According to the ancient proverb, "All roads lead to Rome." But today, all roads lead to everywhere and anywhere. Modern bridges, tunnels, and mountain roads have transformed the impassable into the possible. And nowhere has the potential for a road-trip adventure quite like Europe.

Whichever route you take, it will be heaving with history. You can visit ancient stone circles, stop at battlefields and castles, and drive through mining towns and fishing villages. And that's all before you've even left the UK. On mainland Europe, pick a theme – the Moorish architecture of Andalusia, say, or the Socialist monuments of the former Yugoslavia – or buckle up for a journey that crosses borders and moves from one language to the next. Follow the flow of famous rivers, scale mighty mountain passes, or join the dots between some of the world's most historic cities; have breakfast in Brussels, lunch by Lake Garda, or dinner in Dubrovnik. The scope and variety of a European road trip is thrilling.

Whether you're at the wheel of a racing-red Ferrari, a camper van, or even an electric vehicle, this book will transport you across the continent in 50 extraordinary drives. You'll find classic trips like Iceland's Ring Road and the Lavender Route through Provence, lesser-known journeys such as Albania's unsung Riviera, and roads that the motor-mad will have long marked down on their bucket lists, from Romania's Transfăgărășan Highway to the Atlantic Road in Norway. So whether you're out for a Sunday drive or are hitting the road for weeks on end, getting from A to B has never been so much fun. Enjoy the ride.

Today, all roads lead to everywhere and anywhere. Modern bridges, tunnels, and mountain passes have transformed the impassable into the possible.

OPPOSITE On the Trollstigen road in Norway's fjords

ABOVE RIGHT A bird's-eye view of Anatolia, Türkiye

RIGHT Hitting the road in a classic Fiat 500

PREPARING FOR YOUR ROAD TRIP

ICON KEY

ACCOMMODATIONS

DETOUR

FACT

GREAT VIEW

HIKE

MUSEUM

PHOTO OP

PIT STOP

WILDLIFE

So you're all fired up and ready to put the pedal to the metal. But before you jump behind the wheel and sink into the driver's seat, it's wise to take some time to prepare. Here are some essentials to help get you started.

PLANNING A ROAD TRIP

Spontaneity is a romantic notion, but having a well-thought-out plan—even if you choose to change the route, or circumstances upend it—will likely forge a more successful trip. This is especially true in Europe, where hot spots have defined peak (and off-peak) seasons. Expect busy routes and inflated prices during the July and August school-break boom—particularly evident on the Mediterranean and Adriatic coasts. You should also check weather ahead of time, as northern routes and more remote destinations may be closed in the winter, while high winds can affect mountainous stretches year-round. Frequent breaks will help you drive safely, so pinpoint a few desirable pit stops ahead of time. You should also book accommodations in advance in places where there may be limited options or availability.

CHOOSING YOUR VEHICLE

If you are renting a car, choose a model suitable for the trip—one that's mobile enough for the narrow streets of ancient cities or sturdy enough for rough terrain in the Alps or the Nordics. If you are driving between countries, expect higher costs: car rental companies will usually add a fee for crossing borders and a significant surcharge for returning the car to a different location. Some companies will rent cars only to those over the age of 21, while others may add a charge for any driver under the age of 25. If you are planning an extended trip, leasing a car might be a better option.

If you've got your own vehicle, there are still precautions to take. For instance, if you have a right-hand drive, you will need to use headlight deflectors; British drivers need to display a UK sticker, too. All cars should have their wheels checked before you set off—you may need winter tires or snow chains for Alpine passes, and adequate tread and air pressure for driving on hot roads in the height of summer. All drivers, whether you are renting or not, are required to carry a reflective jacket and a warning triangle, for potential breakdowns, as well as a first-aid kit.

CURRENCY, INSURANCE, AND DOCUMENTS

While many EU countries take card payments, it's wise to carry some cash. Just make sure it's the correct currency: though most nations use the Euro, there are 29 different currencies currently in use across the continent. You will need a valid driver's license from your home country, as well as adequate car and health insurance that covers each of the countries you will visit. Drivers from non-EU countries (UK exempt) will need an International Driving Permit (IDP). However, in some countries, such as Croatia, an IDP is required only if the original document is written in a different script, such as Arabic, Chinese, or Cyrillic.

RULES OF THE ROAD

The road laws differ across Europe, so ensure you read up before you arrive. Across the continent, the minimum age requirement for driving is 18 years old, while in the UK, it is 17. Speeds vary by country—and also by season—so pay close attention to the posted limit. Remember that in continental Europe, kilometers per hour are used, while it's miles per hour in the UK. Likewise, most of Europe drives on the right-hand side of the road, while the UK, the Republic of Ireland, and Cyprus all drive on the left. Keep an eye out for tolls, and note that some European countries have electronic toll stickers or registration systems; you may be issued a penalty charge immediately if you're not signed up.

When it comes to rules, Norway has the strictest laws, and driving fines are around 10,000 NOK ($1,000), so make sure you do your research. In Europe, regulations on drinking vary by country. In most European nations, the blood alcohol content limit is 0.05 percent, while the UK is 0.8 percent. Hungary, Greece, and Slovakia, meanwhile, operate a zero-tolerance policy. Under no circumstances should you drive under the influence of drink or drugs. Emissions rules are a more recent addition to the highway handbook. If you're planning on driving through a major city, check to see whether your car passes and if you need to register your vehicle in advance. There are a few slightly more unusual rules to be aware of, too: for example, no one under 18 is allowed in the front seat in Spain; you need a clean license plate in Bulgaria and Romania; you must keep headlights on in the day in Slovenia and Czechia; and splashing pedestrians with puddles is illegal in the UK. Europe: one continent, many different road rules.

USEFUL WEBSITES

Schengen News An excellent resource, this website broadcasts new updates that travelers should be aware of, such as new visas, tourist taxes and fines. *www.schengen.news*

ETolls Pay for your tolls with this app. *www.etolls.eu*

Your Europe This website has a handy section on driving abroad in Europe. *www.etsc.eu*

TOP A room with a view

ABOVE Mobility is key in the narrow streets of Europe's ancient cities

THE ROAD TRIPS

1. Scottish Highlands
2. Causeway Coast
3. Peak District
4. Eryri and the Bannau
5. Atlantic Highway
6. Wild Atlantic Way
7. D-Day Beaches
8. Loire Valley
9. Route des Grandes Alpes
10. Lavender Route
11. French Riviera
12. Costa Norte
13. Castille and León
14. Andalusia
15. Route 1
16. The Alentejo
17. The Ardennes
18. Zeeland's Delta Works
19. The Elfstedentocht
20. Romantic Road
21. Black Forest High Road
22. Romanesque Road
23. German Alpine Road
24. High Passes of the Swiss Alps
25. Grand Tour of Switzerland
26. Grossglockner High Alpine Road
27. Baroque Trail
28. The Italian Lakes
29. Stelvio Pass
30. Tuscan Hill Towns
31. Emilia-Romagna
32. Amalfi Coast
33. Baltic Capitals
34. Great Bieszczady Loop
35. High Tatras
36. Julian Alps
37. Dalmatian Coast
38. Spomenik Circuit
39. Transfăgărășan Highway
40. Central Mountains
41. Albanian Riviera
42. Peloponnese Peninsula
43. Pindus Mountains
44. Anatolia
45. Atlantic Road
46. Norwegian Fjords
47. West Coast Sweden
48. Finnish Lakeland
49. Viking Trail
50. Iceland's Ring Road

SCOTTISH HIGHLANDS

START/END
Inverness, Scotland

DISTANCE
516 miles (830 km)

DURATION
5–7 days

ROAD CONDITIONS
Paved country roads.

THE BEST TIME TO GO
Spring and summer see long days but busier roads; snow may disrupt winter drives.

OPPOSITE The road, winding down from the Bealach na Bà on Applecross Peninsula

Scotland's north has an end-of-world feel. Sparsely populated, it is a land of castles and clan skirmishes, mountains and moors, white-sand beaches, and whisky distilleries. This showstopping circuit guides you through it all.

Laying claim to the best of Scotland's soul-stirring scenery, the Highlands are ripe for a road trip. Head as far north as you can for this route to remember, a 516-mile (830-km) loop around Scotland's northern Highlands that encompasses the wilds of Caithness, Sutherland, and Ross-shire—parts of the country too remote and untamed for most tour buses. You start in Inverness, at the east end of the Great Glen, where sites such as the Culloden Battlefield and Loch Ness await nearby, but this trip is about venturing beyond local hotspots.

WILD WEST

Once you've completed a quick search for Nessie, it's time to hit the back roads. The road winds between misty lochs and glens on its way to the west coast. Your first stop is only 15 miles (24 km) in, for a dram (if you're not driving) at The Singleton Distillery and, slightly further on, a walk across the suspension bridge at Rogie Falls—a fitting way to begin this Scottish tour. Another 60 miles (100 km) or so along the tarmac, you'll hit the mountains of Applecross Peninsula and the Bealach na Bà, a steeply hairpin single-track road that climbs to 2,054 ft (626 m)—the drive's highest point—and affords views to Skye.

Once you've passed this challenge, you'll be rewarded with the minute communities of Torridon and Shieldaig and the gentle trails of Loch Maree National Nature Reserve, the oldest reserve in Britain.

More seaside villages unspool as you head north. Stop in Poolewe, on

INVERNESS
START

ROGIE FALLS
Cross the bridge here in August or September and you might see salmon leaping upriver.
24 MILES (39 KM)

BEALACH NA BÀ
The wonderful winding road over the "Pass of the Cattle" was completed in 1822.
78 MILES (126 KM)

Loch Ewe, to visit the colorful Inverewe Garden and take a boat trip with local fishers for a chance to spot seals and white-tailed sea eagles. In Ullapool, book a village tour, take a dip in Loch Broom, and feast on hand-dived scallops, fresh crab, and haddock wraps at the award-winning Seafood Shack.

ANCIENT EARTH

As you begin your ascent into the northern reaches of the Scottish Highlands, things take a turn for the ever-more-magnificent. This ancient terrain features some of western Europe's oldest rocks, and some of the world's earliest fossils. To experience it for yourself, don your hiking boots for a walk through Inverpolly Nature Reserve and up Suilven peak. It's a tough 12.5-mile (20 km) out-and-back hike to the top, but the payoff is extraordinary views over Loch Coruisk and out to sea. Alternatively (or as well), pop into the North West Highlands Geopark visitor center—the route's halfway point—where you can learn more about the primordial specimens.

And on you drive, your next stops taking in beautifully sited Durness (make sure to peek into Smoo, Scotland's largest cave) and no shortage of beautiful beaches—standouts include Sango and

TOP Exotics thriving in pretty lochside Inverewe Garden

LEFT Brooding mountains near Inverpolly Nature Reserve

OPPOSITE The needle-sharp sea stacks at Duncansby Head

SUILVEN
The name of this peak comes from the Old Norse *súla fjell*, meaning "pillar mountain".

237 MILES (381 KM)

SANGO BAY
Sango offers golden sands, rippled dunes, and great surf, with a campsite just above.

298 MILES (480 KM)

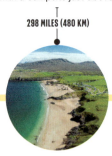

SCOTTISH HIGHLANDS

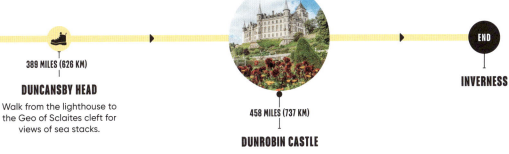

389 MILES (626 KM)
DUNCANSBY HEAD
Walk from the lighthouse to the Geo of Sclaites cleft for views of sea stacks.

458 MILES (737 KM)
DUNROBIN CASTLE
This huge pile also has a falconry, with daily displays from April to October.

END
INVERNESS

AROUND THE BLACK ISLE

Take a loop of this peninsula near Inverness to explore Pictish stones at Rosemarkie and the thatched home of fossil-hunter and folklorist Hugh Miller in Cromarty. You can look for dolphins off Chanonry Point or work up an appetite kayaking the Moray Firth or mountain biking at Learnie Red Rocks.

Ceannabeinne, and the remote Sandwood Bay. Reaching the latter takes a slight detour west of Durness, plus a 4-mile (6.5 km) walk, but it's perhaps the best beach in the country.

EASTERN ADVENTURE
The winding drive eastward along the north coast is a scenic treat. After 30 miles (48 km) of ins and outs, you'll reach the crofting village of Tongue, a historic crossroads used by Gaels, Picts, and Vikings. It sits on the Kyle of Tongue, with the mountains of Ben Loyal and Ben Hope looming above, and with the ruins of Castle Varrich nearby. Farther on is Bettyhill, with its homely cafés and Strathnaver Museum, which explores Sutherland county's 8,000 years of human history. Continuing east, nip up to Strathy Point Lighthouse for windswept cliff walks along a craggy coastline.

The town of Thurso is an obvious stopping point, and home to Wolfburn, the mainland's most northerly whisky distillery. It would be rude not to stop for another wee dram. The mainland's most northerly point is nearby Dunnet Head, an RSPB reserve where puffins, razorbills, and guillemots abound. It's about half an hour's drive to John O'Groats from here—not the UK's northernmost point, as is popularly believed—but still worth visiting for Duncansby Head's majestic sea stacks and raucous birds.

JOURNEY'S END
Finally, it's time to veer south to return to Inverness. You'll pass the precarious ruins of Castle Sinclair Girnigoe, and then Whaligoe harbor, accessible only by navigating 330 zigzagging steps carved into the cliffs. Farther on is 14th-century Dunrobin Castle, an enormous fairy-tale palace of a place, with plush rooms and formal gardens inspired by France's Versailles; Dornoch, meanwhile, is home to a fine cathedral, glorious white-sand beaches, and Loch Fleet National Nature Reserve, home to a bevy of birds, plus otters and seals.

Up for one final dram at journey's end? Continue on to Tain, north of Inverness. The home of the famous Glen Morangie whisky distillery; it's the perfect spot to toast a trip well done.

CAUSEWAY COAST

START/END
Belfast/Derry/Londonderry, Northern Ireland

DISTANCE
121 miles (195 km)

DURATION
2–3 days

ROAD CONDITIONS
Tarmac surfaces, largely A-roads.

THE BEST TIME TO GO
Fall offers fiery colors and quieter roads.

OPPOSITE The iconic hexagonal columns of the mythical Giant's Causeway

Northern Ireland's coast is raw and elemental, with more than a whiff of myth and legend. Here, strange rocks, ruined castles, crashing surf, and remarkable stories combine to deliver one of the UK's greatest road trips.

According to folklore, Finn McCool created the Giant's Causeway so he could reach Scotland to fight fellow giant Benandonner. Seeing how huge his rival was, Finn retreated, but was followed home. Duped into thinking a blanket-covered Finn was actually Finn's baby son—and thus fearing how enormous his father must be—Benandonner fled, destroying the causeway and leaving only a few remnants behind. It's a fine story to explain the bizarre rocks that lie off Antrim today and sets the tone for a magic-tinged drive along the Causeway Coast.

CASTLES AND CLIFFS
The route begins in Belfast, Northern Ireland's rejuvenated capital: from the interactive Titanic Museum to the hip bars of the Cathedral Quarter, there's a real buzz here. But the open road beckons.

Hugging the shores of Belfast Lough, it's a short drive north to Carrickfergus Castle. This Norman bastion is extremely well preserved and allegedly haunted by a wronged soldier. Next stop off is The Gobbins, an Edwardian cliff path clinging to the edge of the Islandmagee Peninsula. Don a hard hat for a guided tour via its suspension bridges, rock-hewn staircases, and secret tunnels.

Just beyond, the route enters the Antrim Coast and Glens National Landscape, where the uplands of the Antrim Plateau are sliced by steep valleys that run into the sea, and the extinct volcano of Slemish Mountain rears up, laced with St. Patrick legends.

Drive half an hour or so along the shore to the mighty Glenarm Castle

BELFAST
START

CARRICKFERGUS CASTLE
Visit this imposing castle, in continuous use since it was built in the 12th century.
11 MILES (18 KM)

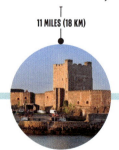

THE GOBBINS
Opened in 1902, this cliffside path features 15 new bridges and 6 raised walkways.
18 MILES (29 KM)

CUSHENDUN
This pretty spot was designed by Clough Williams-Ellis to look like a Cornish village.

55 MILES (89 KM)

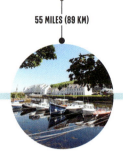

CARRICK-A-REDE
Meaning "Rock in the Road" in Gaelic, this island was a barrier for migrating salmon.

73 MILES (117 KM)

GIANT'S CAUSEWAY
Explore this UNESCO World Heritage–listed site via a network of four walking trails.

80 MILES (129 KM)

to stroll the old walled gardens. A jaunt into the Glenariff Forest Park for mossy waterfall walks is a worthy stop if you have time. Otherwise, continue along the coastal road to Cushendall, "Capital of the Glens," and Cushendun, where you can walk into ancient beach caves used in fantasy series *Game of Thrones*.

ROCKS AND RUINS
As you snake westward for 15 miles (24 km), you'll come to the former Viking settlement of Ballycastle, which makes a good base for exploring the wider area. There are excellent cafés to sample (try Ursa Minor Bakehouse) and folklore to drink in—scout out the sculpture of the *Children of Lir*, who were allegedly turned into swans. From here, hop on a ferry to the wildlife haven of Rathlin Island for a car-free adventure.

Back on the road, and rock-top Kinbane Castle comes next. There's little left of this 16th-century stronghold, but its location on the craggy Northern Irish cliffs is spectacular. In better condition is the Carrick-a-Rede rope bridge, which connects its namesake isle to the mainland. It was first built by fishermen over 250 years ago; today's structure, dangling 98 ft (30 m) above the waves, has been reassuringly well restored.

Just 13 miles (21 km) on, Ballintoy harbor is reached by a steep, twisting road. It's a pretty spot, scattered with sea stacks and craggy islets. From here, you can walk Whitepark Bay beach and feel the sand between your toes.

Turning onto Causeway Road, you'll first pass the ruined Dunseverick Castle (allegedly visited by St. Patrick) and then, only 3 miles (5 km) later, you'll spot the famed hexagonal basalt columns of the Giant's Causeway itself. Formed 60 million years ago, it's a geological wonder. Walk onto the stones—of which there are around 40,000—with an audio guide to learn more; look out for the rock known as the Giant's Boot, said to have been lost by Finn McCool.

Head on your way, but only as far as Old Bushmills, which has been distilling

GO LOOPY
There are nine additional scenic loop drives off the main coastal route. For instance, add on the spectacular Torr Head detour (14 miles/22 km), which takes in the Fairhead Cliffs. Or veer down the Roe Valley (29 miles/47 km) for offbeat exploring, including spooky Dungiven Priory and pretty Carrick Rock Gorge.

CAUSEWAY COAST

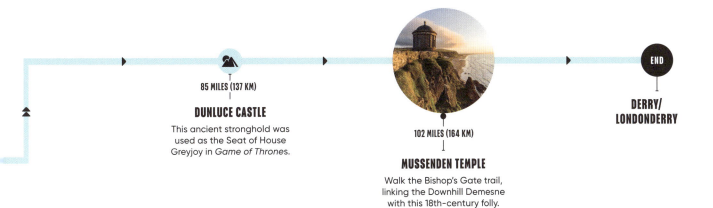

85 MILES (137 KM)

DUNLUCE CASTLE
This ancient stronghold was used as the Seat of House Greyjoy in *Game of Thrones*.

102 MILES (164 KM)

MUSSENDEN TEMPLE
Walk the Bishop's Gate trail, linking the Downhill Demesne with this 18th-century folly.

END

DERRY/ LONDONDERRY

whiskey since 1608, using water that gushes over the basalt bedrock. The perilously perched but spectacular ruins of Dunluce Castle (thought to have inspired Cair Paravel in C. S. Lewis's *Chronicles of Narnia*) await, with their archaeological finds and tales of feuding clans and screaming banshees.

CITY AND SURF
The seaside town of Portrush lies only 3 miles (5 km) ahead. Walk along East Strand beach to the limestone Whiterocks cliffs or hit the waves—this is the surf capital of Northern Ireland. Portstewart, the next bay along, is a quieter spot with another incredible beach: a stretch of golden sand, backed by 6,000-year-old dunes, with views to Inishowen headland and Mussenden Temple. Cross the Bann River and head up to this clifftop summerhouse, from where you can see the mountains of Donegal and, on a clear day, Scotland.

Lonely Magilligan Point, 8 miles (13 km) on, overlooks Lough Foyle—a stroll here is one last immersion in nature before you drive into Derry/Londonderry. The only city in Northern Ireland to retain its medieval walls, it's a history-packed place, not least with reminders of the country's recent Troubles. Walk the walls for one last spellbinding memory of what is a truly magical trip.

ABOVE Dunluce Castle

RIGHT The Peace Bridge, Derry/Londonderry

OPPOSITE Crossing the Carrick-a-Rede rope bridge

PEAK DISTRICT

START/END
Glossop/Macclesfield, England

DISTANCE
42 miles (68 km)

DURATION
6–7 hours

ROAD CONDITIONS
Tarmac roads; winding and occasionally narrow.

THE BEST TIME TO GO
Summer for heather, fall for vibrant color; winter can bring dangerous conditions and road closures.

OPPOSITE Hope Valley near Castleton, its dramatic scenery typical of this drive

The diverse and dramatic nature of the Peak District, the UK's original national park, makes building roads quite the engineering challenge in this wild region of middle England. The result? Some of the country's very finest drives.

The Peak District is ground zero in terms of access to the English countryside. It was here, on Kinder Scout, the area's highest point, that a Mass Trespass was held in 1932, putting people's right to roam on the front pages. Then in 1951, the Peak District became Britain's first national park, protecting this special landscape in perpetuity, for the benefit of the nation. The park reaches into five counties—you could spend weeks exploring, working your way from the striking gritstone edges of the Dark Peak to the limestone dales of the White Peak. But a day's drive, combining two of the region's most thrilling roads, is a great taster.

TAKE THE SNAKE

Begin in Glossop, a market town on the park's western edge that found wealth in the 18th century from the calico trade. Old mill buildings, chapels, and workers' cottages remain today, alongside independent shops and microbreweries. This country town also sits at the foot of the Snake Pass, the more evocative name for the A57, which lies between the moorland plateaux of Kinder Scout and Bleaklow and links the cities of Manchester and Sheffield. The road, which follows the course of the Ashop River, got its nickname from the Snake Inn, which was built as a staging post along the route. But it's also a perfect descriptor of how this lonely road slithers through the brutally beautiful moors, hills, and forest in a gripping series of tight bends.

GLOSSOP START

SNAKE PASS SUMMIT
This 1,673 ft (510 m) high point is where the road crosses the Pennine Way National Trail.

3.7 MILES (6 KM)

KINDER SCOUT
At 2,087 ft (636 m), this iconic moorland plateau is the Peak District's highest point.

4.3 MILES (7 KM)

13 MILES (21 KM)

LADYBOWER RESERVOIR
Enjoy the best panorama of Ladybower from Bamford Edge, near Bamford village.

20 MILES (32 KM)

CASTLETON
Cute Castleton provides access to nearby caves and the village's ruined castle.

ABOVE Patchwork fields above Ladybower Reservoir

RIGHT A gargoyle at St. Peter's Church in the village of Hope

The Snake Inn—sadly, no longer a pub—lies roughly halfway between Glossop and the Ladybower Reservoir at Ashopton. The original village of Ashopton, along with Derwent, were flooded to create this Y-shaped reservoir in the Upper Derwent Valley. Park up to walk a circuit, passing the neo-Gothic dam and surrounding hills; when the water's low, you might spy remnants of the sunken villages.

ROCK ON
Just over 9 miles (14 km) on, and you'll reach the village of Bamford in the valley below. It has a few shops and pubs if you're in need of refreshment. Otherwise, head on to Hope, a handsome village at the meeting of rivers, overlooked by Win and Lose Hill. There's been a settlement here for thousands of years—Neolithic artifacts have been found, as well as a Bronze Age barrow, known as the Folly Ring. Pop into St. Peter's Church and check out its Saxon cross and excellent gargoyles.

Steering west, the A6187 leads to Castleton, a pretty cluster of cottages, cafés, pubs, and tea rooms, and an interesting museum set in striking countryside. This is where the Peak District's distinct personalities meet, northern gritstone hitting southern limestone. The surrounding hills are pocked with caves, including Blue John—descend 245 steps to navigate this network of caverns, the only place in the world where the semiprecious stone is found. The geology is most spectacular, however, at wind-whipped Winnats Pass, where the narrow road squeezes between sheer, craggy cliffs, and drops dramatically—it's an exhilarating drive.

Continuing through the pass, the route traverses billowing sheep-grazed hills, alongside drystone walls—there are 26,000 miles (42,000 km) of these walls (built without any mortar holding them together) in the Peak District. After 9 miles (14 km), you'll reach the elegant spa town of Buxton. The Romans called it Aquae Arnemetiae (Spa of the Goddess of the Grove), and the Georgians built a beautiful sweeping curve of buildings opposite St. Ann's Well; part of this is now the five-star Buxton Crescent Hotel & Spa. Relax here, stroll the Pavilion Gardens, or catch a show at the Grade-II listed Opera House. For something a bit more adventurous, head just outside of town to delve underground and explore the stalactites and stalagmites of Poole's Cavern.

SHORT AND SWEET
The Cat & Fiddle road, linking Buxton and Macclesfield, is 12.5 miles (20 km)

> The geology is most spectacular at wind-whipped Winnats Pass, where the narrow road squeezes between sheer, craggy cliffs, and drops dramatically.

long, but it has achieved icon status. The road scampers across the heart of the Peaks in a series of testing twists and turns; care must be taken, not least because it's easy to be distracted by the breathtaking views. Like Snake Pass before it, the road gets its name from the Cat & Fiddle Inn, perched high on the desolate moor. Opened in 1813, it was once the second-highest pub in Britain; it's now the Forest Distillery, where it crafts gin and whisky.

There are still some scenic bends to manage, past Macclesfield Forest (plenty of walking trails here), before you arrive in Macclesfield itself. This former industrial hub was once famed for its silk industry—visit the Silk Museum and its restored Paradise Mill for a fascinating tour. Macclesfield is also home to passionately run indie shops and restaurants. If you can, time your visit for the last Sunday of the month, when the Treacle Market takes over town, to round off your trip with live music and tasty street food.

ABOVE Regency buildings in the attractive Georgian spa town of Buxton

WINNAT PASS
This dramatic pass is said to be haunted by a young couple murdered here in 1758.
22 MILES (35 KM)

BUXTON
Buxton's thermal waters, rich in magnesium, are thought to have curative powers.
31 MILES (50 KM)

CAT & FIDDLE INN
Charles Rolls once frequented this pub while testing cars with his partner, Mr. Royce.
35 MILES (56 KM)

MACCLESFIELD
END

ERYRI AND THE BANNAU

START/END
Cardiff/Llandudno, Wales

DISTANCE
186 miles (300 km)

DURATION
3–5 days

ROAD CONDITIONS
Paved, mostly single roadway.

THE BEST TIME TO GO
Spring for newborn lambs and lush hills; fall for colors with no crowds.

OPPOSITE A hiker surveying the views from the top of Black Hill in Bannau Brycheiniog

It's simple: drive one road, see Wales from top to bottom. The main north–south route that dissects the country links historic towns; striking castles; two magnificent national parks; and swaths of wild, empty landscapes.

The A470 isn't the most enticing name for a road trip. But the trunk route that connects Cardiff and Llandudno on the Irish Sea is far more thrilling than it sounds. On its way, the road slices through the full gamut of Welsh scenery. And don't be fooled by its highway status—despite being the country's principal coast-to-coast route, much of it has a narrow, windy back roads feel.

HEAD FOR THE HILLS
Before wandering off into the countryside, take time to enjoy the Welsh capital's buzz, joining a behind-the-scenes tour of the BBC studios (where shows such as *Doctor Who* are filmed) and strolling the shops of regenerated Cardiff Bay.

Then hit the road. At first, the A470 is a busy dual-roadway affair. But don't let that dent the romance of Castell Coch, a 19th-century fairy tale of a place that looms on a leafy hillside just outside Cardiff. As you progress through the Taff Valley, and get beyond the town of Merthyr Tydfil, the road narrows to enter Bannau Brycheiniog, or the Brecon Beacons National Park as it was once known. This striking wilderness is a land of sweeping ridges, wild moors, and endless hiking possibilities—the trail up 2,907 ft (886 m) Pen y Fan, the highest point in southern Britain, starts from the Storey Arms on the A470. If it's busy, stop at the visitor center in Libanus for alternative hikes.

Beyond the park, the road delves into rural mid-Wales, variously lined by trees and fringed by hills, picking up the Wye River. Stop for pretty views of the Wye

---

CARDIFF
START

CASTELL COCH
Visit this Victorian take on a medieval castle and be awed by its sumptuous interiors.
7 MILES (11 KM)

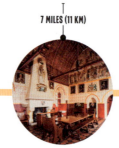

BANNAU BRYCHEINIOG
The name means "peaks of Brychan's kingdom," after the legendary king who ruled here.
41 MILES (66 KM)

BUILTH WELLS
Head to the town's Groe Park for the best views of handsome Wye Bridge, built in 1779.

69 MILES (111 KM)

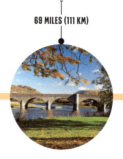

RHAYADER
Rhayader is the gateway town for the Cambrian Mountains and magnificent Elan Valley.

83 MILES (134 KM)

CLYWEDOG RESERVOIR
At 236 ft (72 m) high, the dam here is the tallest mass concrete dam in Britain.

97 MILES (156 KM)

ABOVE The Elan Valley, a highly scenic detour

OPPOSITE TOP Cadair Idris, in southern Eryri National Park

OPPOSITE BOTTOM Castell Dolwyddelan, silhouetted above wintry fields

from Lady Milford's suspension bridge, near Erwood village. Follow the river to the market town of Builth Wells, something of a historic spot. Look out for the mural depicting Llywelyn ap Gruffydd, one of the few Welsh-born Princes of Wales, who entered his final skirmish with the English Marcher Lords here in 1282.

Continue curving alongside the Wye to the crossroads town of Rhayader. This is Cambrian Mountains country, the sparsely populated, nature-rich, history-soaked heartland of Wales. Here, 15th-century Welsh hero Owain Glyndŵr fought many battles; today, majestic red kites and buzzards seem to outnumber people. The Cambrians have long been called the country's "Green Desert." Don't expect a phone signal; do expect plentiful opportunities for experiencing nature: hiking, mountain biking, horseback riding, birdwatching, and more. Detour from here into the spectacular Elan Valley, where a 16-mile (26 km) mountain road rises, falls, and bends around a network of Victorian-built reservoirs to create one of Wales's most scenic short drives.

MOUNTAIN HIGHS
Back on the main road lies Llanidloes, the first town on the Severn River, where there's a handsome timber-framed market hall and the chance to make a twisty loop of Clywedog Reservoir.

The drama increases as you progress north, the earth rising to the soaring summits and sheer valleys of Eryri (Snowdonia) National Park. The road wriggles and squirms, dips and falls as it enters this untamed land. As you drive the 10-mile (16 km) roller coaster to the town of Dolgellau, look for stern Cadair Idris mountain looming to the south.

Take a breather at Coed y Brenin Forest Park, Britain's first purpose-built mountain biking center and a good

ERYRI AND THE BANNAU

158 MILES (254 KM)
CASTELL DOLWYDDELAN
This moody 13th-century castle is one of several bastions built to defend the mountain passes.

177 MILES (285 KM)
BODNANT GARDEN
Don't miss the rare Champion Trees at this Italianate mansion with a glorious Victorian garden.

END
LLANDUDNO

place to pause for woodland walks and coffees. Past Trawsfynydd Lake, the A470 twists into Blaenau Ffestiniog, a former slate-mining town tucked beneath mountains. This is the place to learn more about Snowdonia's industrial past and see how the town has moved on. Old coal pits and quarries have been repurposed, offering mining tours, cavern crawling, and zip-line rides. You can also hop aboard the Ffestiniog & Welsh Highland Railway here, to explore Snowdonia by steam train.

SUMMIT TO SEA
From Blaenau Ffestiniog, it's an exhilarating drive over the Crimea Pass and down past Castell Dolwyddelan into Betws-y-Coed, an Alpine-like village, surrounded by forest, that serves as an adventure hub: climb the 3,560 ft (1,085 m) high Yr Wyddfa (Snowdon) mountain or try climbing or kayaking at Plas y Brenin, the National Outdoor Center.

Continuing north, the road winds through the foothills and farmland of the lush Conwy Valley, past Llanrwst's Tudor-era Gwydir Castle (allegedly haunted). Then, follow the A470 along the river's east bank for 15 miles (24 km) past the National Trust's colorful Bodnant Garden, to reach Llandudno and the Irish Sea. Promenade the Victorian pier, nip across the bridge to stroll the ramparts of Conwy Castle, and look back inland to the mountains to realize how far you've come.

NORTH WALES WAY
Llandudno is halfway along the 75-mile (120 km) North Wales Way. This driving route heads west to lively Bangor, then crosses the Menai Suspension Bridge over the straits to Anglesey to visit 13th-century Beaumaris castle, infamously long-named Llanfairpwllgwyngyllgo-gerychwyrndrobwlll-lantysiliogogogoch and the port of Holyhead, road's end.

ATLANTIC HIGHWAY

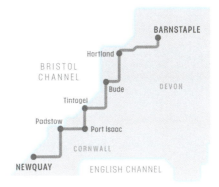

START/ENDS
Barnstaple/Newquay, England

DISTANCE
76 miles (122 km)

DURATION
2–3 days

ROAD CONDITIONS
Paved, often narrow and winding, with tight bends.

THE BEST TIME TO GO
Outside peak summer and school breaks, to avoid tourist traffic.

OPPOSITE Boats moored at the seaside village of Clovelly, in North Devon

Few roads penetrate the northern coasts of Devon and Cornwall in England's South West. But follow the ones that do, and you'll uncover witches and wizards and some of the world's finest walks.

There's something about the West Country's northern shore. Yes, it gets busy in the summer months, but this quaint region retains a magic nonetheless. The A39, aka the UK's Atlantic Highway, has long been the principal route into Cornwall from North Devon. But it's a trunk off which you must branch: drive it straight, and you'll miss the best parts.

STEER AND STROLL

This 76-mile (122 km) journey offers constantly twisting contours, staggering views of the Atlantic Ocean, plunging cliffs, ancient legends, and epic beach stop offs along the way. The drive begins in the bustling port town of Barnstaple, on the Taw River, where historic Pannier Market—trading since the 1600s—makes a picturesque starting point. West, across the Torridge River, you'll drive into the seaside village of Appledore, where pastel-hued cottages line bunting-clad streets. This comely fishing village, with its independent shops, pubs, and tea rooms, is a taste of what lies ahead. While roads have trouble reaching much of this shoreline, the South West Coast Path does a much better job, tracing the land's dramatic extremities as closely as it can. Park often and walk sections of this spectacular route. The unspoiled hamlet of Buck's Mills is a noteworthy leg-stretching pit stop, where a lovely 5-mile (8 km) loop to Peppercombe valley passes shingle beaches and red sandstone cliffs.

Just a short drive on, the car-free fishing village of Clovelly might seem an odd choice for an automobile focused

BARNSTAPLE
START

APPLEDORE
Catch the ferry from Appledore to pretty Instow, just across the estuary.
9 MILES (15 KM)

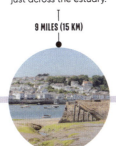

BUCK'S MILLS
This hamlet was allegedly settled by survivors of a galleon wrecked in the Spanish Armada.
17 MILES (28 KM)

26 MILES (42 KM)

CLOVELLY
Owned by the Hamlyn family since 1738, this village is all steep cobbled streets.

34 MILES (55 KM)

BUDE
Explore Bude Castle, built in 1830 alongside Bude Canal and now a heritage center and café.

adventure. But when you park at the top of the village and teeter down the cobbled pathways, past whitewashed cottages into the working harbor below, you'll understand why. Take a moment to gaze at the emerald waters and the views across tethered fishing boats and the Atlantic Ocean.

Head back onto the A39 and, almost immediately, turn off again to navigate the twists and turns to Hartland. This peninsula has some of the wildest edges in England. Plot another walk, or simply marvel at the rugged rocks from the pub at Hartland Quay.

CORNISH CAPERS
Welcome to Cornwall, where the thriving seaside resort of Bude, 16.5 miles (27 km) from Hartland Quay, is your first stop. The sandy beach has a huge sea pool for calmer swimming—and warmer waters for a dip off-season. Eager surfers should travel a little farther along the coast to Widemouth Bay for miles of Blue Flag sand and waves that suit both novice and seasoned boardriders.

From here, continue south along the A39, cruising through farmland, woods, and villages, with occasional glimpses of the sea, until the turn to Boscastle. This ancient harbor, built around a natural cleft in the cliffs at the end of the steep Valency Valley, couldn't be prettier.

The ruins of a castle rise on a wave-bashed headland—a romantic vision made all the more intriguing by its purported links to King Arthur.

Here, you'll find one of the area's quirkier attractions, the Museum of Witchcraft and Magic—an emporium of all things folkloric and occult.

More magic lies along the coast in Tintagel. The ruins of a castle rise on a wave-bashed headland—a romantic vision made all the more intriguing by its purported links to King Arthur. It's said the legendary ruler was born here. True?

BELOW Waves lapping the beach at Bude

ATLANTIC HIGHWAY

LEFT Fishing boats in the attractive harbor at Boscastle

abandoned Port Quin affords hikes up to nearby Doyden Castle or kayaking around wild Pentire Point.

CATCH OF THE DAY

The Camel Estuary slices into the coast beyond Port Isaac. This is where you'll find the fishing village of Padstow, known for its gastronomic delights. Fine-dining fiends can refuel at Michelin-starred No.6 Padstow or Rick Stein's renowned eatery, though nothing quite beats beer-battered fish and chips on the seafront.

You're approaching the end of the coastal route, but there's one last detour: Bedruthan Steps. This is one of the most magnificent beaches on the Atlantic Highway, where—at the bottom of a stairway—mussel-crusted rock stacks are smashed by the ocean's waves.

Just 5 miles (8 km) farther, and with one final right-hand turn off the A39, you reach your destination: Newquay, the surfing capital of Britain. Stay awhile to enjoy the epic beaches, packed events calendar, and a Cornish ale or two.

TEA TIME

In both Devon and Cornwall, you can indulge in cream teas: scones, fruit jam, clotted cream, and a pot of tea. However, be sure to change behavior when you cross the county border. In Devon, spread the cream first, followed by jam; in Cornwall, it's jam then cream.

Probably not. But it's still a fantastical place: cross the vertiginous footbridge, explore the remains of the 13th-century castle and earlier medieval buildings, and climb down to Merlin's Cave.

Back on the A39, soak up more recent history at the Cornwall at War Museum, on Davidstow Moor, a decommissioned World War II airfield. It's packed with artifacts charting the role the region played in 20th-century conflicts.

Farther on, beyond Camelford, turn off for Port Isaac, yet another idyllic fishing village. Much seen on screen—notably in British TV series *Doc Martin*—it's a glorious cluster of cottages. Squeeze down the alleys, watch the boats bob, and listen to sea shanties (the folk music group Fisherman's Friends was formed here in the 1990s); continuing to near-

CORNWALL AT WAR MUSEUM
The museum's airfield is littered with eerie abandoned buildings from World War II.
49 MILES (78 KM)

PORT ISAAC
Set off on a sea safari from this former pilchard-fishing village.
55 MILES (89 KM)
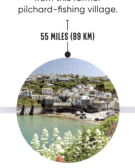

PADSTOW
Dine at fine seafood restaurants or visit the National Lobster Hatchery.
65 MILES (105 KM)
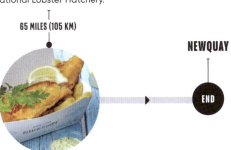

NEWQUAY
END

WILD ATLANTIC WAY

START/END
Muff/Kinsale, Ireland

DISTANCE
1,600 miles (2,500 km)

DURATION
2–3 weeks

ROAD CONDITIONS
Narrow, winding country lanes; well signed.

THE BEST TIME TO GO
June to September for optimal weather, winter for wildness; be prepared for rain year-round.

OPPOSITE Capturing sunrise at Fanad Head Lighthouse from the cliffs at Malin Head

Running the length of Ireland's west coast, the Wild Atlantic Way is epic in both proportions and scenery. This spectacular route traces the Atlantic, a formidable force that has shaped the country's landscapes and heritage.

The Wild Atlantic Way isn't just a drive; it's a route to understanding Ireland. It traces every nook and cranny from the Inishowen Peninsula to West Cork, linking nine counties—and with them beaches, sea cliffs, stone circles, monasteries, pretty villages, and, of course, lively pubs.

There are countless detours to take, places to linger, and activities to try. The roads—which are narrow, twisty, sometimes potholed, or populated by sheep—don't lend themselves to speed. This is a route to take slowly and savor.

GNARLY NORTH

You'll be hopping from one county to the next as you journey south, beginning in County Donegal at the village of Muff, the start of the Way. Your first official stop is Malin Head, the Irish mainland's northernmost point. Park up and hike from Banba's Crown, at the tip of the headland, past Hell's Hole chasm, for views that stretch to the Irish islands, Scottish hills, and across to Fanad Head.

As you begin wiggling south, hugging some 186 miles (300 km) of craggy coast, you'll pass Doe Castle, Glengesh Pass, and Slieve League. The latter has long been a place of pilgrimage, and at 1,972 ft (601 m) high, constitutes some of Europe's mightiest cliffs. The best spot to gaze at this granite is at sea level on a boat trip from nearby Teelin Harbour.

Some 25 miles (40 km) farther lies the lively town of Donegal. Take a tour to learn of the clans and Vikings who made their homes here—it was the Vikings who gave the town its name in the 8th century. Before you move on,

MUFF
START

MALIN HEAD
This remote headland at the end of Europe makes a fine place to watch the sunset.
50 MILES (80 KM)

SLIEVE LEAGUE
Hike knife-edge One Man's Pass to reach the cliffs' highest viewpoint.
250 MILES (402 KM)

330 MILES (531 KM)

MULLAGHMORE HEAD

The coast around this headland offers some of Ireland's best surfing.

550 MILES (885 KM)

CROAGH PATRICK

Thousands of pilgrims climb this holy mountain on "Reek Sunday," the last Sunday in July.

TICKET TO RIDE

Want proof of your road trip? Buy a Wild Atlantic Way Passport (€10; available from selected post offices) and get it stamped en route. There are 188 official "discovery points" on the Way; local post offices hold the relevant stamps. Complete your passport to earn a Wild Atlantic Way Certificate.

visit the area's beautiful beaches: dune-backed Murvagh; Rossnowlagh, for the surf; and horse-friendly Tullan Strand.

The Way then whisks you along the short Country Leitrim coast for 37 miles (60 km) into Sligo, where the area around Mullaghmore village offers a fishing harbor, a fine Neolithic tomb, impressive surf, and views to the flat-topped Benbulben rock formation. It was this iconic coast and countryside that inspired poet W. B. Yeats, who is buried in nearby Drumcliffe cemetery.

BAYS AND BOGS

As you leave Sligo, the route enters magnificent Mayo, meandering west into every nip and tuck along the county's coast. Downpatrick Head is especially breathtaking. Suck in the salty sea air on a hike along the coast here to a multicolored sea stack swirled by seabirds and a holy well that marks the site of a church founded by St. Patrick; locals hold mass here on Easter Sunday in his honor.

It's a dreamy drive around islet-spattered Clew Bay, where the magnificent peak of Croagh Patrick looms large over the scenery, a mountain with a history as tall as its 2,507 ft (764 m) height: legend has it that Ireland's patron saint fasted for 40 days and nights on its summit in 441 CE. It's a tough climb, but with a pair of walking boots and a few hours to spare, you, too, can make it to the chapel at the top and soak up the views that sweep back across Clew Bay.

With Croagh Patrick in your rearview mirror, you'll drive along a fine stretch of coast before reaching the Doolough Valley, where the poignant Famine Memorial commemorates the souls who perished here in 1849. The road through the valley leads to Killary Harbour, Ireland's only fjord, a sliver of inlet ending at the village of Leenaun. To the south lie the Maumturk Mountains and Twelve Bens and the prehistoric bogs and heaths, hills and hiking trails of Connemara National Park.

ABOVE Waves washing Tullan Strand beach, near Donegal

WILD ATLANTIC WAY

Twenty kilometres (12.5 miles) down the coast is the better-than-it-sounds Derrigimlagh Bog. Not only is this swathe of lakes and peatland rich in wildlife, it's where, in 1907, Italian inventor Guglielmo Marconi established the first trans-atlantic radio service. In another first, but not such a good one, the first nonstop flight across the ocean crashed here in 1919; a memorial marks the site.

ALL THE WAY TO GALWAY

The run through County Galway rewards drivers with an unspooling of pretty beaches, tiny harbors (like ravishing Roundstone), and the scattered isles of Kilkieran Bay. If you have the time, drive out among them past the Lettermore Causeway. Or hop on a ferry in Rossaveal to explore the three windswept Arran Islands, lying just offshore.

As you arrive into Galway, rugged landscapes make way for an entirely different Ireland. Here, the craic is strong with traditional bars pulsing with folk musicians—an experience not to be missed. You won't want to leave this jovial city behind but continue around the bay into County Clare and perhaps the Wild Atlantic Way's biggest draw: the Cliffs of Moher. Rising to 702 ft (214 m) above the raging waves, this bulwark of shale and sandstone is a popular stop. For a quieter take, hike the cliff-edge trail from Doolin to Hag's Head and

ABOVE The dinky harbor in pretty Roundstone in County Galway

ABOVE LEFT Admiring the dramatic Cliffs of Moher

KYLEMORE ABBEY
Stop at this castle north of Derrigimlagh Bog, a monastery since the 12th century.

600 MILES (966 KM)

ARRAN ISLANDS
Take the ferry from Rossaveal to Inis Mór, Inis Meáin and Inis Oirr, all home to ancient sites.

GALWAY
For Irish trad music, try Tig Coili, Tigh Neachtain, An Púcán, or the Crane Bar.

820 MILES (1,320 KM)

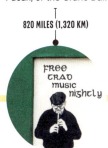

BLENNERVILLE WINDMILL
Ireland's largest working windmill, on Tralee Bay, has a display on Irish emigration.

1,000 MILES (1,609 KM)

DINGLE
Murphy's hand-makes excellent ice cream here; its sea-salt flavor uses Dingle sea water.

1,100 MILES (1,770 KM)

VALENTIA ISLAND
The island's lighthouse keeps watch over this stretch of the wave-battered Skellig coast.

ABOVE Limerick's 13-century King John's Castle

OPPOSITE TOP Winding coastal road on the Dingle Peninsula

OPPOSITE BOTTOM Kinsale's colorful town center

Liscannor. Continuing on the coast from here will take you all the way along the rocky edges of Loop Head, ending at a lighthouse and cliffs thronged by seabirds at the rocky peninsula.

A car ferry from Killimer to Tarbet, in County Kerry, saves you driving all the way around the Shannon Estuary, although that would mean missing out on Limerick; roughly 80 miles (130 km) away, it offers a strapping 13th-century castle and a sporty vibe. Catch that car ferry, and beyond some fine beaches, including 6 miles (10 km) of uninterrupted sand at Ballyheigue, you'll eventually reach Tralee. This small town, famed for its roses, is a gateway to the wild, sea-salty Dingle Peninsula and its superb coastal scenery: variously soft and golden or thrillingly craggy. Highlights include Brandon Point, at the foot of Mount Brandon, for fine hikes and bay views, and driving the Conor Pass, at 1,496 ft (456 m), the highest mountain road in Ireland. The scattered Blasket Islands lie off the peninsula's tip—look across to them from Dunmore Head and Carrignaparka Beach. Then follow the snaking Slea Head Road along the shore to Dingle town, keeping an eye out for *clochán*, stone "beehives" where monks once lived.

FEELING THE FORCE
It would be easy to lose days in Dingle. It's that kind of town—effortlessly affable, with many good boozers. But the Ring of Kerry will tempt you on, an iconic drive that outlines the Iveragh Peninsula. Tag on the Skellig Ring, a far-west add-on that reaches some of the most pristine parts of the country, and you'll get to traverse Coomanaspig Pass, marvel at the angular Kerry Cliffs, and drive over the bridge from Portmagee to Valentia Island. A boat trip to the Skelligs, a group of islands once inhabited by monks but more recently by Jedi (they were a filming location for two recent *Star Wars* films) is worth time away from the wheel.

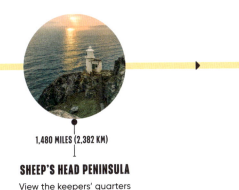
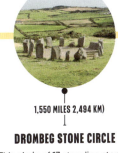

1,480 MILES (2,382 KM)

SHEEP'S HEAD PENINSULA
View the keepers' quarters in the lighthouse at the tip of Sheep's Head.

1,550 MILES 2,494 KM)

DROMBEG STONE CIRCLE
This circle of 17 standing stones, known as the Druid's Altar, dates from around 150 BCE.

END

KINSALE

Having rounded Iveragh Peninsula, you're straight onto Beara, a lowly populated peninsula with a time-warp feel and a wealth of Bronze Age remains. For the spectacular Healy Pass, a hairpinning route created in 1847 as a work relief program during the Great Famine, you'll need to venture inland, a gripping drive that merits the detour.

FAR-SOUTH FAREWELL

As you reach Healy Pass, you'll enter the route's final county: Cork. It's certainly not the least, though. Drive around Sheep's Head Peninsula, stopping at Ahakista's tiny Tin Pub for fortifying refreshments. On your way to Mizen Head, you'll pass pretty fishing harbors and jaw-dropping cliffs, from where you've got a good chance of spotting dolphins and whales, including fin whales, minke whales, and (if you're very lucky) a pod of orcas. The town of Baltimore is a lovely place to watch boats bobbing in the harbor before continuing east to Drombeg, where you can circuit the small ring of stones that was erected here over 3,000 years ago.

West Cork's good looks continue as you move onto handsome Red Strand and Inchydoney beaches and then Clonakilty, Cork's "Music Capital" and a fine spot in which to catch a live session by a local folk band. Eventually, you'll reach Kinsale and your uplifting ending. Wander the colorful streets, stroll the harbor and the formidable fortress by its side, and sink a pint or two of the dark stuff in its lively bars.

SOUTHERN SORROW

The Irish mainland's southernmost point is at Brow Head, just east of Mizen Head. Its absolute southernmost point, however, is Fastnet Rock. Dominated by the country's tallest lighthouse, Fastnet is known as "Ireland's teardrop"—it was the last place seen by 19th-century emigrants sailing for the New World.

D-DAY BEACHES

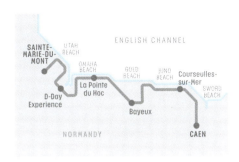

START/END
Sainte-Marie-du-Mont/Caen, France

DISTANCE
78 miles (126 km)

DURATION
2–3 days

ROAD CONDITIONS
Well-maintained paved roads.

THE BEST TIME TO GO
Around June 6, for the annual D-Day events.

OPPOSITE Ruined German bunkers on Utah Beach

Millions visit France's northern coast every year, paying tribute to the Allied troops who fought on D-Day. On this poignant trip along Normandy's fringe, you'll visit informative museums, orderly cemeteries, and scattered war relics.

Operation Overlord, launched on June 6, 1944, and better known as D-Day, was the largest amphibious invasion in the history of warfare. Featuring around 6,000 ships and 156,000 troops, it kickstarted the campaign to liberate northwest Europe from Nazi occupation. By the end of that first day, however, more than 4,000 American, British, and Canadian servicemen, among others, had lost their lives. When World War II ended, the landing sites—all beaches—became places of remembrance and symbols of the price of peace.

REMEMBERING THE FALLEN

You'll start your journey at the sobering Plage de la Madeleine near Sainte-Marie-du-Mont. This beautiful beach, code-named Utah, was the westernmost of the Allied forces' landing sites, and the first to be stormed. On a calm, sunlit day, it's hard to imagine the terror that unfolded when more than 23,000 American soldiers began disembarking on that summer morning in 1944.

Giving visitors an insight into what happened are two nearby museums. The first, overlooking the beach, is the Musée du Débarquement Utah Beach, which tells the story of the invasion and the meticulous behind-the-scenes preparation that preceded it. Taking pride of place is a US Army Air Force B-26 Marauder, painted to represent a famous bomber called Dinah Might. Inland, is the D-Day Experience, a contemporary museum with a 1940s cargo plane flight simulator, just off the N13 near Carentan-les-Marais.

SAINTE-MARIE-DU-MONT — START

MUSÉE DU DÉBARQUEMENT UTAH BEACH
Learn about the US Army's role in Operation Overlord.
1 KM

D-DAY EXPERIENCE
This immersive attraction uses 3D films to evoke the events of June 6, 1944.
7 MILES (11 KM)

COLLEVILLE-SUR-MER
With row upon row of graves, the Normandy American Cemetery is a moving sight.

35 MILES (56 KM)

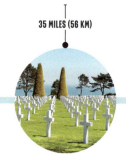

BAYEUX
Visit the museum and cemetery, then unwind over a glass of calvados (apple brandy).

47 MILES (76 KM)

ARROMANCHES-LES-BAINS
The remains of a Mulberry Harbor can be seen offshore at this quiet seaside resort.

57 MILES (92 KM)

When you're ready, follow the road as it curves east, then take the quiet, rural D514 north for 18.5 miles (30 km) to La Pointe du Hoc. This clifftop spot has fine views of both Utah Beach and Omaha Beach, where a few German bunkers survive. Early on June 6, 1944, a team of US Army rangers scaled the cliffs at Omaha to seize enemy weapons that would have decimated the Allied Forces. The Pointe du Hoc Ranger Monument commemorates their courage.

Continue east to Colleville-sur-Mer to visit the excellent Overlord Museum, where military equipment and personal recollections help paint a picture of events at Omaha. The nearby Normandy American Cemetery and Memorial, one of the most visited sites on this stretch, offers a graphic reminder of the bitter sacrifices that were made. Immaculately kept, its 9,300 white marble grave markers stand in silent rows.

COMMONWEALTH GRAVES
From Omaha Beach, drive 12.5 miles (20 km) southeast to Bayeux. Famous for its UNESCO-listed tapestry depicting the Norman Conquest of England in 1066, this historic city is also home to the Musée Mémorial de la Bataille de Normandie, covering D-Day and its aftermath. The Bayeux War Cemetery, the largest of the region's British and Commonwealth graveyards, is the resting place for 4,848 soldiers from the UK and elsewhere. Poignantly, there's also a memorial to 1,807 more Commonwealth soldiers whose remains were never found.

Back on the road, head north through a patchwork of fields, meeting the coast once again at Longues-sur-Mer, where a formidable artillery battery, part of Nazi Germany's Atlantic Wall coastal defenses, still points out to sea. From here, follow the D514 to Arromanches-les-Bains and the impressive Musée d'Arromanches, which focuses on the landing beaches assigned to Commonwealth forces: Gold, Juno

EXTEND YOUR TRIP
Around 31 miles (50 km) east of Caen and the D-Day landing sites is a clutch of Normandy's most appealing coastal towns. The twin resorts of Deauville and Trouville offer belle-époque villas, stylish hotels, and splendid sandy beaches, edged with boardwalks. Further east, Honfleur is a pretty port with oodles of historic charm.

D-DAY BEACHES

62 MILES (100 KM)

GOLD BEACH
Thousands of British troops landed here on D-Day, liberating Bayeux the next day.

66 MILES (106 KM)

JUNO BEACH
Juno was the focus for Canadian forces, now honored at the Juno Beach Center.

END

CAEN

and Sword. Offshore, at low tide, the bulky concrete remains of Arromanches' Mulberry Harbor, a floating dock that was crucial to the Allies' landing strategy, can be seen.

Arromanches lies at the western end of Gold Beach, the central zone in an 11-mile (18 km) landing area stretching from Port-en-Bessin in the west to Ver-sur-Mer in the east. Despite its dark history, this dune-spotted, white-sand beach is a beautiful spot for a stroll.

CANADA'S D-DAY LEGACY
Courseulles-sur-Mer, and Juno Beach, lie 3.5 miles (6 km) east along the D514. The fourth and final beach you'll visit on this trip was stormed by the Canadian Army on D-Day. More than 45,000 Canadians died in France during World War II, 381 of them on D-Day, and the Juno Beach Center, a nonprofit museum, commemorates their service.

To bring your trip to a powerful close, take the D79 southeast for 12.5 miles (20 km) to Caen. The horizon seems wider than ever as you drive past seemingly endless fields. Just north of the city's ring road is one of Europe's leading war museums, the monumental Le Mémorial de Caen. Behind its austere concrete frontage, you'll find a wealth of World War II artifacts, lasting reminders of that fateful day.

OPPOSITE Rusted barbed wire at clifftop La Pointe du Hoc

RIGHT Rows of gravestones in Bayeux Cemetery

BELOW The remains of a Mulberry Harbor, in the waters off Arromanches-les-Bains

43

LOIRE VALLEY

START/END
Angers/Orléans, France

DISTANCE
174 miles (281 km)

DURATION
4–5 days

ROAD CONDITIONS
Well-maintained paved roads.

THE BEST TIME TO GO
Spring, for wildflowers, or the September-to-November grape harvest, when the region hosts fall festivals.

OPPOSITE Château de Chambord, one of the Loire's many magnificent châteaux

Historic and utterly romantic, the Loire Valley is one of France's most beguiling regions. Rich in opulent aristocratic estates and wineries, this is the perfect setting for a classy adventure.

Roaming the Loire Valley is like stepping back in time. Hundreds of châteaux dot the horizon, while medieval villages, rolling vineyards, and magnificent castles await seemingly around every corner. You could spend weeks here, but four or five days is the perfect amount of time to take in the region's romance.

The area that perches along the Loire River blossomed into a cradle of architectural grandeur during the French Renaissance of the 15th and 16th centuries. The valley became a rural retreat for royals and nobles, who commissioned Italian-inspired châteaux with gleaming towers, glittering halls, and grand ornamental gardens surrounded by peaceful farmland. Today, the stretch from Chalonnes-sur-Loire in Pays de la Loire to Sully-sur-Loire in Centre-Val de Loire is a vast UNESCO World Heritage Site—and makes for a stunning road trip.

MEDIEVAL TEXTURES

There's no set route here, so travel east to west or west to east—whatever takes your fancy. If you're heading upstream, Angers is an excellent place to begin. Its stocky medieval castle houses the remarkably colorful 14th-century *Tapestry of the Apocalypse*, the largest surviving set of medieval woven panels in the world.

For your first glimpses of the Loire, head southeast to join the D952, a winding route that hugs the north bank. As you drive through the Loire-Anjou-Touraine regional nature park to Saumur, the glossy water feels close enough to touch. Saumur's striking medieval

ANGERS

START

ANGERS
Soak up the atmosphere of medieval France in this characterful town.
0 MILES (0 KM)

SAUMUR
This riverside town is famous for its 12th-century château, wines and horse shows.
31 MILES (50 KM)

CHINON
This picturesque small town in the historic region of Anjou has a splendid fortress.

51 MILES (82 KM)

AZAY-LE-RIDEAU
Steeped in romance, Château d'Azay-le-Rideau is one of the region's loveliest castles.

65 MILES (105 KM)

TOURS
Base yourself in the cathedral town of Tours, known for its fine Vouvray wines.

80 MILES (129 KM)

RIGHT The lavish interior of the Château d'Azay-le-Rideau

OPPOSITE The tranquil Jardins de Roquelin in Meung-sur-Loire

BELOW Afternoon sunlight casting a glow over Saumur

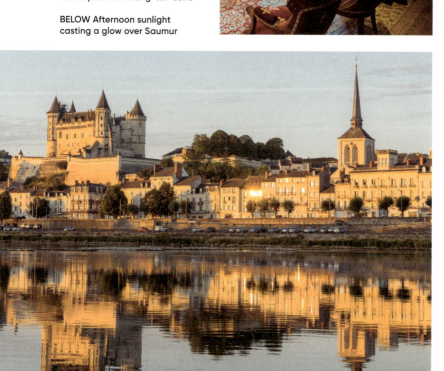

château presides over the town center, and there's a gastronomic treat waiting on the outskirts: Le Musée du Champignon, where a fascinating array of edible mushrooms mature in underground caves, a peasant tradition dating back centuries.

There's more medieval majesty at Chinon, 18.5 miles (32 km) southeast of Saumur. Set on the Vienne, a tributary of the Loire, Chinon is a pretty place of stone and half-timbered houses, dominated by its royal fortress.

RENAISSANCE ROMANCE

From Chinon, the tree-lined D751 leads to Azay-le-Rideau, an appealing little town on another Loire tributary, the Indre. Its romantic turrets reflected in the water, the Château d'Azay-le-Rideau is a gem: the writer Honoré de Balzac called it "a faceted diamond." After visiting the sumptuous salon and apartments, treat yourself to a table at Auberge Pom'Poire in town, a lovely restaurant with a Michelin star.

Before you reach the city of Tours, there are two more castles to admire: the ancient Château de Langeais and Château de Villandry, with its magnificently laid-out gardens. Tours itself lies in the heart of the Touraine wine region, famous for its Cabernet Franc and Chenin Blanc wines. There are excellent cellars and vineyards on the city's fringes, including Domaine Marc Brédif, which offers rare Vouvray wines dating back to 1874, and Château de Fontenay, established in 1680.

Heading east, the scenic D751 hugs the Loire's southern bank all the way to Amboise, a town associated with Leonardo da Vinci. The great man spent his final years in the Château de Clos Lucé, which is now an absorbing museum of his life and work, stuffed with models of his inventions, from a revolving bridge to a prototype armored tank. His tomb lies in the Chapel of Saint-Hubert at Château d'Amboise. Before leaving town, seek out its celebrated patisserie and chocolatier, Maison Bigot, for indulgent handmade chocolates or a ribbon-tied *gâteau de voyage*, a delicious rum and almond biscuit.

IN THE FOOTSTEPS OF KINGS

While this trip is all about the Loire, it's well worth tearing yourself away to visit the Château de Chenonceau on the Cher River, southeast of Amboise, with its gorgeous interior and rooms adorned with flowers from the gardens. From Chenonceau, you'll rejoin the Loire at Blois, an attractive medieval town that was home to several French kings. Today, it's gourmet heaven. Restaurant Christophe Hay, which has won two Michelin stars for its deliciously light

cuisine, and Assa, with a Japanese-inspired menu, are wonderful places to splurge. Both use local ingredients, such as fish from the Loire, to great effect.

One of the grandest châteaux in the entire region is also one of your last. The Château de Chambord is an architectural tour de force, with more than 400 rooms, several hundred fireplaces, and dozens of staircases, including a double-helix staircase designed by Leonardo da Vinci.

Brimming with scented roses, Jardins de Roquelin in charming Meung-sur-Loire, northeast of Chambord, is the perfect spot for a relaxing interlude before you draw your journey to a close in the historic city of Orléans, nestled—suitably—in a nook on the mighty Loire River.

GUINGUETTES

When the sun shines in the Loire Valley, there's only one place to go: a Guinguette. Appearing usually in the summer months, these open-air riverside bars are an ideal place to spend the evening, sipping wine, dining on fresh fish, and listening to live music. There are plenty of options in Angers, Tours, and Orléans.

CHENONCEAU
Explore this delightful château, with its gleaming white stone walls and graceful arches.

BLOIS
Indulge in gourmet dining in this medieval, food-loving, riverside town.

131 MILES (212 KM)

CHAMBORD
A knock-your-socks-off blockbuster château, with hundreds of rooms.

145 MILES (233 KM)

ORLÉANS
END

ROUTE DES GRANDES ALPES

START/END
Thonon-les-Bains/Menton, France

DISTANCE
432 miles (696 km)

DURATION
5–6 days

ROAD CONDITIONS
Paved roads; possible hazardous conditions from late fall to late spring.

THE BEST TIME TO GO
Summer to midfall, as many passes close in winter.

OPPOSITE Mountain huts on the Col des Aravis

Linking Lake Geneva and the Mediterranean, the Route des Grandes Alpes is an epic expedition across Europe's greatest mountain range, taking in countless jaw-dropping views along the way.

Hannibal crossed the Alps on an elephant, but all you need is a car with a bit of torque. From Thonon-les-Bains, on the shores of Lake Geneva (or Lac Léman to the French), the Route des Grandes Alpes climbs to nearly 9,200 ft (2,800 m) and crests 17 mountain passes as it wiggles relentlessly south.

FIRST PASSES

Not long from Thonon, you'll spy the Gorges du Pont du Diable, cut in antiquity by subglacial rivers. You're then soon traversing the first of those mountain passes at the Col des Gets and gliding south into Cluses, where the glacier-fed Arve River flows a steely blue. Here, gearheads of another sort can visit a museum dedicated to the Alpine tradition of clock making.

About 9 miles (14 km) from Cluses is the Chartreuse du Reposoir, founded by Carthusian monks in 1151. The setting alone is enough to convince you to take your vows: a handsome cream building, the monastery sits secluded on a small lake amid forested slopes that cycle through deep green, blazing red, and pure white with the seasons.

The drive continues to Le Grand-Bornand, where you'll discover century-old chalets, art studios, and the local delicacy: Reblochon cheese. Then it's on to the Col des Aravis, where, on a clear day, you can make out towering Mont Blanc in the distance. After tackling the Col des Saisies, and many more switchbacks, you'll pull into Beaufort, where more cheese awaits, this time the town's famed eponymous variety.

THONON-LES-BAINS
START

GORGES DU PONT DU DIABLE
Ancient subglacial rivers cut out these devilishly dramatic gashes in the limestone.
9 MILES (14 KM)

CHARTREUSE DU REPOSOIR
Say a prayer of thanks for the views from this 12th-century monastery.
43 MILES (69 KM)

From Beaufort, forests and hairpin bends lead to the Col de Méraillet and, just beyond, the sparkling Roselend Lake. Dam construction created the reservoir in 1962, flooding a farming village in the process. What was spared provides one of the most sumptuous scenes on the entire drive: a tiny chapel of rough-hewn stone and twin bells that looks out over turquoise water, highland pastures, and gently rolling mountain ridges.

THE HIGH POINT

Barely 5 miles (8 km) from the last mountain pass, you traverse another, the Cormet de Roselend. From there, aim southeast, passing avalanche shelters in the Haute-Tarentaise Valley, and then Lac du Chevril, before pulling into the ski resort of Val d'Isère, where lifts head up the slopes on the edge of town.

Just a few minutes from the resort, you'll hit the heavens at the Col de l'Iseran, at 9,068 ft (2,764 m) the highest pass on the drive. Even in summer, there are often piles of snow here, and from the summit, you'll be treated to views of the Pisaillas Glacier. Once you make it over, you'll briefly cruise through the Parc national de la Vanoise, where ibex, chamois, and black grouse roam.

Natural splendor is the drive's main draw, but the next 93 miles (150 km) or so feature plenty of human-made

ABOVE Picturesque chapel on the edge of Roselend Lake

LEFT An ibex in Parc nacional de la Vanoise

OPPOSITE The intimidating walls of Fort Victor-Emmanuel

ROSELEND LAKE
A tiny chapel gazes out over mountain ridges, pastures, and the lake's turquoise water.
99 MILES (160 KM)

COL DE L'ISERAN
Spot cyclists trying to tackle this famous stage of the Tour de France.
145 MILES (233 KM)

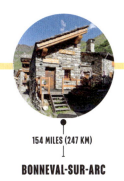

154 MILES (247 KM)

BONNEVAL-SUR-ARC

Take some time to appreciate the local homes' traditional Alpine construction techniques.

176 MILES (283 KM)

FORT VICTOR-EMMANUEL

This striking fort was built to defend the kingdom of Piedmont-Sardinia.

236 MILES (379 KM)

BRIANÇON

This is the highest fortified town in Europe, with walls that date to 1734.

HANNIBAL'S CROSSING

The crossing of the Alps in 218 BCE by Hannibal, a Carthaginian general, is considered one of the greatest military feats in history. With 30,000 troops, 15,000 horses, and (most famously) 37 elephants, he took just 16 days to cross the Alps in order to attack Rome from the north.

beauty, too. Twenty minutes from the Col de l'Iseran lies Bonneval-sur-Arc, a stunningly pretty village of gray stone houses with dark wooden shutters that looks as if it was chiseled out of the encroaching mountain peaks. It's one of the few places where you can still see these house-building techniques.

GREAT WALLS

The descent from Bonneval to Modane largely follows the edge of Parc national de la Vanoise. Shortly before you get to Modane, you'll pass Fort Victor-Emmanuel and the Marie-Thérèse Redoubt. Part of the Esseillon Barrier, they were built by the kingdom of Piedmont-Sardinia in the early 1800s to defend against French invasions. The fort in particular is an intimidating presence, a series of impregnable buildings ascending a mountain slope like a giant's staircase.

After a relatively straight bit of road along the Arc River, you'll head south on a stretch of the D902 that weaves like a drunken sailor on its way up to the Col du Télégraphe and then down again to Valloire, nestled in a valley where France's northern and southern Alps meet. Shift into a low gear as you begin the steep climb up from here to the Col du Galibier, where you can indulge in preposterous views of mountain peaks and glaciers. Then it's not even 6 miles (9 km) to the next pass, the Col du Lautaret, and its rather unexpected botanical garden, Le jardin du Lautaret, a collection of more than 2,000 alpine plant species from around the world.

A straightforward drive down the D1091 through the Guisane Valley brings you to Briançon, the highest fortified town on the continent. Designed by Louis XIV's excellent military architect, the Marquis of Vauban, the old town's ramparts were completed in 1734. Inside the walls, it's as if the fortifications have kept out not just invaders but time as well; cobbled streets wind past pastel houses, and the layout of the main road, the Grande Rue, hasn't changed since 1345.

BELOW The colorful Old Town of Menton, on the French Riviera

On the southern side of the Col d'Izoard from Briançon lies the Casse Déserte, a barren swathe of mountainside that looks as if someone has poured ash down the slope, burying everything except the spiky stone pinnacles at the summit.

The road continues south through the Parc Naturel Régional du Queyras and on to the imposing Fort de Tournoux, and then Barcelonnette, one of the most unique towns along the whole route. Beginning in the mid-1800s, the area saw a wave of emigration to Mexico. Some of those emigrants returned, bringing with them New World influences; today, you'll find several dozen "*villas mexicaines*" displaying Mexican architectural characteristics.

Immediately south of Barcelonnette, you enter Parc national du Mercantour, a refuge for gray wolves and ibex; the park's Col de la Cayolle is the last pass above 6,500 ft (2,000 m) on the drive.

TO THE SEA

You're on the home stretch now. Descend through the Val d'Entraunes, and then up and over the Col de la Couillole en route to Roubion, where hulking masses of rock threaten to topple onto the rustic stone houses. Zig and zag your way to the Col de Turini before motoring south to Sospel. Established in the 5th century CE, the town enjoys a lovely setting amid low, green mountains and astride the Bévéra River. The architecture here feels decidedly more Mediterranean than Alpine. Take time to visit the graceful Sospel Cathedral and the remains of the 14th-century city walls.

From Sospel, the road will carry you over the Col de Castillon, the last pass of the drive, and into Menton. Where the road ends, palm trees line the shore, warm French Riviera waves lap at the beach, and the forbidding Alpine peaks of the last 435 miles (700 km) are suddenly just a memory.

MARQUIS OF VAUBAN

Many of France's most important defensive fortifications were the work of Sébastien Le Prestre, Marquis of Vauban (1633–1707). Military architect to King Louis XIV, he conceived of citadels, sea forts, mountain batteries, and even entire towns along France's borders. In 2008, his fortifications were collectively recognized as a UNESCO World Heritage Site; included among these are Briançon and the fortified Alpine village of Mont-Dauphin.

CASSE DÉSERTE
This eerily arid mountain slope offers some spectacular hiking.
250 MILES (402 KM)

BARCELONNETTE
Time your visit for the town's annual Dia de los Muertos festival.
298 MILES (479 KM)

SOSPEL
Feel the vibe shift from Alpine to Mediterranean in this delightful 5th-century town.
420 MILES (677 KM)

MENTON
END

CONNECTING THE CONTINENT

It's an age-old conundrum: how to get from A to B. For the earliest Europeans, the only answer was to walk, hoofing it over paths laid out by those who'd traveled before them. Then came the Romans, the continent's first great road builders, who laid 49,700 miles (80,000 km) of paved roads to link their capital with Britain, Byzantium, and Iberia. Since then, the quest to make travel faster and more convenient on the continent has continued unabated.

One of the 20th century's first great road-building projects involved turning a centuries-old mule track used by smugglers and peddlers to cross the Alps into the highest road pass in Europe. It took seven years to construct a road over France's Col de l'Iseran, which was finally opened by French President Albert Lebrun in 1937.

It was a triumph, but engineers soon figured out that they didn't have to go over mountains. They could go through them. From 1995 to 2000, workers blasted out over 88 million cubic feet (2.5 million cubic meters) of rock to create the Lærdal Tunnel, which eases travel between the Norwegian cities of Oslo and Bergen. At 15 miles (24.5 km), it's the longest road tunnel in the world. It even incorporates artificial caves for drivers to take a break at.

Equally impressive is the series of 20 tunnels that carry motorists around the Faroe Islands. Most cut through the archipelago's mountainous terrain, but three run beneath the sea. Completed in 2020, the network includes the first-ever underwater roundabout, which circles an illuminated blue pillar by the Faroese artist Tróndur Patursson.

Though these are relatively new constructions, the ideas are surprisingly old. In 1865, Claes Adelsköld proposed the construction of a submerged train tunnel beneath the Øresund strait. It never materialized as Adelsköld had intended, though the year 2000 saw the opening of the Øresund Bridge in its place, joining Malmö in Sweden with Copenhagen in Denmark. From the Swedish side, a bridge connects to an artificial island, where the roadway plunges into an underwater tunnel for the remainder of the trip to Denmark.

ABOVE A frozen tunnel on the Col de l'Iseran, opened in 1937

> One of the 20th century's first great road-building projects involved turning a mule track used by smugglers and peddlers to cross the Alps into the highest road pass in Europe.

LAVENDER ROUTE

START/END
Avignon/Sault, France

DISTANCE
173 miles (278 km)

DURATION
3–5 days

ROAD CONDITIONS
Well-maintained paved roads.

THE BEST TIME TO GO
Late June to the end of July, when the lavender fields are in full bloom.

OPPOSITE Rows of lavender at picture-perfect Abbaye Notre-Dame de Sénanque

In summer, the fields of Provence turn a vivid purple as row upon endless row of lavender blooms. Ditch the GPS and follow your nose down charming country lanes as you soak up the region's dreamy sights and scents.

Provence is lovely at any time of year, but it's particularly transfixing in summer, when the annual lavender crop blooms and the fields surrounding the region's hilltop villages become beautifully bruised in shades of purple and blue. A fine way to experience this event is with a slow drive from town to town, stopping at lavender farms, distilleries, and boutiques—and taking plenty of deep breaths as you go.

Avignon serves as a convenient point of departure for flower chasing, but don't be hasty about hitting the road. This city on the Rhône deserves some appreciation for its architecture and lively squares. Pay a visit to the Palais des Papes, the seat of papal power for seven decades in the 1300s, and the Pont d'Avignon, which has reached partway across the river since most of it washed away in the 17th century.

TWIN CROWNS

From Avignon, head 18.5 miles (30 km) east to Coustellet. The town itself is rather bland, but it's home to the excellent Musée de la Lavande Luberon, where you can gain a deeper understanding of lavender and the common hybrid lavandin. Set amid lavender fields and olive trees, the museum explains the history, harvest, and distillation of lavender; just as importantly, it serves lavender ice cream.

The drive to Gordes offers one of the most dramatic approaches to a town in Provence, if not all of France. While fields and vineyards carpet the valley below, a jumble of cream-colored buildings

AVIGNON
START

COUSTELLET
Learn all about lavender—and try lavender ice cream—at the Musée de la Lavande Luberon.
19 MILES (31 KM)

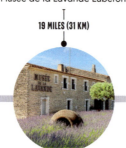

VILLAGE DES BORIES
This restored settlement of centuries-old huts lies just outside the town of Gordes.
24 MILES (39 KM)

ABBAYE NOTRE-DAME DE SÉNANQUE
Lavender fields front this pretty 12th-century abbey.

28 MILES (45 KM)

ROUSSILLON
This lovely town is painted in shades of sunset, thanks to its historic ocher quarry.

37 MILES (59 KM)

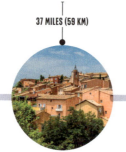

VALENSOLE
Marvel at vast fields of lavender as you drive around the Valensole Plateau.

81 MILES (130 KM)

climb a rocky hillside to the Château de Gordes and Eglise Saint-Firmin. The town is just as alluring up close, with petite bakeries and shops selling local lavender and honey lining its streets.

Before leaving Gordes, make the short drive to Abbaye Notre-Dame de Sénanque, founded in 1148. In summer, brilliant purple lavender plants run in tidy rows up to the stone abbey, a soothing off-white just a shade deeper than the resident Cistercians' cowls.

Double back through Gordes and make your way to Roussillon. Driving into the village is like driving into the sunset, its buildings a palette of reds and golds and burnt oranges, a legacy of the area's ocher deposits.

ACROSS THE PLATEAU
Leaving Roussillon, make your way east to Valensole, but do so slowly. This portion of the journey finds you in the heart of the Luberon, a region of mountains and valleys, lavender fields, vineyards, and hilltop villages that deserves unhurried exploration. In Lacoste, you can visit the crumbling Château de Lacoste, once home of the infamous Marquis de Sade. The perched villages of Bonnieux and Saignon both provide stunning vistas of lavender fields in the valleys below. Apt's candied fruits have been famed throughout France for centuries. In Manosque, you can tour the plant of cosmetics giant L'Occitane en Provence, whose roots are in the local lavender. Whether you visit these towns or others is immaterial, though—you'll find delight anywhere you go.

When you do finally make it to Valensole, you'll find the Provence of your purple dreams. The roads running across the Valensole Plateau, particularly the D6, D8, and D56, are flanked by seemingly boundless fields of lavender, with violet rows stretching off to the horizon. Complementing them are fields of another local specialty: sunflowers. As you drive between the gold and purple, be sure to stop at the seasonal roadside stands to pick up some locally made lavender products.

EXTEND YOUR TRIP
Instead of aiming straight for Digne after crossing the Valensole Plateau, head southeast for a truly dramatic change of scenery. Cruise through the center of the Parc Naturel Régional du Verdon to take in the monumental Verdon Gorge, a 15.5-mile (25 km) gash in the limestone that's 2,297 ft (700 m) deep in places.

LAVENDER ROUTE

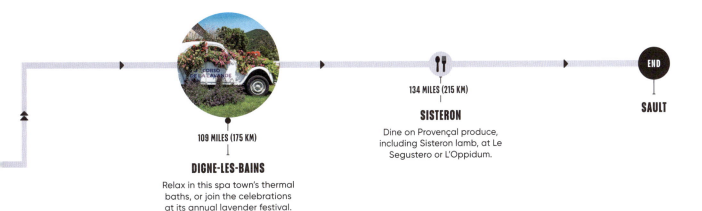

109 MILES (175 KM)

DIGNE-LES-BAINS
Relax in this spa town's thermal baths, or join the celebrations at its annual lavender festival.

134 MILES (215 KM)

SISTERON
Dine on Provençal produce, including Sisteron lamb, at Le Segustero or L'Oppidum.

SAULT

After crossing the plateau, aim for Digne-les-Bains, long an important center for lavender distillation. If your boot isn't already full, pop into Les Lavandières en Provence or one of the town's other boutiques for lavender room spray, lotion, or eau de toilette.

A 40-minute drive northwest of Digne is Sisteron, whose majestic Sisteron Citadel dates, in parts, to the 1100s. For part of the lavender season, it's the venue for the Nuits de la Citadelle festival.

PURPLE GAZE
Lavender and sunflower fields guide you out of Sisteron on your way west to Sault, which rivals Valensole for the title of Provence's lavender capital. In town, shops like La Maison des Producteurs de Sault and La Loubatière sell fragrant cosmetics and fresh bunches of lavender, while the surrounding countryside is dotted with farms and distilleries like Arôma'Plantes and Sarraud that have been in the same families for generations. Before ending your journey, spend whatever time you have left cruising the country roads and basking in the pastoral beauty of it all. Be sure to pause at the Belvédère de Saint-Jean overlook, 2.5 miles (4 km) south of Sault, to take in the patchwork of purple in the valley below, while Mont Ventoux rises up in the distance.

RIGHT An archway in orange-tinted Roussillon

OPPOSITE A monk wandering the cloisters at the Abbaye Notre-Dame de Sénanque

BELOW Sisteron, home to a 12th-century citadel and the imposing Rocher de la Baume

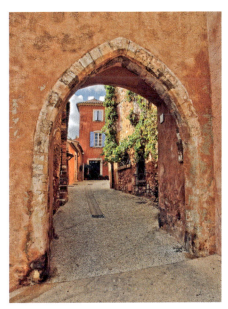

FRENCH RIVIERA

START/END
Monaco/Saint-Tropez, France

DISTANCE
91 miles (147 km)

DURATION
3–4 days

ROAD CONDITIONS
Well-maintained, though narrow, two-lane roads.

THE BEST TIME TO GO
Summer, for peak Riviera, or February, for the Nice Carnival.

OPPOSITE Blue-and-white striped umbrellas fill Nice's Publique de l'Opéra beach

The Côte d'Azur has long been a playground for the rich and famous, and its inimitable mix of chic beaches, très exclusive hotels, and glistening Mediterranean blues makes this stretch one of Europe's most glamorous drives.

Your riviera road trip starts with a quick cross-country drive. You could make it from one end of Monaco, the world's second-smallest nation, to the other in under 10 minutes. But slow down and take it all in. The city-state sets the mood for the miles ahead with its affinity for autos. The Collection de Voitures Anciennes displays Prince Rainier III's haul of classic cars—everything from a Lamborghini Countach 5000 to a World War II Weasel 1943. The city is also the venue for the famed Monaco Grand Prix, which roars through the narrow streets each May. Drive the course at the speed limit of 19 mph (30 km/h), and then imagine tearing through at 130 mph (200 km/h).

CLIFF-HANGERS

You'll spend most of this trip by the sea, but, for now, climb up the D6007/M6007 to the enthralling clifftop town of Èze. Its stone buildings, 14th-century churches, and quaint galleries seem to dangle directly over the Mediterranean, encouraging both rapt seagazing and a tight grip on the nearest railing.

From Èze, head to Saint-Jean-Cap-Ferrat. Once a fishing settlement, the peninsula became a favored retreat for the likes of Marc Chagall, Winston Churchill, and Pablo Picasso. In fact, the notable beach Plage Paloma was named for the Spanish painter's youngest daughter. You'll pass the cotton-candy pink Villa Ephrussi de Rothschild, which holds the Baroness Béatrice Ephrussi de Rothschild's art collection—just some dusty old things like a carpet from the Palace of Versailles

MONACO
START

ÈZE
Pull yourself away from the coast ever so briefly to take in this charming clifftop town.
6 MILES (9 KM)

SAINT-JEAN-CAP-FERRAT
Pretty in pink, the Villa Ephrussi de Rothschild boasts amazing art as well as themed gardens.
12 MILES (19 KM)

19 MILES (30 KM)

NICE
Soak up sun, style, and art history in the Riviera's biggest city.

35 MILES (57 KM)

ANTIBES
Of all the Côte d'Azur's resorts, none does glamour quite like the Hôtel du Cap-Eden-Roc.

TOP The forested peninsula of Saint-Jean-Cap-Ferrat

ABOVE Nice's Promenade des Anglais is lined with luxe hotels

and a fire screen whose previous owner was believed to be Marie Antoinette.

From Saint-Jean-Cap-Ferrat, follow the M6098 around the Pointe du Gaton, and you'll soon find yourself in Nice, the Riviera's largest city. The drive will take you down the Promenade des Anglais, which runs around the Baie des Anges and past venerable five-star hotels Le Negresco and Palais de la Méditerranée. One glance is enough to understand why Henri Matisse and Marc Chagall spent their last decades nearby, crafting canvasses that are now on display at the Musée Matisse and Musée National Marc Chagall. The sun never seems to set on Nice, but the old town's tiny alleyways exist mostly in shadow—all the better for unearthing its atmospheric bars, restaurants, and cafés.

MODERN MASTERS

After communing with artists in Nice, visit Cagnes-sur-Mer. Pierre-Auguste Renoir bought a home here in 1907; it's now the Renoir Museum, which hosts his paintings and sculptures. The Musée Picasso is just 6 miles (10 km) down the coast in Antibes. Displaying a selection of the Spaniard's works, it occupies a 14th-century château that housed the Grimaldi family, military troops, and, for a few months in 1946, Picasso himself.

Antibes is as emblematic of the Riviera as anywhere on the drive: alluring beaches, an atmospheric old town, megayachts in the harbor, and lounging A-listers. You'll likely find the latter at the Hôtel du Cap-Eden-Roc, a grand dame at the tip of Cap d'Antibes. It's hosted everyone from Anatole France to Ella Fitzgerald and Elizabeth Taylor.

Follow the D6007 around the bay to Cannes, where drivers will be rewarded with a cruise along La Croisette, the iconic palm-tree-lined boulevard. At its end is the Palais des Festivals et des Congrès, the structure that hosts the Cannes Film Festival each spring. Le Suquet, the town's oldest part, sits across the yacht-packed port. Here, cobbled streets curve along the steep topography on their way up to the Château de la Castre. Its position offers the perfect vantage point for counting the stars—the ones in the sky and those chasing the Palme d'Or.

THE CÔTE'S QUIETER SIDE

The next stretch is light on glitz, at least by the Côte d'Azur's standards. On your way to Saint-Raphaël, cruise down the ancient Roman Corniche d'Or, which curves along the coast tracing the rocky red headlands. Swing by the Cap du Dramont for stunning views of Île d'Or, a rugged islet, complete with a stone

> **The Château de la Castre offers the perfect vantage point for counting the stars—the ones in the sky and those chasing the Palme d'Or.**

tower, thought to have inspired *The Black Island* from Hergés' comic series *The Adventures of Tintin*.

Five miles (8 km) on is Saint-Raphaël, a relaxed resort town where villas from the late 1800s share space with a 12th-century church and daily flower market. Neighboring Fréjus boasts the ruins of a Roman aqueduct and amphitheater, along with some of the drive's best beaches. South of town are the picturesque ponds of Villepey.

Finish with a flurry at Saint-Tropez, Riviera resort town par excellence. There's maritime history at the 17th-century Citadelle and artistic legacy at the Musée de l'Annonciade. And while the coast's earthy roots still poke through in the old fishing quarter and the Place des Lices—the central square where old-timers play pétanque—today's Saint-Tropez is very much the realm of the moneyed classes. If you can't join their ranks just yet, don't worry. The sunshine, salty air, and sea coolly lapping at your toes are all free.

ABOVE The narrow streets of Cannes' Le Suquet old town

CANNES
Watch the sunset from Plage du Midi, or stargaze at the world's premier film festival.
44 MILES (70 KM)

ÎLE D'OR
Head to the Cap du Dramont to spot this crenellated tower from across the sea.
63 MILES (102 KM)

PONDS OF VILLEPEY
These brackish waters just south of Fréjus are home to some 270 bird species.
72 MILES (115 KM)

SAINT-TROPEZ
END

COSTA NORTE

START/END
San Sebastián/Santiago de Compostela, Spain

DISTANCE
515 miles (828 km)

DURATION
10-12 days

ROAD CONDITIONS
Paved, ranging from highways to narrow country lanes with switchbacks.

THE BEST TIME TO GO
High summer for the best weather; for less congestion, visit in June and September.

OPPOSITE Verdant rolling vineyards, where the grapes for *Txakoli wine* are grown

Spain's windswept, cliff-lined coast is famed for its Michelin-starred cities. But there's more to explore. Delve deeper and you'll discover charming fishing villages, natural landscapes, and dazzling architecture along the way.

Begin your journey of Spain's northern coast 12 miles (20 km) from the French border in San Sebastián. The Basque city has more Michelin stars per square yard than anywhere else in the world. And the best and most efficient way to get a taste of the city is on a food tour. After a whiz around the culinary hot spots, stroll La Concha beach. Then it's time to hit the road.

As you head west through the northern Spanish countryside, you'll see the vines that crisscross the landscape, ready to make *Txakoli*, a softly sparkling Basque white wine. It would be tempting to while away the day in a shorefront *enoteca* (wine bar) in Zarautz, where the road meets the sea, but continue along the coast to Getaria and, if you're early enough, you'll be able to watch local fishermen hauling in the day's catch.

BASQUE IN THE GLORY
From the beaches of Getaria, head to Bilbao where visitors are greeted with the shimmering contemporary curves of the Guggenheim art museum. Designed by Frank Gehry, the bold building was part of a revitalization project that put the once-industrial Bilbao on the proverbial map. Today, the city is as much a cultural hub as it is a foodie one. Build up an appetite with a stroll around the contemporary center and finish with a flavorsome finale on the bar—and restaurant-dotted Calle Santa Maria. Here, you can sample the region's small bites known as *pintxos*.

More art and architecture await in Santander. To get there, navigate the

---

SAN SEBASTIÁN
START

SAN SEBASTIÁN
Take a stroll on La Concha, the city's gorgeous half-moon shaped beach.
0 MILES (0 KM)

BILBAO
Fuel up on bite-sized *pintxos*, which are a quintessential part of Basque cuisine.
63 MILES (102 KM)

ROAD TRIPS IN EUROPE

127 MILES (205 KM)

MOURO ISLAND
The island's lighthouse has been steering ships away from the rocky dangers since 1860.

209 MILES (336 KM)

PICOS DE EUROPA
Home to brown bears and Iberian wolves, the park spans Asturias, Cantabria, and León.

EXTEND YOUR TRIP

Continue on the coast from A Coruña and you'll hit the Costa da Morte ("Coast of Death"). The rocky stretch got its name for the many shipwrecks that have occurred in its treacherous waters. It's safe to explore by road, though, and offers pretty villages, lush forests, and epic views.

narrow roads that loop toward the popular surfing spot of Somo. Resist the temptation to ride the waves, if you can, and cruise along the curving coastline, tracing Santander's beach-dotted bay. In the harbor, the futuristic Renzo Piano-crafted Centro Botín arts center is hard to miss. Continue on to La Magdalena Peninsula for unspoiled views of the isolated Mouro island, where the waves crash and the wind whistles.

It's difficult to tear yourself away from this dramatic spot, but more sublime art awaits just along the road. With two architectural masterpieces under your belt, head to Comillas where the work of one of Spain's most iconic visionaries, Antoni Gaudí, resides. El Capricho is a whimsical 19th-century chalet and one of the few examples of Gaudí's design outside of Catalonia. An early build by the Spaniard, the flamboyant, nature-inspired design includes styles later perfected in Barcelona's Park Güell and Basílica de la Sagrada Família sites.

BUILDING MOMENTUM
In spectacular contrast to Gaudí's human-made grandeur is the Picos de Europa mountain range. The N-621 winds its way inland among beech and oak trees. Here, valleys peppered with high pastures and scree slopes rise to become rugged mountaintops. Shoot uphill to Fuente Dé, where a cable car whisks you even higher for a bird's-eye view of the surrounding peaks.

On your way to Santiago, you'll pass through bucolic Asturias. The region is home to the Lakes of Covadonga, where cows roam freely, the jingling bells around their necks piping a song out across the slopes. Leave the car behind and hike around the glacial lakes, or simply sit back and enjoy the views. Once you've had your fill of this natural beauty, it's time to make your way to the regional capital of Oviedo. Cider-making is a deep-rooted Asturian tradition, so when you pull into the city, a crisp glass poured with flourish from

ABOVE The limestone cliffs of the Picos de Europa

COSTA NORTE

LEFT Santiago de Compostela's basilica is a UNESCO-listed site

BELOW The towering rock formations of As Catedrais

on high is just the ticket. Refreshed and raring to go, visit Iglesia de Santa María del Naranco, a pre-Romanesque 9th-century church on Oviedo's hillside.

Return to the Asturian coastline and trace the shore, where wild beaches and unspoiled inlets are frequent. When you cross the Ribadeo o del Eo, you've reached Galicia. Continue on the road, dipping in at As Catedrais beach. During low tide, 100 ft (30 m) high geological formations made of slate and schist can be seen arching above the sand.

KEEPING IT RÍAS

Delve deeper into Galicia where the Rías Altas—long sea inlets that are similar to Nordic fjords—are rich with *almejas* (clams) and *nécoras* (velvet crabs). Sticking to the coast, follow the narrow roads that wind across the clifftops. Though challenging, they will reward drivers with glimpses of towns such as Cariño and Ferrol. In A Coruña, pause at the Torre de Hércules lighthouse.

From here, bid farewell to the sea as you snake inland toward Santiago de Compostela. Not only is this city the endpoint for your road trip, but it is also the culmination of the Camino de Santiago pilgrimage. Join the steady stream of modern-day worshippers who visit the famed basilica. As you wrap up your grand tour, you too can share the sense of accomplishment that pervades this sacred site.

AS CATEDRAIS
See the towering rocky columns of this beach on the Galician coast.
355 MILES (571 KM)

A CORUÑA
Head to the Torre de Hércules, an atmospheric spot to watch the waves roll in.
467 MILES (751 KM)

SANTIAGO DE COMPOSTELA
END

CASTILE AND LÉON

START/END
Segovia/Burgos, Spain

DISTANCE
365 miles (589 km)

DURATION
6-8 days

ROAD CONDITIONS
Paved roads and cobblestones in historic centers.

THE BEST TIME TO GO
Avoid the peak summer crowds by visiting in spring or fall.

OPPOSITE The Roman-built Aqueduct of Segovia, which runs through the city's old town

Forget the coastal high-rises and crowded beaches, Spain's Castile and Léon is an entirely different ballgame. This interior region is home to an impressive selection of impeccably preserved castles and cathedrals.

Spain's sparsely populated, central plateau, known colloquially as the *meseta,* is packed with beautifully preserved fortifications. History buffs could while away a few weeks crisscrossing these epic plains and mountain peaks, springing from one historic site to another. For a snappy weeklong tour of the highlights, though, start in the UNESCO-listed Segovia and traverse the fort-filled route to Burgos.

IN WITH THE OLD
Segovia's pinnacle, looming large over the terracotta-topped houses and cobblestone streets, is the Alcázar de Segovia. Complete with fairy-tale towers, the fort is rumored to have inspired the castle in Walt Disney's *Sleeping Beauty*—along with Germany's Neuschwanstein Castle, of course *(p99)*. The regal site has served as residence to 22 kings and dates back to Roman times. Only a five-minute drive away is another Roman configuration—the Aqueduct of Segovia. This soaring bridge cuts a spectacular line straight through the old town's center. Crane your neck to spot the top of this architectural feat—which stands at 90 ft (28 m) tall and 2,600 ft (813 m) long—before then steering your way out of town.

Before you reach the center of Ávila, you'll first need to pass through the city walls, or *muralla*. Like something out of Tolkien's *Lord of the Rings*, the 1.5-mile (2.5 km) long defensive perimeter features eight imposing gates, 88 watchtowers, and more than 2,500 turrets. Park outside the

SEGOVIA

START

PARADOR DE SEGOVIA
A Brutalist icon in central Spain, this hotel boasts a foliage-filled indoor pool.
0 MILES (0 KM)

ÁVILA
The fortified walls protect the bustling city within, including an impressive cathedral.
44 MILES (70 KM)
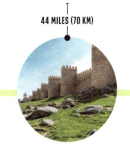

SALAMANCA
The city's Bambú tapas bar is known for its modern take on Spanish classics.

108 MILES (173 KM)

ZAMORA
Gaze at the Romanesque cathedral's unusual Byzantine-style dome.

150 MILES (241 KM)

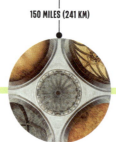

LAGUNAS DE VILLAFÁFILA NATURE RESERVE
Spot kestrels and eagles swooping over the wetlands.

185 MILES (298 KM)

ABOVE The "new" 16th-century Salamanca Cathedral

OPPOSITE TOP The pretty village of Covarrubias

OPPOSITE BOTTOM Inside Burgos Cathedral

medieval center, and walk the walls to see the grandeur of this ancient city up close.

HEAVEN SENT
With the magnificent fortifications of Ávila behind you, turn your thoughts to Salamanca. Nicknamed the Golden City for its yellow-stone buildings, it is the proud owner of two stately basilicas. The *Nueva* and *Vieja*—new and old—are only a stone's throw from one another and feature architectural styles ranging from Romanesque to Baroque.

This is one of the region's liveliest cities—which might have something to do with it being home to Spain's oldest university. Stop to drink in the atmosphere—as well as a couple of *cañas*, for the nondrivers—before heading back on the road.

After some 40 miles (70 km), you'll reach the city of Zamora, straddling the Douro River. As well as its 24 churches and its cathedral, Zamora is known for its full-bodied, delicious wines, which are produced just off the river's banks.

With many human-made wonders under your belt, take a moment to appreciate a natural phenomenon: the Lagunas de Villafáfila Nature Reserve. This important wetland features several bird hides where you can glimpse Central and Northern European avian species during the spring and fall migrations.

After some peaceful birding, hit the northbound A-66 to León—a key city in medieval Spain—to visit the Gothic cathedral and marvel at its striking kaleidoscopic stained glass.

This wouldn't be a complete itinerary of Spain's extraordinary castles and cathedrals without a visit to Burgos's religious masterpiece. But first, you must navigate 110 miles (180 km) of Castile and León's idyllic countryside, passing

CASTILE AND LÉON

335 MILES (539 KM)

FUENTE AZUL
Take a dip in this natural swimming hole, and discover its surprising cinematic links.

366 MILS (589 KM)

BURGOS
Sitting pretty atop the Parque de Castillo, Burgos Castle offers far-reaching views of the city.

END

BURGOS

a flurry of charming villages as you edge ever closer to the ancient city. Stop often and you'll be rewarded with the region's lesser-visited gems. In Castrojeriz, you can spend a night off-grid among the ruins of the 12th-century Convento de San Antón. Covarrubias, meanwhile, is considered one of Spain's prettiest villages, with 15th-century houses sporting exposed timber frames and adobe façades. Drivers who detour to Covarrubias can also discover the Fuente Azul swimming hole—a refreshing place to take a dip. Cinephiles with an eager eye might recognize this spot: across the road is the Monastery of San Pedro de Arlanza, where gruesome scenes from the Western *The Good, The Bad and The Ugly* were filmed.

HOLY REST
From here, it's a final 30 miles (50 km) to Burgos, where the city's cathedral, an important pilgrimage church, awaits. Another UNESCO-listed site, it was once a modest Romanesque church that was upgraded in the 1200s to the Gothic triumph that stands today. There are extraordinary ceilings, vaulted domes, tall turrets, and a peaceful cloister to wander.

Before you leave the cathedral, visit the tomb of folk hero El Cid. He has long been considered the ideal medieval knight since his adventures were immortalized in a 12th-century Castilian poem. It's a grand end for a grand trip.

CASTLE COUNT

The Middle Ages were a tumultuous time on the Iberian Peninsula. Kingdoms in the north regularly warred with one another, while also battling the Muslim caliphates and kingdoms in the south. The result—a plethora of castles—means that Castile and León has more UNESCO-listed sites than any other region in the world.

ANDALUSIA

START/END
Seville/Córdoba, Spain

DISTANCE
411 miles (663 km)

DURATION
10–12 days

ROAD CONDITIONS
Paved roads that range from highways to steep mountain lanes.

THE BEST TIME TO GO
Any time except (the blazing) summer; watch out for icy roads on mountain passes during the coldest months.

OPPOSITE Seville's spectacular Royal Alcázar palace

There is more to Andalusia than its majestic cultural capitals. As well as the historical sights of Seville, Granada, and Córdoba, there are whitewashed villages perched on hilltops of dizzying heights to discover.

When people think of Spain, often it's images of flamenco dancers artfully spinning in polka-dot frocks, or pictures of poised bullfighters that come to mind. Andalusia is the birthplace of both. This delightful drive through a region still richly steeped in tradition is a highlight reel of archetypal Spain, bookended at either end by the magnificent Moorish monuments of Seville and Córdoba.

JUMPING TO IT

Seville, Spain's former gateway of maritime trade, makes a natural starting point for your Andalusian adventure. The city's Triana district has for centuries been home to flamenco musicians, potters, and seafarers—and it's a great place to discover Seville's more authentic side. Head into the bustling center to visit the Royal Alcázar, the enthralling palace complete with palm-tree-shaded gardens.

Steer past Seville's aristocratic mansions and ornate plazas as you leave the city and head into the countryside. Thanks to the area's stable climate, Algodonales has become known as a skydiving and parapenting center. Here, daredevils are rewarded with a perspective of the Sierra de Grazalema park that very few see. Take the leap yourself—or watch in awe from the ground below—and then make the steep, narrow climb to the whitewashed hilltop villages, or *pueblos blancos*, of the Grazalema Natural Park. Around 6 miles (10 km) from Algodonales, you'll reach the picturesque lakeside village of Zahara de la Sierra. From here, take the CA-9104,

SEVILLE
START

ROYAL ALCÁZAR OF SEVILLE
Snap a selfie in the city's gilded palace complex, which featured in *Game of Thrones*.
0 MILES (0 KM)

ALGODONALES
Watch skydivers glide across the sky from the whitewashed town of Algodonales.
56 MILES (90 KM)

63 MILES (101 KM)

ZAHARA DE LA SIERRA
A gateway to the Sierra de Grazalema, this village sits on a reservoir of blue-green waters.

85 MILES (137 KM)

RONDA
Set in the town's Plaza de Toros arena is a museum dedicated to bullfighting.

steering south to Grazalema. Wander the quaint streets, stopping to watch local artisans weave woollen blankets.

BRIDGING THE GAP
The drive out of Grazalema will take you down a spectacular but challenging mountain route (and up again). Drive slowly, stopping to admire the views from the Puerto de las Palomas road, which reaches out over the Guadalquivir valley. Keep an eye out for the occasional vulture swooping through the sky.

Soon you will arrive in Ronda, a white town that perches dramatically on rugged limestone cliffs. Known as the home of modern bullfighting, Ronda's 18th-century Plaza de Toros is an important site for the controversial tradition. The arena is no longer active, aside from once a year when the town dons traditional dress and the bullring erupts once more for the Feria Goyesca.

Less contentious is the Puente Nuevo, the city's spectacular "new bridge," which (despite its name) was completed in 1793. The stone structure connects Ronda's two halves, which are split by a gorge that descends 400 ft (120 m). Explore the bridge by foot, peering over the edge if you dare, before motoring across the ancient overpass.

A 10-mile (20 km) drive delivers you to Setenil de las Bodegas, one of the area's

> Known as the home of modern bullfighting, Ronda's 18th-century Plaza de Toros bullring erupts once a year for the Feria Goyesca.

most unusual *pueblos blancos*. Here, the houses are built into caves along the Guadalporcún gorge, with overhanging sections of rock. The design hints at Andalusia's roots: Romans introduced the color scheme, while medina-like alleyways and hilltop fortresses were inspired by Muslim caliphates (Islamic states) and taifas (independent Muslim kingdoms of the Iberian Peninsula).

BELOW Mountaintop Ronda's Puente Nuevo bridge

ANDALUSIA

LEFT Walkers crossing a bridge on the El Caminito del Rey

EL CAMINITO DEL REY

Named for Alfonso XIII, who walked the route in 1921, the "King's Path" was built in the 20th century to facilitate maintenance of a nearby hydroelectric plant. The boardwalks, which were fully renovated in 2015, reach heights of 330 ft (100 m). A guided tour is recommended.

Pass through Olvera before driving east to El Caminito del Rey, a route of vertiginous walkways that offers an exhilarating adventure through Desfiladero de los Gaitanes' gorge. Although the access point for those attempting the three-hour hike is at the gorge's northern end, drive the MA-5403 past pine forests and ocher rock formations to the southern exit. When you reach the outskirts of El Chorro, you'll be able to glimpse the route's arched bridges and suspended walkways from the road—and the tiny hikers slowly snaking their way along them. If you're tempted to give it a go yourself, double back to the start, at the Conde del Guadalhorce Reservoir.

SHORE THING

Leave Andalusia's mountainous interior behind and head for the seaside city of Málaga. The adventurous A-7075 route runs past the neolithic dolmens and limestone towers of Torcal de Antequera Natural Park. It's a longer journey but well worth the rocky spectacle. If you're in a hurry, you can speed across Spain's interior taking the A-357.

When the turquoise waters of the Costa del Sol appear on the horizon, so too will the glitz and glamour of revitalized Málaga. There's plenty to see, do, and eat here, with contemporary museums, artistic venues, world-class bars, and restaurants.

For the next leg of the journey, you can either follow the coast for 60 miles (100 km), past pretty seaside towns such as Salobreña and La Herradura on your way to Motril, or you can head for the rugged hills and detour to the sugarcube villages of Las Alpujarras, located in the foothills of the Sierra Nevada mountains. Either way, it'll act as a pleasant interlude before the next major stop on your journey, further inland: the storied city of Granada.

OLVERA
Visit the dramatic castle in Olvera, which sits atop a rock in the town's center.

116 MILES (187 KM)

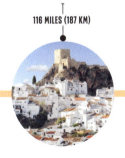

TORCAL DE ANTEQUERA
For an alternative to El Caminito del Rey, try a hike in this park's ethereal landscape.

171 MILES (275 KM)

MÁLAGA
Sample the city's typical fare at El Pimpi, which has links to actor Antonio Banderas.

203 MILES (327 KM)

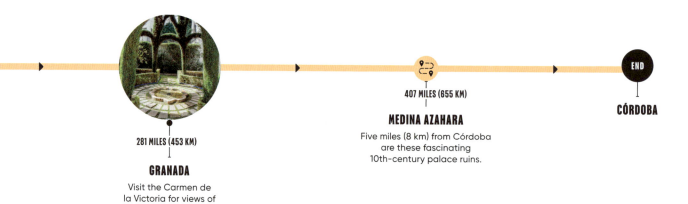

281 MILES (453 KM)

GRANADA
Visit the Carmen de la Victoria for views of the Alhambra.

407 MILES (655 KM)

MEDINA AZAHARA
Five miles (8 km) from Córdoba are these fascinating 10th-century palace ruins.

END

CÓRDOBA

EXTEND YOUR TRIP

On Spain's southernmost tip sits the popular surfing town of Tarifa. From here, you can board the ferry, car and all, to cross the 20 miles (33 km) of water to Tangier, Morocco. Let your Africa exploration begin.

ABOVE The mesmerizing arches of Córdoba's Mezquita

THE REAL ESPAÑA

Set across three hills in the shadow of the snow-topped Sierra Nevada mountains, Granada is the perfect place to break a journey. Start with a stroll in the Albaicín district, whose steep, cobbled lanes are lined with traditional *carmenes*, two-storey houses that were established by the Nasrid Empire in the 14th and 15th centuries. You can get a glimpse inside one at the Carmen de la Victoria, whose walled garden offers unbeatable views of the Alhambra, Granada's clifftop palace and fortress that served as the seat of power for Spain's last Muslim ruler. Once you've admired it from afar, visit the gilded palace itself, joining a guided tour to unlock the secrets of the Alhambra's intricate decorative motifs. Finish with a flourish at a flamenco show – for the most authentic experience, visit one of the city's *peñas*, clubs that attract the best flamenco artists.

High on the kicks and flicks of the traditional Spanish dance form, skip on to the last leg of your journey. At its cultural apex in the 10th and 11th centuries, Córdoba served as a global model of modernity and learning. But first, a quick detour, to the 10th-century Medina Azahara – or, at least, what's left of it. The palace, now in ruins, was built by Caliph Abd-al Rahman III at the foot of the Sierra Morena mountains.

Drive the final 8 km (5 miles) from here to Córdoba to visit another mesmerizing site: the city's Mosque-Cathedral, or Mezquita. Incredibly preserved, the UNESCO-listed site depicts how Islamic and Christian artistic influences have intertwined over the centuries. As evening settles over this jewel in Andalusia's crown, make your way to the three-Michelin-star Noor. Its menu focuses on a culinary retelling of Córdoba's history, while using modern techniques and ideas. It's a unique way to explore the past while remaining rooted in the delicious present, the perfect toast to the region – and a trip well done.

HOSPITALITY ON THE ROAD

Europe has a notable reputation for hospitality, boasting historic hotels and restaurants so good that people will cross borders to sample the cooking. But attention to travellers' needs isn't just a product of modern tourism.

The word "hospitality" can be traced to the Latin term *hospes*, which could mean either "guest" or "host", and has been a concept since ancient Greek and Roman times. In fact, the first hotel chain (or what most resembled one) appeared during the Roman Empire: *mansiones* were government-run villas where officials could find a room and board. Private facilities known as *cauponae*, meanwhile, catered to the lower classes, with *mutationes* acting as the era's service stations.

As the Roman Empire disintegrated, the Church became Europe's primary provider. Monasteries offered shelter, meals and medical treatment to pilgrims, travellers and the destitute. They were joined by hospitals that, in the Middle Ages, functioned as religious and charitable institutions. In what's now known as Turkey, *caravanserai* were established to shelter caravans on trade routes such as the Silk Road. They spread with Muslim travellers, eventually arriving in Andalusia. Today, visitors to Granada can still find the 14th-century Corral del Carbón, a warehouse and inn that mainly served grain merchants.

By this time, what we would consider "inns" had started opening up across Europe, though none would make anyone's "Best of" lists. Guests often slept on the floor, with basic food served.

> The word "hospitality" can be traced to the Latin term *hospes*, which could mean "guest" or "host", and has been a concept since ancient Greek and Roman times.

And the less said about hygiene, the better. Gradually, however, things started to improve. By the early 1800s, tourists could avail themselves of luxury hotels, ski resorts and the like. In the 1920s, the Michelin brothers enticed the public onto the road with the first fine-dining guide.

Today, new hotels and restaurants pop up all the time, though road trippers keen to travel through time can still experience properties around in the early days: Spain's Parador de Santiago de Compostela has been serving pilgrims since it opened in 1499, while the Gasthaus Zum Roten Bären in Freiburg, Germany, welcomed its first guests way back in 1120.

ABOVE People socializing at a *caravanserai* in Urfa, Turkey

ROUTE 1

START/END
Porto/Lisbon, Portugal

DISTANCE
238 miles (384 km)

DURATION
7-10 days

ROAD CONDITIONS
Well-paved roads; occasionally steep and cobblestoned.

THE BEST TIME TO GO
From May to September; avoid summer if you'd like to beat the crowds.

OPPOSITE Porto's Dom Luis I bridge is a grand double-decker affair

With vibrant monuments, impressive castles, and sleepy fishing villages turned surfing hubs, Portugal's lengthy top half has a lot to offer. But only if you're brave enough to ditch the country's uninspiring main artery.

A nonstop drive from Portugal's second city to its capital is doable in just over three hours. But to take the Autoestrada do Norte, the A1 highway, that stretches between the two, would mean bypassing every gem in between.

GRAPE EXPECTATIONS

This elongated journey starts in Porto, the city that gave the country its name and which has a long-standing importance as a global trade hub. It all started with the Romans, who planted vines upstream in the Douro Valley and began exporting wine. It wasn't until the 17th century, however, that port was first produced, shipped into the city and stored along the river banks—where the historic port houses are still based today. But there's more than fortified wine available.

Make your way to the Douro River's southern side and walk across the Dom Luis I bridge, a striking double-decker structure that's 150 ft (45 m) tall. The top deck, and its far-reaching views, are reserved for the city's trams and pedestrians, while cars can motor along the lower level. From here, it's an uphill battle—literally. Though Lisbon's moniker may be the City of Seven Hills, Porto has a few dizzying inclines of its own. And you'll need to conquer them, and the cobblestone streets, to get to your first stop: the azulejo-clad São Bento Railway Station. Instead of boarding a train, linger in the main hall to admire the 20,000 painted tiles that depict scenes from Portuguese history.

Azulejos are intricately painted ceramic tiles that have historically been used

PORTO
START

SÃO BENTO RAILWAY STATION
Watch out for the commuters as you gaze at this train station's beautiful azulejos.
0 MILES (0 KM)

AZULEJO
The term *azulejo* comes from the Arabic word *azzelij*, meaning "little polished stone."

to clad buildings since the 14th century. Twenty-five miles (40 km) south of Porto is another tiled beauty: the Igreja Matriz de Santa Maria de Válega church boasts dazzling, and unusually colorful, ceramic scenes.

ON THE TILES

Portugal's reputation for world-class pottery extends further than façades, and there's no better place to learn of the country's handicraft heritage than Aveiro. The charming, canal-dotted city, a 20-mile (35 km) drive due south, is home to the Vista Alegre Porcelain Museum, where you can learn all about the crafty business. There's plenty more to explore in this technicolor city—and the best way is aboard an *abarco moliceiro*, the city's answer to the Venetian gondola. Before you leave Aveiro on, make a quick detour to Praia da Costa Nova beach. Here, you can take a dip in the bracing Atlantic waters and gaze at the seafront's picturesque striped houses.

Wind down the coast past Praia da Vagueira and Poço da Cruz before heading inland to Coimbra. The country's former capital is often overlooked in favor of the country's first and second cities. It's a lively spot, however, one that's home to the oldest university in the Portuguese-speaking

IGREJA MATRIZ DE SANTA MARIA DE VÁLEGA
See the vibrant tiles at this vibrant church.
25 MILES (40 KM)

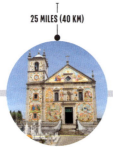

VISTA ALEGRE PORCELAIN MUSEUM
Visit this Aveiro site to learn of the city's crafty heritage.
52 MILES (83 KM)

219 MILES (352 KM)

QUINTA DA REGALEIRA
Walk the winding stone staircase at this unique Sintra estate.

239 MILES (384 KM)

LISBON
See live *fado*, Portugal's melancholic music, at the popular Tejo bar.

END

LISBON

world. The university's Baroque Joanina Library is a bibliophile's dream and is home to tens of thousands of ancient volumes, many of them priceless.

After exploring Coimbra, hop back in the driver's seat and drive toward the fishing village of Ericeira. It's a long 130-mile (200 km) stretch so break up the journey along the way: the literary town of Óbidos boasts 14 bookstores, while Pombal features an impressive hilltop castle.

SURFING, SINTRA, AND SOULFUL SOUNDS

Watersports enthusiasts may have heard of Peniche and Nazaré, the latter known for its 80 ft (25 m) high waves. But give them a miss and continue to Ericeira instead. The fishing village, and its 2.5 miles (4 km) of cliff-lined coast, is one of only two World Surfing Reserves in Europe. Unlike Nazaré, there are surf breaks here for every level—plus the opportunity to dip into the bracing Atlantic waters—but watching from the golden shore is an equally enjoyable pastime.

When you can pull yourself away from the waves, drive south to magical Sintra, known for its notable castles and palaces. After a tour, Lisbon and its hills are in sight. Take the panoramic N247 past Cascais, a quaint town where Portuguese royals vacationed in the summer months.

The fishing village of Ericeira, and its 2.5 miles (4 km) of cliff-lined coast, is one of only two World Surfing Reserves in Europe.

Once in Portugal's capital, park and then stroll the Alfama district's warren of narrow lanes to the Miradouro de Santa Luzia for spectacular views over the Tagus River. To close out your trip, seek out a *fado* bar—lively Tejo is a reliable choice—to enjoy the artful longing of Portugal's national music. The soulful sounds are sure to strike a chord, and you'll soon be longing for the chance to to be back behind the wheel and out on the road again.

ABOVE Lisbon's Miradouro de Santa Luzia's viewpoint

OPPOSITE TOP Praia da Costa Nova's pretty seaside houses

OPPOSITE BOTTOM Praia de Ribeira d'Ilhas beach in Ericeira

THE ALENTEJO

START/FINISH
Lisbon/Odeceixe, Portugal

DISTANCE
350 miles (564 km)

DURATION
10–12 days

ROAD CONDITIONS
Paved roads with bumpy and narrow paths deep in the countryside.

THE BEST TIME TO GO
Spring or fall; during the summer, there are breezes along the coast, but the interior sizzles with heat waves.

OPPOSITE Typical whitewashed houses and cobblestone streets in Évora

Rolling along Portugal's untamed coast and cutting deep into its hilly interior, this route serves up everything from whitewashed fishing villages to modern vineyards. Welcome to the Alentejo, Portugal's rustic, lesser-trodden region.

Driving across the Alentejo countryside is like traveling to a bygone era. For long stretches, only the copper-hued trunks of cork oaks lean into the road to greet you. After the coastal areas near Lisbon, which feel lively and glitzy in comparison, it seems like time has stood still in the region's sleepy hamlets and hilltop villages. Peace reigns supreme here, as it does on the seemingly endless sandy stretches farther south, where Atlantic rollers pummel beaches bereft of crowds.

ALONG THE ATLANTIC COAST

Your journey starts in the country's capital, Lisbon. Pick up a couple of *pastéis de nata* from the famed Pastéis de Belém bakery for the drive and leave the thronging crowds behind you as you cross Portugal's magnificent answer to San Francisco's Golden Gate Bridge, the magnificent Ponte 25 de Abril.

The winding coastal route journeys south from here, entering the Parque Natural da Arrábida, which is famed for its white cliffs and dense vegetation. Make sure you stop at the *miradouros*, or viewpoints, along the way to admire the breathtaking ocean views, and follow indistinct dirt roads to discover the park's hidden beaches.

Curve around the peninsula and, after 40 miles (60 km) on the road, you'll reach the hamlet of Portinho da Arrábida. Pause for a splash in the cool turquoise waters and a lunch of grilled fish at O Farol. Once you're fully sated, and you've dried off in the sun, continue the scenic route inland.

LISBON
START

LISBON
Pastéis de Belém has been making custard tarts since 1837 using an ancient recipe.
0 MILES (0 KM)

PARQUE NATURAL DA ARRÁBIDA
Look out for wildcats and eagle owls in the dense vegetation.
28 MILES (45 KM)

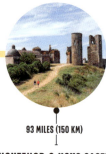

93 MILES (150 KM)

MONTEMOR-O-NOVO CASTLE

This ruined castle perches on the hilltop overlooking the town it once ruled over.

114 MILES (183 KM)

ÉVORA

Sample the best of Évora's sweet treats at the ornately tiled Conventual Pão de Rala.

It's a lengthy but worthwhile stint of some 80 miles (130 km) before you hit the medieval city of Évora, the capital of Alentejo, so consider stopping in Montemor-o-Novo to wander its majestic castle ruins.

As soon as you pull up in Évora, you'll realize that this historic spot was worth the mileage. Home to Portuguese kings in the 15th century, its past also includes periods of Celtic, Visigothic, and Islamic rule. And while Lisbon boasts custard tarts, Évora has its own selection of sweet treats. The best place to get your sugar fix is at the *pastelaria* Conventual Pão de Rala. Try the spot's namesake bake—a sweet bread made from a recipe that dates back to the 16th century. It's best washed down with an espresso in the bakery's *azulejo*-clad interior.

Following your tasty pit stop, a stroll through the old town reveals a diverse collection of monuments: among others, the Temple to Augustus, built by the Romans in 1 ce, and the 16th-century Chapel of Bones, a macabre site where the walls are lined with the bones and skulls of around 5,000 people.

FROM ANCIENT WONDERS TO MODERN MARVELS

Swap chilling chapels for chilled wine with your next stop, at the Herdade do Freixo winery. While Porto's historic fortified wine receives much of the nation's grape-based buzz, Alentejo's fertile lands are home to some award-winning wineries. This rural spot offers tastings of wines made from Arinto, Alvarinho and Touriga Nacional, but there's also a contemporary feat here that even designated drivers can appreciate: a grand curving concrete staircase that looks quite spectacular.

Purchase a bottle to sip later and continue southwest to medieval

LEFT View of Évora from the city's cathedral

BELOW The eerie Chapel of Bones in historic Évora

THE ALENTEJO

LEFT The whitewashed houses of Porto Covo

EXTEND YOUR TRIP

Driving the Atlantic coast is seen as a right of passage for many Portuguese. Families pack up their cars, surfboards in tow, and spend their summers moseying south, dipping into the pretty towns and beaches along the way. Finish this familiar route by continuing to the town of Sagres, which sits at Europe's edge.

Monsaraz. Here, you can admire views over the Alqueva Reservoir, the largest artificial lake in Europe., and the sky above. The Dark Sky Alqueva observatory takes advantage of the area's prime stargazing conditions, making this an inevitable overnight stop.

THE WILD PORTUGUESE WAY

Back on the road, you'll traverse Alentejo's countryside for your return to the coast. Break up the 90-mile (150 km) journey at Alcácer do Sal, where a pretty promenade makes for a nice stroll.

Soon you'll arrive in coastal Comporta, a glamorous spot known for its endless sandy stretches and gastronomic offerings. There are more beaches and pretty towns to discover as you travel south through the Santo André

e da Sancha Nature Reserve and the Vicentine Coast Natural Park. The latter is a 60-mile (100 km) stretch of pristine coastline marked by dramatic clifftops and traditional fishing villages.

As you motor along the Costa Vicentina, as locals refer to it, you'll pass Praia da Samoqueira, with its towering rock formations and the hidden inlet of Praia de Porto Covinho. Before long, you'll reach the town of Porto Covo, with its brilliant-white buildings trimmed with sky-blue and forest-green paint.

It's a final 40 miles (60 km) to the very edge of Alentejo, where the region meets its sunny southern sibling, the Algarve. Sandwiched between the two is the town of Odeceixe, which was named after the Seixe River that winds past the village and into the Atlantic, creating a unique horse-shoe-shaped beach.

Head to Odeceixe beach for a fitting goodbye to this wild coastline. When the tide is coming in, choose a place along the Seixe River to jump in, where you will be propelled beachward by the channel's current. Linger here to gaze at the mighty Atlantic as it laps the shores.

DARK SKY ALQUEVA
Take advantage of the area's low light-pollution levels and book a night of stargazing.
163 MILES (262 KM)

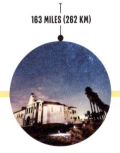

SANTO ANDRÉ E DA SANCHA NATURE RESERVE
Observe flamingos wading in saltwater lagoons here.
295 MILES (474 KM)

ODECEIXE BEACH
This wide-shored beach is a great place for novice surfers to practice the art.
351 MILES (564 KM)

ODECEIXE
END

THE ARDENNES

START/END
Liège, Belgium

DISTANCE
216 miles (349 km)

DURATION
4–5 days

ROAD CONDITIONS
Well-maintained paved roads.

THE BEST TIME TO GO
Fall, for gorgeous colors in the forest.

OPPOSITE Kayakers paddling down the Ardennes's verdant Semois River

A combination of natural forested beauty, rich history, and cultural variety makes a road trip through the Belgian stretch of the Ardennes one of Europe's ultimate countryside drives, and a blissful way to pass a few days.

One of the continent's most enchanting regions, the Ardennes offers a vast network of deciduous, mountainside forests where Belgium meets with Germany, France, and Luxembourg. Your journey begins (and ends) in Liège, which is known as the Fiery City, both for its lively atmosphere and history as a cradle of revolutionary thought. For a snapshot—and to get the count up on your pedometer—ascend the Montagne de Bueren 374-step staircase for wide-reaching views of Liège's old town and its historical architecture. Leave the Belgian beer flight for the end of your trip, though—it's time to hit the road.

SPAS AND FAST CARS

As you leave Liège, the city gives way to a patchwork of green fields before the forests of the Ardennes close in, just outside the town of Spa. People have been bathing here since Roman times—in fact, spas around the world were named for this Belgian town.

But despite the impressive facilities of the area's Les Thermes de Spa complex, travelers to this wooded corner of Europe don't just visit for the warm waters—and especially the car-minded types. Five and a half miles (9 km) out of town lies the Circuit de Spa-Francorchamps, an iconic Grand Prix race track that hosts motorsport competitions most days. Formula One fans should time their visit for when the Belgian Grand Prix comes to town in the summer, or when the track opens to the public for their chance to whistle

---

LIÈGE
START

LIÈGE
This spirited city is full of revolutionary history and tempting brewery taprooms.
0 MILES (0 KM)

SPA
The thermal town is home to luxurious baths—as well as Agatha Christie's Hercule Poirot.
25 MILES (40 KM)

FRANCORCHAMPS

Thrill seekers rejoice: there are regular motorsport events at this famous racecourse.

31 MILES (49 KM)

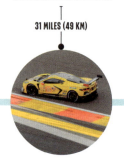

LA ROCHE-EN-ARDENNE

Sample Belgian delicacies from Maison Bouillon & Fils butchers.

63 MILES (101 KM)

BASTOGNE

Stark reminders of the cost and heroism of World War II exist in this Walloon city.

80 MILES (129 KM)

around the Francorchamps circuit that has seen legends Lewis Hamilton and Ayrton Senna take the checkered flag.

From here, winding roads snake through oak and birch woodlands toward the pretty medieval town of La Roche-en-Ardenne. As well as its picturesque location on the Ourthe River, La Roche is known for its local delicacies. Sample Ardennes ham and saucisson from Maison Bouillon & Fils butchers, and pair with a boulangerie baguette for an idyllic riverside picnic.

TAKING IN THE HISTORY

The drive from La Roche-en-Ardenne takes you along quiet country roads, lined with stone walls crawling with ferns, to Bastogne, a site of World War II significance. The Battle of the Bulge saw German forces unsuccessfully attempt to drive the Allies backward through the wooded hills of the Ardennes. A moving stop, the Bastogne War Museum documents the period in poignant detail, with displays of tanks, uniforms, and soldiers' personal effects.

As you continue southwest, through forest, farmland, and small villages, another historical site sits on the horizon: Bouillon and its mighty medieval fortress. The castle, which dates back 1,000 years, perches dramatically on the ridge of a hill overlooking the town below. Park in Bouillon, shake off your legs, and climb the 300 steps to the castle's highest point. Incredibly, it is still a place of industry: once you've explored the eerie tunnels and taken in the views, seek out the cellar—you'll smell it before you see it—where wheels of sheep's cheese ripen in the cool caverns.

It's worth sticking around until the sun sets on the town, when the castle is illuminated for all to see and Bouillon's restaurants open their doors. This is a great place to taste the local Ardennes fare—a hearty, German-influenced cuisine that features dishes such as red turkey cooked in beer, and bacon and dandelion salad.

BATTLE OF THE BULGE

The Ardennes Offensive, also known as the Battle of the Bulge, was a counterattack mounted by the German army in the winter of 1944–1945. German tank divisions punched through the US and British lines, creating a frontline in the shape of a bulge, but were pushed back by the end of January 1945.

THE ARDENNES

149 MILES (239KM)

HAN-SUR-LESSE

A vintage tram carries you deep beneath the earth into a wondrous network of caves.

217 MILES (349 KM)

LIÈGE

Toast your road trip at Brasserie C, a Liège local with 46 brews on tap.

END

LIÈGE

GOING UNDERGROUND

Darkness of a different kind awaits in Han-sur-Lesse, 29 miles (47 km) north of Bouillon. You'll have to pocket your car keys for this next experience as you board a century-old tram that carries you deep into the hillside. Here, the Lesse River has carved out an ethereal network of caves. Inside, stalagmites and stalactites furnish the interior where, amid the icicle-like formations, archaeologists have recovered spearheads and jewelry dating from 10,500 years ago. Just as enchanting are the caves of Hotton, a 20-mile (30 km) drive northeast, where an underground river surges through a limestone landscape resembling a skeletal coral garden.

Once you've resurfaced, it's time to round off your grand tour of the Ardennes. The impressive Gothic arches of Liège's cathedral await your return— as does a Belgian brew. Beer lovers have their pick in this gastronomic city: the Jupiler is one of the country's biggest breweries, but Brasserie C is best for a local toast, with 46 draft lines to choose from. As you take in the hoppy, heady scents, the words of novelist and Liège legend Georges Simenon might resonate: "The smell of a freshly opened bottle of beer is the smell of my country." *Santé*!

RIGHT The spectacular interiors of the Han-sur-Lesse caves

OPPOSITE The quaint town of La Roche-en-Ardenne

BELOW The Gothic interior of Liège Cathedral

87

ZEELAND'S DELTA WORKS

START/FINISH
Volkerakdam/Rotterdam, the Netherlands

DISTANCE
158 miles (255 km)

DURATION
2–3 days

ROAD CONDITIONS
Flat, well paved—and plenty of bridges.

THE BEST TIME TO GO
Spring, to spot the highest concentration of seabirds.

OPPOSITE Zeeland's Delta Works series, comprising 13 dams, completed in 1997

Zeeland's flood defenses are a feat of engineering, protecting vast areas of the Netherlands from being swallowed by the sea. This trip connects these stellar structures with medieval towns, windmills, and habitats for rare seabirds.

A symbol of human ingenuity, the Delta Works is the Netherlands's largest series of flood defenses. The collection of dams and flood barriers were built following the destructive North Sea Flood of 1953, which drowned the provinces of Zeeland and South Holland. This route focuses on this monumental spectacle—with a slice of Dutch charm, and the odd windmill, for good measure.

DAM GOOD

The first in the Delta Works series that you'll visit is Volkerakdam, a system of dams, locks, and bridges overlooking the fortified town of Willemstad. Immediately, you'll notice the landscape: pancake-flat, with the horizon constantly shifting between land and sea. Though it may have a heightened risk of flooding, this sprawling terrain is a haven for wildlife. Park often, and you'll be rewarded with panoramic vistas with sights of majestic birds and plenty of larger animals. Be sure to pack your binoculars.

As you drive west from Volkerakdam, your next nature-focused pit stop is the birdwatching hide, Vogelkijkhut de Kluut. From this peaceful sanctuary, which gazes out over the wetlands, you'll glimpse shelducks, spoonbills, and ospreys nestled within the reeds. Farther down the N59 highway, there's a chance to spot more animals in Hellegatsplaten nature reserve, where dun-colored fjord horses and heck cattle, their heads crowned with curving horns, reside.

Philipsdam, another sea defense, awaits 15 miles (25 km) down the road, so it's back in the car. As the N59 veers left

VOLKERAKDAM

VOLKERAKDAM
This impressive complex of dams and bridges lies in the shadow of a hilltop fortress.

0 MILES (0 KM)

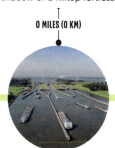

START

PHILIPSDAM
The wetlands of Oosterschelde National Park were created by this huge water barrier.

16 MILES (25 KM)

GREVELINGEN
This vast saltwater lake is the largest body of saltwater in Europe.

53 MILES (85 KM)

MIDDELBURG
Gothic architecture and Frisian cuisine await in the capital of Zeeland province.

67 MILES (108 KM)

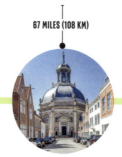

OOSTERSCHELDEKERING
The mightiest of the Delta Works is a wildlife haven home to seals and porpoises.

78 MILES (126 KM)

RIGHT The pretty town of Middelburg, Zeeland's capital

OPPOSITE Kitesurfers on the windy Strand bij Ouddorp

BELOW The Netherlands's longest bridge, Zeeland

onto the N257, you'll be caught between two immense bodies of water, Krammer on your left and Grevelingen, Europe's largest saltwater lake, on your right. The Delta Works soon comes into the picture again: Philipsdam separates the Krammer and Volkerak lakes from the Eastern Scheldt estuary. A happy by-product of the Delta Works is the creation of swimming beaches—Strand Laagbekken, next to the dam, provides a refreshing pause from the journey.

COASTAL DRIVES AND FRESH SEAFOOD
The route heads inland for a while before returning to the coast and emerging onto what may be the most remarkable stretch: a 6-mile (10 km) road along the top of Oesterdam. It is a meditative and slightly surreal section, as if you're driving out into the middle of the sea.

Soon enough, though, you're back on terra firma, passing pretty medieval towns, such as the picturesque Goes, on your way to Zeeland's capital, Middelburg. The city's Gothic town hall, completed in 1520, is an architectural gem in the center. You'll find plenty of lunch spots in Middelburg's old town— laid-back Basalt is recommended for its mouthwatering seafood.

A short drive north of Middelburg lies the Oosterscheldekering, a 5-mile (8 km) long series of huge gates that

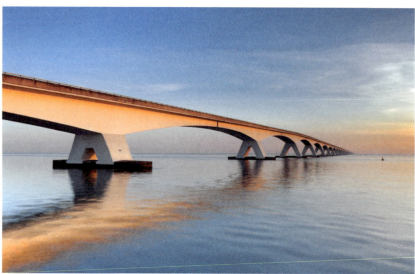

open and close to repel storms. Beyond this is the Zeeland Bridge—the longest bridge in the Netherlands at 16,500 ft (5,200 m)—which carries you above the water, sandbanks, and marshes of the Oosterschelde National Park. This is one of the wildlife hot spots of the Delta Works region, home to wading birds and a colony of seals, which you might spot lolloping on beaches or spits of sand. Another mammalian inhabitant of the national park is the dolphinlike porpoise, which playfully leaps in and out of the water.

THE LAST PORT OF CALL

With a fair share of defenses under your belt, it's a fitting point to learn about the area's history, which you can do at Watersnoodmuseum in Ouwerkerk. The museum documents the havoc of the 1953 North Sea Flood. It's a poignant moment in the trip and emphasizes exactly why the protections were put in place.

This touching stop is best lightened with a trip to the seaside. Feel the sand between your toes at Renesse Strand, a dune-lined arc that stretches for 10.5 miles (17 km) and has beach bars and restaurants aplenty. Otherwise, holiday resort Port Zélande opens onto Strand bij Ouddorp, a golden crest popular with kitesurfers, thanks to the area's stiff winds. Lessons are available on the beach if you fancy picking up a new skill.

Forty miles (65 km) along the coast is Rotterdam. As its name suggests, the Netherlands's second city has its own sea defenses—the first of which was built in the 12th century. Before you can see the ancient structure for yourself, you'll have to navigate the Dutch countryside, a windmill or two, and the last of the Delta Works—the Haringvlietdam. Your arrival in the city's port will be signaled by industrial cranes and shipping containers. Leave the car behind and continue by water taxi into Rotterdam itself, where you can explore this cultural hub and all it has to offer.

THE NORTH SEA FLOOD

On January 31, 1953, disaster swept in: a high tide with a violent storm saw the North Sea spill into the Netherlands and northwest Belgium, as well as the UK. The storm prompted the three countries to update their flood defenses. The Netherlands, most prominently, built the Delta Works.

PORT ZÉLANDE
Sea, sand, and (sometimes) sun are on the cards at the region's premier beach resort.
109 MILES (176 KM)

HARINGVLIETDAM
Cross the route's final bridge into a land of wading birds and whirring windmills.
121 MILES (195 KM)

PORT OF ROTTERDAM
An awesome industrial landscape of cranes and looming ships marks this stop.
136 MILES (218 KM)

ROTTERDAM
END

THE ELFSTEDENTOCHT

START/FINISH
Leeuwarden/Dokkum, the Netherlands

DISTANCE
112 miles (180 km)

DURATION
1–2 days

ROAD CONDITIONS
Well-maintained roads.

THE BEST TIME TO GO
Summer, to hear the ceremonial cannons booming above Sloten.

OPPOSITE The Elfstedentocht, an ice-skating race across Friesland's frozen waterways

Follow in the tracks of legendary ice-skating route, the Elfstedentocht, on this scenic drive through Friesland's 11 picturesque cities. Cruise past grassy plains and vast lakes, spotting windmills, tulips, and ferries on the way.

What could be more thrilling than donning your ice skates and whizzing along the frozen canals, lakes, and rivers of Friesland, stopping off at medieval cities for a mug of cocoa? Though the world's largest ice-skating tour, the Elfstedentocht, or Eleven Cities Tour, hasn't been held since 1997, there's a much more convenient way to complete this historic route: in the comfort of your car. Thankfully, subzero temperatures aren't a prerequisite of the road-based option, which means motorists can drive the Elfstedentocht year-round.

HIDE AND SNEEK
A great starting point is the regional capital of Leeuwarden, a laid-back city of cyclists, cafés, and eye-catching architecture. The pleasingly wonky Oldehove, a tilted church tower, is said to be the Netherlands's answer to Pisa's leaning legend.

The Netherlands's watersports capital, Sneek, is the second city on your route. Cruise through flat farmland—this is the Netherlands after all—to reach the canal-dotted center. Sneek's waterways connect directly to the Frisian Lakes (of which there are 24 in total), so a sailing tour is always an option—assuming, of course, that the water hasn't frozen over. The best known lake is Sneekermeer, where you can dip your toe into a host of watersports before heading to the third stop on your journey.

Windmills are a Dutch icon—there are around 1,200 across the country—and one of the most famous is located in the

LEEUWARDEN
START

LEEUWARDEN
The capital of Friesland is a place of leaning towers, canal cruises, and bar-lined plazas.

0 MILES (0 KM)

SNEEK
A Renaissance water gate marks your arrival into Sneek, a launchpad for lake cruises.
17 MILES (27 KM)
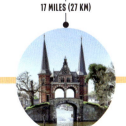

IJLST
One of Friesland's most photogenic windmills resides in this chilled-out city.

19 MILES (31 KM)

SLOTEN
Clustered around a canal, this city boasts militaristic medieval architecture.

31 MILES (50 KM)

STAVOREN
The once-powerful city remains a lovely spot for lunch and a stroll.

46 MILES (74 KM)

nearby IJlst. The 300-year-old De Rat windmill hasn't always graced the city; it was first built in Zaanstreek and was moved to Friesland in 1828.

GOING DUTCH
As you navigate the country's grassy plains, it's hard to imagine that this was once a place of war. But you can see relics of the turbulent medieval period at Sloten. The fortified town was fought over for its strategic position between Sneek and other trading cities. Today, it's one of the area's sleepier stops.

Leave the interior cities behind in search of the Netherlands's coastline. Stavoren, which sits on the banks of the IJsselmeer bay, is Friesland's oldest city. It illustrates just how much the Dutch coastline has been shaped by the sea: Stavoren was a wealthy port in medieval times, until a sandbank began to form in the bay, blocking the city from trading ships. It fell into obscurity and the city was swallowed by a flood in 1657. The mini-city's pretty harbor is lined with colorful houses and Stavoren's two famed statues: *The Lady of Stavoren* and *The Fish* fountain. The latter was designed by Mark Dion as part of the 11Fountains project, which saw 11 artists from 11 countries design water features for the Elfstedentocht cities. Keep your eyes peeled for the remaining 10, which include *The Whale*, *The Bat,* and *The Oort Cloud*.

Back in the car and 6 miles (10 km) north is Hindeloopen, where pretty seafarers' cottages, decorated with anchors, recall the glory days of the Dutch shipping trade. From here, board the passenger ferry that takes you across the IJsselmeer lake to charming Enkhuizen. Visit the Zuiderzee Museum to learn about the area's seafaring history, and the intriguing Flessenscheepjes Museum, which displays the world's largest collection of ships in bottles.

THE LADY OF STAVOREN
Stavoren legend tells that a rich but greedy medieval woman commissioned a sea captain to bring her the world's greatest treasure. When he returned with a supply of wheat to feed the city's poor, she was enraged, throwing it overboard into the harbor. A huge sandbank grew around it, cutting prosperous Stavoren off from trade and sending it into ruin.

THE ELFSTEDENTOCHT

57 MILES (92 KM)

WORKUM
The home of Jopie Huisman is also a place of pretty churches and traditional fishing boats.

84 MILES (135 KM)

FRANEKER
The city's 18th-century mechanical solar system is a UNESCO-listed wonder.

END

DOKKUM

When you see church spires, you're nearing your eighth Frisian city, Workum. This small center is best known as the home of Jopie Huisman, a 20th-century artist who, interestingly, refused to sell his paintings. The museum dedicated to his life and work, set in a striking industrial building, is an illuminating stop.

A TASTE OF FRIESLAND

Continuing north, the road passes through the city of Bolsward and on to Harlingen, where harborfront restaurants serve classic Frisian fare. Sample tasty local dishes, such as *snirtjebraten*, pork shoulder roasted with allspice and cloves. Friesland's fare reflects its multicultural influences, brought over during its seafaring past.

With only two cities remaining, the home stretch is within your grasp. Before you hang up your keys in Dokkum, though, pause in Franeker to see the Eise Eisinga Planetarium—the world's oldest working orrery (mechanical model of the solar system), dating from 1781.

It's a final 30 miles (45 km) through the Dutch interior to Dokkum. The nation's northernmost city is best known for two things: its hexagonal defenses, which include a 80 ft (24 m) wide moat and 15 ft (5 m) high ramparts, and its breweries. A little Dutch courage, and you've reached the finish line.

RIGHT The Eise Eisinga Planetarium in Franeker

OPPOSITE A statue of the famed *Lady of Stavoren* looks out over the once wealthy port

BELOW Workum is the eighth city of the Elfstedentocht

ROMANTIC ROAD

START/END
Würzburg/Füssen, Germany

DISTANCE
206 miles (333 km)

DURATION
4-6 days

ROAD CONDITIONS
Easily navigable and well maintained.

THE BEST TIME TO GO
Visit in fall once the crowds have gone home, the colors have changed, and the medieval towns are at their coziest.

OPPOSITE Cycling through Rothenburg ob der Tauber

Journey through the rich history of Bavaria on this storied tour, taking in the medieval splendor of ancient villages, Baroque exuberance of grand churches, and the fantastical castles designed by the Bavarian kings of yore.

This popular tourist route cuts a line straight through the heart of Bavaria. It's not hard to see why it has become so beloved by vacationers. The Romantic Road (or *Romantische Straße*) is a handy way to experience the region's most famous landmarks in one fell swoop. It combines an impressive blend of medieval towns and ancient castles with majestic Alpine scenery, so beloved by visitors to this part of Germany. So what are you waiting for?

THE BAVARIAN WAY

Based loosely on the track of an old Roman road, the trail was first marketed as a tourist route in the 1950s. Its intention was to draw visitors to the region and revive economic activity in the wake of World War II.

Today's Romantic Road begins in the historic city of Würzburg, best known for its UNESCO-listed Würzburg Residence. This grand, 350-room palace was constructed in the mid-1700s by architect Balthasar Neumann as the home of the local prince-bishops. It is a particularly opulent example of Bavarian Baroque, with manicured gardens to match.

From here, hop in the car and head due south along the leafy Tauber valley toward Rothenburg ob der Tauber. This medieval town has kept its historic charm remarkably intact, with its half-timbered homes and spindly spired churches. Its town hall offers the perfect leg-stretching activity: climb the 220 steps to the tower's top for stunning views across

WÜRZBURG

WÜRZBURG
Visit Würzburg Residence, an 18th-century UNESCO-listed palace.
0 MILES (0 KM)

START

ROTHENBURG OB DER TAUBER
Fairytale spires and neo-Gothic churches grace this beautiful medieval town.
38 MILES (61 KM)

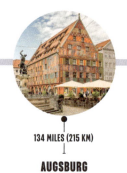

86 MILES (139 KM)

NÖRDLINGEN
Perfectly oval-shaped, this ancient town was built in a meteorite impact crater.

96 MILES (155 KM)

HARBURG CASTLE
This impeccably preserved medieval castles soars above the small town of Harburg.

134 MILES (215 KM)

AUGSBURG
This historic city was founded by the stepchildren of Roman emperor Augustus.

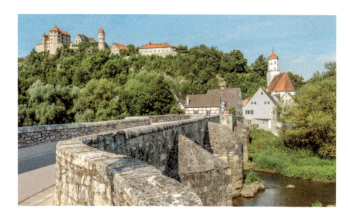

TOP Medieval Harburg Castle overlooks the town

ABOVE The stuccoed interior of the Pilgrimage Church of Wies

the settlement's picturesque warren of worn-down cobbled streets.

Leave Rothenburg and meander south through dense woodland to another impressive medieval marvel, Nördlingen. Built in the impact crater of a meteorite that hit the earth about 15 million years ago, the town has a perfect oval-shaped footprint. Walk the ancient walls and covered parapet paths to get a bird's-eye view of the orange-roofed settlement. The town is a good place to fuel up on Bavarian cuisine, too; visit one of its cozy taverns for hearty portions of *Schweinshaxe* (roast pig's knuckle) and *Leberknödelsuppe* (liver dumpling soup).

AS YOU LECH IT

Continue your drive south along the rolling Swabian plains until you reach Harburg, a small town towered over by a lofty medieval castle—famed for being one of the largest and best-preserved of its kind in Europe.

From here, the road curves along verdant farmland before crossing over the Donau and tracing the course of the Lech River into Augsburg. Bavaria's third-largest city is a rich symphony of architectural wonders from across the centuries; look out for the Renaissance St. Anna Kirche, an imposing 10th-century cathedral and the

16th-century town hall, with its twin onion-domed spires.

Beyond, the Romantic Road runs parallel to the Lech River from Augsburg, and down into the majestic foothills of the Bavarian Alps. The farther south you travel, the higher the peaks rise above the clouds, like distant, snowcapped pyramids. Continue motoring past Landsberg am Lech to reach a region known as the Pfaffenwinkel. This area is famed for its high concentration of churches and monasteries, dotted between the towns of Schongau and Ettal. The most notable of these is the Pilgrimage Church of Wies, which represents one of the most exuberant examples of Bavarian Rococo interiors. The light-filled chapel is filled with elaborate frescoes, intricate stucco work, and plenty of dazzling gilded details designed by acclaimed German architect Dominikus Zimmermann in the 1700s.

FAIRY TALE IN FÜSSEN

Back on the road, head toward the mountainous horizon. On the outskirts of Füssen, an awe-inspiring marvel sits on the hillside, its tall, gleaming towers rising above the tree line: Neuschwanstein. As impressive in real life as it is in pictures, this castle was built for Bavarian King Ludwig II, who had a penchant for elaborate feats of fantastical architecture. Its turreted, fairy-tale structure was the vision of the king himself, who worked with a stage designer rather than an architect to make his dream castle a reality. It's no wonder it (reportedly) provided the inspiration for the castle in Disney's *Sleeping Beauty* animation from 1959. And there's more for fantasy fans: another picture-perfect palace is just around the corner. The slightly more modest Schloss Hohenschwangau is where King Ludwig II grew up. The palace was built by his father atop the 12th-century ruins left by Schwangau knights.

Following the gilded grandeur of the regal residences, Füssen is a welcome finale. Steeped in Alpine charm, the scenic cobblestoned old town sits on the banks of the Lech River and makes for a peaceful stroll. Treat yourself to your own fairy-tale ending and find a bed for the night at one of Füssen's snug B&Bs. Who knows where your dreams will take you next?

> **Neuschwanstein was the vision of the king himself, who worked with a stage designer rather than an architect to make his dream castle a reality.**

ABOVE The enchanting turrets of Schloss Neuschwanstein

PILGRIMAGE CHURCH OF WIES
One of Bavaria's finest Baroque churches, with gilded stucco work and marble balustrades.
188 MILES (303 KM)

SCHLOSS HOHENSCHWANGAU
Füssen's lesser-known castle is just as majestic as its Disney-inspiring cousin.
204 MILES (329 KM)

FÜSSEN
END

BLACK FOREST HIGH ROAD

START/END
Baden-Baden/
Freudenstadt, Germany

DISTANCE
42 miles (68 km)

DURATION
1–2 days

ROAD CONDITIONS
Well paved, with some fast, arching corners.

THE BEST TIME TO GO
Weekends are rather busy, so go midweek if possible.

OPPOSITE The spa town of Baden-Baden, the gateway to the Black Forest

Germany's oldest scenic route winds through the depths of the Black Forest National Park, along deep valleys and across high mountain peaks. Expect breathtaking views, quaint villages, and plenty of Alpine charm.

It's easy to imagine why this mountainous corner of western Germany was named the *Schwarzwald*, meaning Black Forest. Its rolling landscapes are blanketed in some of Europe's deepest and darkest forests, which are said to have inspired the Brothers Grimm fairy tales.

The Black Forest High Road—officially known as the Schwarzwaldhochstrasse—cuts a path through the heart of the Black Forest National Park, rising to more than 3,250 ft (1,000 m) above sea level. The route was formalized in the 1930s when older roads in the valley were connected to a series of grand hotels built at high altitude. On a clear day, you can enjoy views that stretch all the way across the Rhineland Plain to the Vosges Mountains in France, and sometimes even as far as the Swiss Alps. But when the weather closes in—which it often does—the famed fables all but spring to life in the wood's misty, atmospheric clutches.

HEALING WATERS

The road begins in Baden-Baden, an elegant spa town that's been attracting a particularly well-heeled set of vacationers for centuries. It's still steeped in old-world splendor, with opulent Art Nouveau villas, lush parks, and plenty of luxurious spas where you can test the curative waters for yourself.

Once you've luxuriated for just long enough, hit the road and head for the national park, taking the Black Forest High Road south. Around 5 miles (9 km) from Baden-Baden, stop to visit Geroldsauer waterfall. Follow a short

BADEN-BADEN
START

BADEN-BADEN
The spa town is also home to the contemporary art-filled Museum Frieder Burda.

0 MILES (0 KM)

GEROLDSAUER WATERFALL
Take a short hike through the dense Black Forest to reach this pretty cascading waterfall.

6 MILES (9 KM)
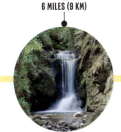

SCHLOSSHOTEL BÜHLERHÖHE
This elegant, now closed, hotel tempted a glitzy set of Black Forest travelers in the 1920s.

10 MILES (16 KM)

UNTERSTMATT
Tuck into typical Alpine fare, such as *Käsespätzle*, at cozy Zur grossen Tanne.

16 MILES (25 KM)

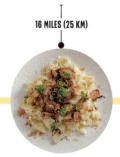

MUMMELSEE
Stay the night at Mummelsee Hotel and wake up with views across the lake.

21 MILES (33 KM)

ABOVE Mehliskopf ski resort in full winter swing

OPPOSITE ABOVE The view across glacial Lake Mummelsee

OPPOSITE BELOW The vast central square in Freudenstadt

footpath that leads from the road, along a series of small ascents and wooden footbridges, to get there. The waterfall itself is a majestic cascade that spills down the hill amid thick greenery and vibrant rhododendrons in spring.

OLD-SCHOOL COOL
Back on the road and you'll quickly find yourself cutting through dense woodland. Continue south along the Grobbachtal Valley to pass Schlosshotel Bühlerhöhe. This grand hotel, which opened its doors in 1920, is the design of acclaimed German architect Wilhelm Kreis. During its heyday, the site was the go-to accommodation for aristocratic vacationers in the region. Since 2010, however, it has stood empty and now towers above the road like a monument to the route's glamorous past.

Once you pass the village of Sand, the Northern Black Forest's Mehliskopf mountain soars to the left of the road. In winter, it's a lively center for snow sports; in the summer, it's a popular spot for hikers and bikers who clamber up its pine-coated sides to reach the 3,300 ft (1,007 m) peak. The stone observation tower, built in 1880, that sits atop it provides a glimpse of the wild, untamed nature for miles around.

Back on the road, the route curves past craggy mountain peaks before arriving in Unterstmatt, another small ski resort that makes for a good lunch spot. For generous servings of local specialities, including the famed Black Forest gateau, head to restaurant Zur grossen Tanne to relax within cozy wood-paneled interiors.

From Unterstmatt, the road snakes upward to reach the highest—and the route's halfway—point, Mummelsee. Those who decide to bed down here for the night (Mummelsee Hotel is an excellent shoreside option) will wake

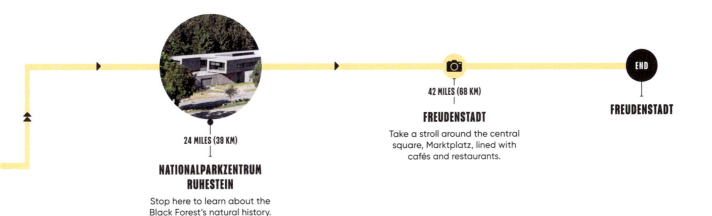

24 MILES (39 KM)

NATIONALPARKZENTRUM RUHESTEIN

Stop here to learn about the Black Forest's natural history.

42 MILES (68 KM)

FREUDENSTADT

Take a stroll around the central square, Marktplatz, lined with cafés and restaurants.

END

FREUDENSTADT

up with views across the mirrorlike glacial lake, which is also a relic of the last Ice Age. According to legend, Mummelsee is home to mermaids who live in a crystal castle at the bottom of its depths. You'll even spot a statue of one of the resident mermaids gazing out from a rock in the water.

OUT OF THE WOODS

Drive south along the forest-shrouded section to reach the Nationalparkzentrum Ruhestein. This state-of-the-art museum has interactive exhibitions on the history and ecology of the Black Forest and is housed within an impressive timber structure built in 2014. It even features a treetop bridge that guides visitors to an observation tower, which offers panoramic views across the mountains.

The road begins to slide southwest along steep mountainsides before dropping down into the Murg Valley, passing through the pretty chalet-filled towns of Obertal and Baiersbronn, before reaching the Black Forest High Road's end point in Freudenstadt. The town was founded in 1599 by Duke Frederick I of Württemberg as a refuge for Protestants fleeing Salzburg during the Thirty Years' War. The Duke enlisted famed architect Heinrich Schickardt to design the town and its vast central square (or Marktplatz). It's a pleasant place for a stroll, with its Renaissance-style arcades and Stadtkirche church. It's also an admirable spot to sip a stein of beer, an appropriate toast to the trip.

EXTEND YOUR TRIP

The Black Forest runs along the Franco-German border, with the French city of Strasbourg located just on the other side. It's a characterful city with a scenic, medieval core, tree-lined avenues, and plenty of cozy bistros serving hearty Alsatian fare.

ROMANESQUE ROAD

START/END
Jerichow/Leipzig, Germany

DISTANCE
260 miles (417 km)

DURATION
4–6 days

ROAD CONDITIONS
This flat route along well-kept highways is very easy to follow.

THE BEST TIME TO GO
Christmastime, when small towns become richly illuminated and their streets fill with traditional markets.

OPPOSITE The grand facade of Merseburg Cathedral

This route encompasses some of Germany's most impressive medieval architecture, from staggering Gothic cathedrals to quaint, half-timbered towns. It offers unbeatable insight into the early days of German history, too.

More than a thousand years ago, the Holy Roman Empire, which ruled much of central and western Europe, was presided over by German emperor, Otto the Great. He hailed from the Saxony-Anhalt region, and it remained his seat of power during his rule, as well as that of his successors. As a result, this corner of central Germany is filled with grand feats of Romanesque design.

While the buildings might look simple from the outside, the Romanesque style aimed to demonstrate the omnipotence of God and the emperor through their immense scale and lavish interior decorations. Romanesque buildings can be easily spotted, thanks to a few key features, such as towering, semicircular arches, small windows, thick stone walls, and graphic biblical depictions.

BUILDING A LEGACY
Germany's Romanesque Road is just one section of the 600-mile (1,000 km) Transromanica, which connects Romanesque buildings across nine European nations. Jerichow town and its majestic 12th-century monastery is a good place to start. The imposing site is Northern Germany's oldest brick building and features two towering spires and a pretty garden ideal for a short stroll.

From here, it's a 45-mile (72 km) drive through rolling fields to Magdeburg. The capital of Saxony-Anhalt, this city is home to Germany's first Gothic cathedral, where Otto and his first wife, Edith, are buried. The structure took more than 300 years to complete and is a mishmash of architectural styles, which

JERICHOW
This town is home to Northern Germany's oldest brick building, Jerichow Monastery.
0 MILES (0 KM)

JERICHOW
START

MAGDEBURG
Otto the Great and his wife, Edith, are buried in this storied city's cemetery.
45 MILES (72 KM)

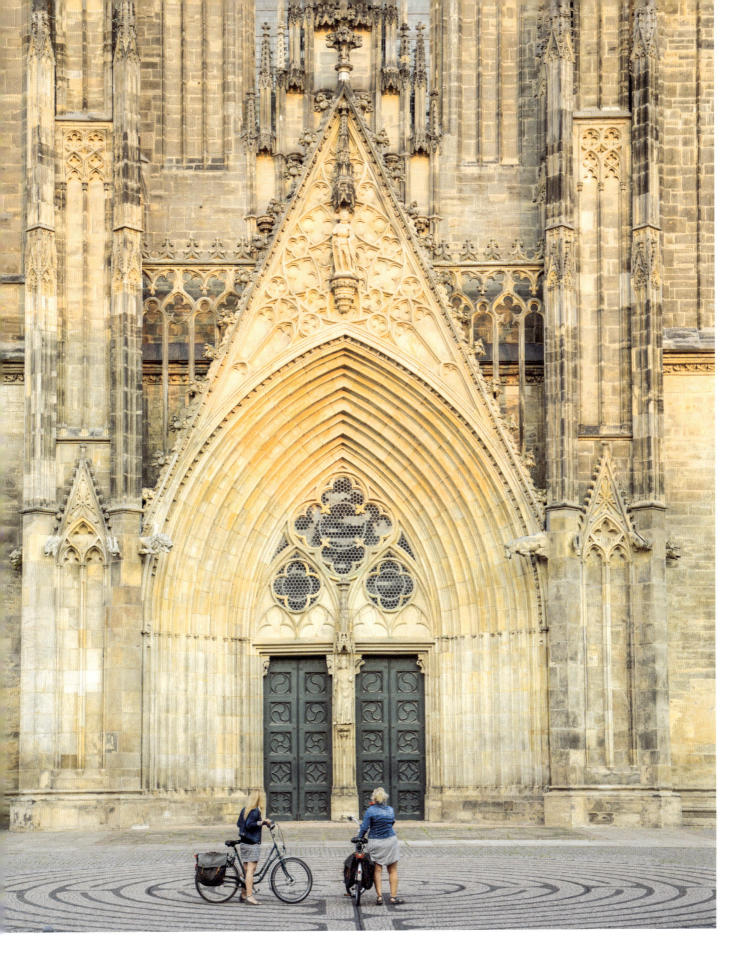

were incorporated over the centuries. Most striking are its elaborately ornamented twin spires, which visitors can climb for panoramic views of the city.

There are more teetering towers to come so drive southwest until you reach Halberstadt, an ancient town in the northern foothills of the Harz Mountains. The historic center was heavily bombed during World War II. Thankfully, most of the half-timbered houses have since been restored and the town makes for an excellent leg-stretching stroll. Meander past the epic Gothic-style cathedral and peek inside to see its original 13th-century furnishings. Despite its exterior, there are plenty of Romanesque marvels to be found within its treasury, which makes up the world's most extensive collection of medieval art. It displays more than 650 artifacts from the 5th to the 18th centuries, including famous tapestries, paintings, and sculptures.

FIT FOR A KING

After a 75-mile (120 km) stint, the town of Merseburg comes into view. Founded in the 9th century, it has been home to a string of German kings. In fact, you'll find many of them resting in the grand stone cathedral, which is renowned as another of the country's finest Romanesque monuments. The castle is also a grand sight to see in this quaint town.

ABOVE The rising spire of Burg Querfurt

LEFT Halberstadt's pretty half-timbered houses

OPPOSITE Schloss Neuenburg in scenic Freyburg

HALBERSTADT
Most impressive in the town's lofty cathedral are the stained-glass windows.

75 MILES (120 KM)

MERSEBURG
This pretty town is home to an impressive cathedral and onion-domed castle.

150 MILES (241 KM)

ROMANESQUE ROAD

173 MILES (278 KM)

BURG QUERFURT

See the staggering stone towers of Central Germany's largest medieval fortress.

186 MILES (299 KM)

MEMLEBEN

The historic ruins of Memleben's Benedictine monastery built to commemorate Otto the Great.

209 MILES (336 KM)

NAUMBURG

See the life-size—and very lifelike—statues that decorate the UNESCO-listed cathedral.

EXTEND YOUR TRIP

The route's start in Jerichow is close to Potsdam—the largest city in the German state of Brandenburg. Its major highlight is Schloss Sanssouci, a palace built by Frederick the Great that constitutes one of the most exuberant examples of German Rococo.

With two of the region's most impressive religious houses under your belt, it's time to visit Burg Querfurt, the largest castle in Central Germany. The venerable medieval fortress is encircled by a moat, with high walls punctuated by dramatic stone towers. Dating from the 9th century, it has served various roles over the years, from a noble residence to a military stronghold. Today, visitors can gain an insight into medieval life through its tours and historical reenactments.

Back on the road, journey through the dense forest of Saale-Unstrut-Triasland Nature Park to reach Memleben. It's here that Otto the Great died in 973, his death marked by a Benedictine monastery that his son constructed.

It's mainly ruins today, but you can still see the original wall fragments of the church, as well as an intact Late Romanesque crypt. Take a stroll under the ancient arches—it's easy to imagine you're in a bygone era.

GRAND DESIGNS

Hop back in the car and drive eastward along the B176. Eventually, you'll see the Schloss Neuenburg perched on a hilltop. Rising high above the small town of Freyburg and the vineyards below, the 11th-century building was once the center of the medieval court and later a hunting residence. Saint Elizabeth of Thuringia lived here in the early 1200s, and a Romanesque chapel was built in her honor. There's a museum here, too, exploring the castle's colorful history and the region's wine-growing heritage. Before you head out in search of the next Romanesque beauty, pause to explore the pretty town.

Fully refreshed, steer ahead to the nearby town of Naumburg. An important trading center during the 12th and 13th centuries, Naumburg is now known for its UNESCO-listed cathedral. Though impressive from the outside, its biggest draw is hidden within: 12 life-size, and unnervingly realistic, sculptures that depict important nobles from when the cathedral was conceived.

BELOW Local Leipzigers cool off in the artificial Cospudener See

CAPTURING THE ZEITZ-GEIST

From Naumburg, the road dips through Saale-Unstrut, one of Europe's northernmost wine-growing regions. Steer past the steep terraces, stone walls, and orchards on your way to Zeitz, the German capital of children's strollers. The town dates back to medieval times, but in the 20th century, it became an industrial hub, thanks to the Zekiwa factory, which produced more than 500,000 strollers annually. Visitors can learn more at the German Stroller Museum. Perhaps unsurprisingly, Zeitz's biggest attraction is, in fact, the Schloss Moritzburg, which was built in an opulent, Baroque-style around a Romanesque nave.

Say goodbye to Zeitz and follow the course of the White Elster River northeast toward your final stop, Leipzig. Before you hit the city, you'll pass a series of lakes surrounded by lush forests. Cospudener See is popular among Leipzigers looking to escape the urban bustle; it's an artificial lake that used to be an open-cast mine and is now a serene spot lined with sandy beaches. Stop for a quick splash with the locals before making your way into the city.

Pretty Leipzig is home to your last Romanesque beauty: St. Nicholas Church. Wander inside and gaze at the cavernous, pastel-hued interior complete with Neo-Classical pillars and a checkerboard tiled floor. The city's cultural venues, such as the fine arts Museum der Bildenden Künste and Gewandhaus concert hall, are also worth exploring. But it's not just history and culture in this lively and creative student city, which is known as "The New Berlin." When day turns to night, Leipzig's moniker becomes apparent as the streets begin to pulse and the city's underground music scene comes alive. It's a modern end to a route steeped in history.

PEACE PLEDGE

Leipzig's Nikolaikirche, or St. Nicholas Church, is as pretty as a picture. It has a powerful history, too. In the 1980s, the site's then pastor, Christoph Wonneberger, initiated weekly "peace prayers," which helped lead to the fall of the East German government in 1989.

ZEITZ
Wheel into Zeitz for the unusual Deutsches Kinderwagenmuseum.
227 MILES (365 KM)

COSPUDENER SEE
This artificial lake is a hub of activity where you can walk, swim, and do watersports.
252 MILES (405 KM)

LEIPZIG
The city's contemporary Museum der Bildenden Künste is well worth a visit.
259 MILES (417 KM)

LEIPZIG
END

AUTOMOBILE MILESTONES

If you're driving the Romanesque Road, you may be lucky enough to spot one of Europe's most elusive, and infamous, cars. After all, it was just 37 miles (60 km) from Zeitz, in Zwickau, that VEB Sachsenring Automobilwerke Zwickau manufactured the Trabant. Often called the worst car ever made, it was an indelible symbol of the German Democratic Republic. This was in no small part because it was one of the only vehicles East Germans could get.

But while these wagons frequently lacked things like turn signals and brake lights, and had a top speed of just 62 mph (100 km/h), Trabants were cutting-edge in one regard: they were the first car to have a body made completely from recycled materials. A mix of phenol resin and cotton fibers, the composite, called Duroplast, was sufficiently durable, and the average "Trabi" lasted 28 years.

The Trabant, which was made from 1957 to 1991, can trace its lineage 199 miles (320 km, or 3.2 hours, as the Trabant speeds) southwest to Mannheim. It was here that Karl Benz drove his Patent-Motorwagen, the first car, in 1886. Naturally, this was the vehicle of choice for the inaugural road trip. Two years after her husband had patented and driven his Motorwagen, Bertha Benz piled the couple's two teenage sons into a new version and, without telling Karl, went to visit her mother in Pforzheim, 56 miles (90 km) away.

It wasn't long before people decided to use these new contraptions for sport and, in 1894, there was another first. This time it was a race. The route was a 50-mile (80 km) drive from Paris to Rouen, with the winner averaging a precise 10.2 mph (16.4 km/h). It was viewed mainly as a reliability test, however. The first *proper* race was held the following year: a 732-mile (1,178 km) round-trip dash between Paris and Bordeaux.

The event paved the way for the Automobile Club de France's very first Grand Prix, held in 1906. The race saw 32 drivers complete 12 laps, split over the course of two days, around a triangular 65-mile (105 km) circuit near Le Mans. Each lap took about an hour—a far cry from the times clocked today.

ABOVE East Germany's iconic Trabant

> Though they had a top speed of just 62 mph (100 km/h), Trabants were cutting-edge in one regard: they were the first car to have a body made completely from recycled materials.

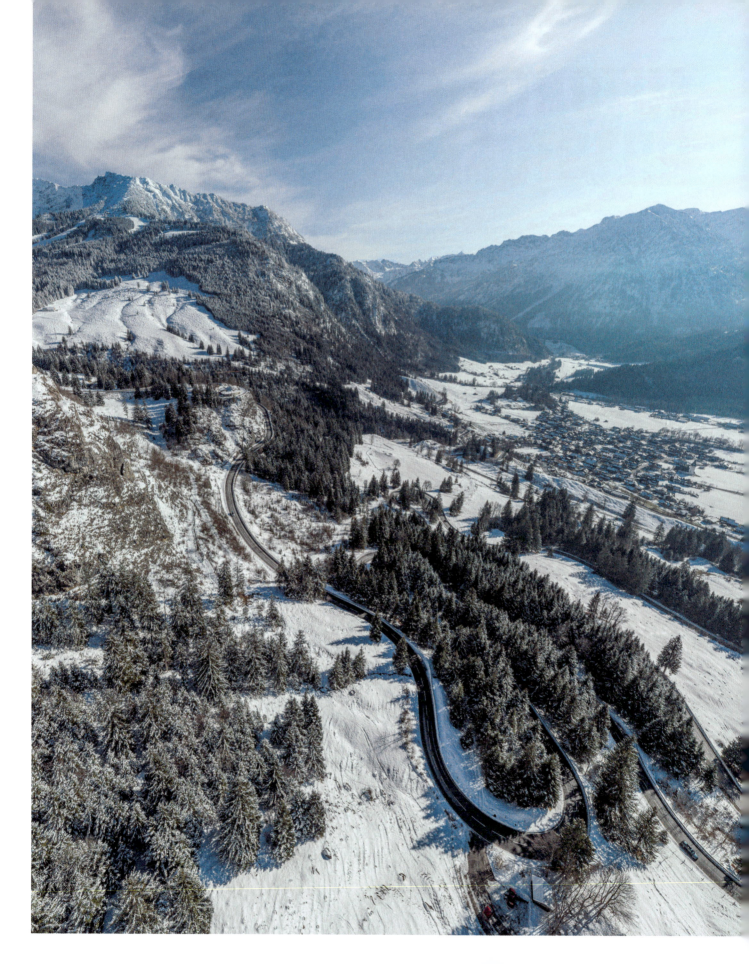

GERMAN ALPINE ROAD

START/END
Lindau/Berchtesgaden, Germany

DISTANCE
200 miles (330 km)

DURATION
5–7 days

ROAD CONDITIONS
Well-signposted routes but with plenty of twists and turns along the mountain passes.

THE BEST TIME TO GO
In spring, when wild flowers form a vibrant blanket over the mountain meadows.

OPPOSITE The twists and turns of the snowy Oberjoch Pass

This exhilarating Alpine road snakes a trail along Germany's southernmost tip. As well as encompassing historic marvels, the route passes swaths of unspoiled nature featuring idyllic mountain views that are hard to beat.

The German Alpine Road is the country's oldest touring route, first mentioned in a travel log by Bavarian King Maximilian II who traipsed along the path by horse and carriage in 1858. Today, the road is a lot more accessible and an ideal course to meander through and admire the Bavarian Alps. What's remarkable about the journey is the sheer variety of landscape: this historic passage skirts past dense forests, mountain meadows, craggy valleys, and towering peaks.

SWITCHING IT UP

This epic route starts in the village of Lindau on the northeastern shore of Lake Constance, where you'll begin your first climb into the Allgäu mountains via the Rohrach ascent. It's a route that rises 1,300 ft (400 m) across a sequence of seven hair-raising hairpin bends. If you need a break after all the excitement, make a quick stop to take in cascading Scheidegger Wasserfälle. Continue on to the town of Lindenberg, where you'll be treated to stunning panoramic views of the Allgäu and Vorarlberg mountains.

With Lindenberg in your rearview mirror, it's time for another winding switchback: the Oberjoch Pass. Swing through the curving corners and then past lush pastures with lazily grazing cows and the small town of Wertach in your sights. From here, it's farewell to the Allgäu region as you cross into Upper Bavaria, an area peppered with lavishly decorated Baroque churches. Stop often to admire these architectural marvels. Back on the road, it's time to cross the Ammer River—and in

LINDAU

LINDAU
On the banks of Lake Constance, this appealing town has a historic lighthouse.

0 MILES (0 KM)

SCHEIDEGGER WASSERFÄLLE
Take the short walk from the roadside stop to see this roaring waterfall.

65 MILES (104 KM)

ROAD TRIPS IN EUROPE

110 MILES (177 KM)

LINDERHOF PALACE
One of three ornate castles built by Bavarian King Ludwig II.

134 MILES (216 KM)

GARMISCH-PARTENKIRCHEN
Pull up a table at Gasthaus zur Schranne, which serves seasonal Bavarian cuisine.

spectacular fashion. In a route that comprises exhilarating switchbacks, it's only fair that the infrastructure matches such grand proportions—and the Echelsbach Bridge is no disappointment. Take a moment to observe the impressive arched construction that rises 250 ft (76 m) above the pine-tree-lined valley floor.

BAROQUE AND ROLL
On the other side of the suspended track is the idyllic mountain town of Oberammergau, which is filled with elaborately painted buildings. From here, a short but very worthwhile detour takes you to Linderhof Palace. Built in the 1870s, it was the smallest but most sumptuous residence belonging to the eccentric Bavarian King Ludwig II. Behind its ornate Baroque façade lies heavily ornamented interiors inspired by the Palace of Versailles. Linderhof's surrounding parkland is equally lavish in its landscaping, filled with neatly manicured beds, grand fountains, and colorful follies. Incidentally, the design-minded monarch conceived two further castles—Hohenschwangau and Neuschwanstein *(p99)*, of Disney fame.

Return to the road, and reality, and travel east to Garmisch-Partenkirchen. Here, you can enjoy sweeping views of the Wetterstein's jagged mountain

The lake's sapphire waters appear first. Walchensee is a true mountain oasis, where swimming, kayaking and windsurfing are commonplace.

peaks—and a plate of hearty Bavarian cuisine at typically Alpine Gasthaus zur Schranne.

Look out for chocolate-box villages, Krün and Wallgau, on your way to the watersports hub of Walchensee. As you round the corner, the lake's sapphire waters appear first. It's a true mountain oasis, where swimming, kayaking, and windsurfing are commonplace.

BELOW Oberammergau is known for its intricately painted houses

GERMAN ALPINE ROAD

LEFT Königssee, overlooked by the Berchtesgaden Alps

EXTEND YOUR TRIP

From Berchtesgaden, it's only a half-hour drive across the Austrian border to Salzburg, the birthplace of Mozart. This pint-sized city sits prettily on the banks of the Salzach River and is filled with impressive Baroque architecture.

Tear yourself away, if you can, as another lake—and the winding mountain passes to get there—is next. Snake past the waterside town of Gmund am Tegernsee, which is a great base for exploring the surrounding countryside. Continue along the scenic path, cutting through the rolling mountain landscapes until you reach Chiemsee. One of the region's largest, the lake is home to three islands, and its clean, crystalline waters make for an idyllic swimming spot.

RAISING THE SPA

After 35 miles (55 km), stop just short of the Austrian border in the lively spa town of Bad Reichenhall. For more than a century, it's been a hot spot for Alpine wellness, thanks to its saline springs. Some are still in operation and offer an invigorating dip. Also worth a trip is the town's historic cable car that has been transporting visitors up the adjoining Predigtstuhl mountain since 1928. The 5,000 ft (1,600-m) peak calls for rapt gazing across the Watzmann mountain range and is a nexus of hiking trails.

Descend into the valley, first by cable car and then by road, only to climb the Schwarzbachwacht Pass on the other side. You'll be rewarded with yet more spectacular mountain views. This time, you'll glimpse Austria's Berchtesgaden Alps in the distance, flanking the lakeside town of Berchtesgaden, the road's majestic end point. Cradled by steep mountain walls, and overlooking the emerald waters of serene Königssee, it's a hard view to beat in terms of picturesque positioning. The town is steeped in traditional Bavarian charm. There are onion-domed churches, wooden chalets with window boxes overflowing with bright blooms, and a cute cobblestone town square. After the twists and turns, steep climbs, and dizzying declines, it's a gentle—and welcome—end to the trip.

CHIEMSEE
You can visit the three islands of this crystalline lake by boat.

166 MILES (267 KM)

PREDIGTSTUHL
Board the 1920s cable car to scale this 5,000 ft (1,600 m) peak.

199 MILES (320 KM)

BERCHTESGADEN
This idyllic mountain town next to Königssee is filled with Bavarian architecture.

205 MILES (330 KM)

BERCHTESGADEN

END

HIGH PASSES OF THE SWISS ALPS

START/END
Lucerne/Locarno, Switzerland

DISTANCE
190 miles (300 km)

DURATION
1-2 days

ROAD CONDITIONS
Hairpin twists and turns that demand careful navigation.

THE BEST TIME TO GO
Summer is the perfect season to explore this route—the sun melts away the snow to reveal vibrant colors and stunning vistas.

OPPOSITE Hotel Belvédère on the Furka Pass, with Rhône Glacier in the distance

This route deserves a place in the road trip hall of fame—and not just because of its cinematic heritage. With twisting passes that round forested valleys, majestic peaks, glaciers, and lakes, it offers views worthy of the wide screen.

Switzerland's mountainous interior is features on many a drivers' bucket list. The Alpine region has close to 70 high-altitude passes, each with hair-raising switchbacks and scenery that will have you pulling up on the roadside more than once. And those attempting the thrilling corners and descents are in good company: the iconic Furka Pass saw Sean Connery's James Bond nip around the mountainsides in *Goldfinger*. Not just for daredevils, this route features views that are just as exhilarating as a high-speed car chase.

THE WILD MOUNTAINSIDE

Begin your journey in the city of Lucerne, where the lake's glittering waters stretch into the distance, flanked on either side by mountain peaks. It's an appropriate start to a road trip known for its striking scenery. Take a wander of the Swiss city, stopping by the well-preserved old town and the waterfront promenade. Sample a slice of Swiss cheese before ascending into the Emmental Alps and the UNESCO-protected natural reserve, Entlebuch Biosphere. Switzerland's largest Alpine moorland, the area is crisscrossed by small mountain streams and scattered with rugged rock formations. The roving Ibex goat can often be seen on the roadside, so passengers should keep their eyes peeled for the large, curving antlers of this Swiss native.

The jagged limestone ridges of the Schrattenfluh mountain lie ahead of you, signaling the true beginning of this Alpine affair. From here, pick up the

LUCERNE
START

ENTLEBUCH BIOSPHERE
Keep your eyes peeled for the curving antlers of the Ibex goat in this Alpine nature reserve.
19 MILES (30 KM)

SCHRATTENFLUH
The mountain's rocky ridges offer experienced hikers a thrilling 6-mile (10 km) route.
31 MILES (50 KM)

CHÄLRÜTIRANK VIEWING POINT
This is the best spot to glimpse this panoramic stretch of Alpine road.

54 MILES (87 KM)

MEIRINGEN
Visit the town's Sherlock Holmes Museum to converse with the detective (or, rather, his statue).

61 MILES (98 KM)

HOTEL HOF UND POST
Bed down for the night at this quaint, family-run hotel, which boasts views across the Alps.

65 MILES (104 KM)

Glaubenbielen Pass, a single-lane road that plunges through tree-lined meadows toward the small town of Giswil, a quaint hamlet sandwiched between the shores of Sarnersee and Lungernersee. Continue toward Lungern, tracing the eastern shore of Sarnersee to your right, with the Huetstock mountain peak on your left. On your way, you'll drive past the Chälrütirank viewing point, which offers spectacular views of the route you've just completed.

When the road begins to steepen, you've reached Brünig Pass. Construction of this high-altitude route began in 1857 in an effort to link Meiringen with Lungern. It's a particularly scenic stretch that runs a curving course through constantly shifting scenery with rocky gorges, storybook wooden chalets, and towering pine trees.

BETTER THAN FICTION
Brünig's end point is the pretty town of Meiringen, which is curiously filled with references to the famed fictional detective Sherlock Holmes. There's a statue and museum dedicated to Arthur Conan Doyle's character, who staged his own death at Reichenbachfälle, plunging into the thundering water in *The Final Problem*. In reality, it's a pretty cascade of seven streams, which is reached by a small, wooden funicular. The area makes a good place to stay the night, with traditional Swiss charm found at nearby Hotel Hof und Post.

Well rested and with a hearty Swiss breakfast fueling you on, follow the course of the Aare River along the Grimsel Pass, through a lush, forested valley flanked by high mountainsides. Just before you reach the small hamlet of Gletsch, a series of narrow hairpin bends snake their way down the mountain, with panoramic vistas across the verdant Goms valley.

From Gletsch, you'll join one of Switzerland's most legendary Alpine routes—the 45-mile (70 km) long Furka

EXTEND YOUR TRIP
From Locarno, it's a smooth journey along the A2 highway to Milan. The drive takes just under two hours and offers plenty of picturesque pit stops along the way, including Lake Como and the historic city of Lugano.

HIGH PASSES OF THE SWISS ALPS

167 MILES (268 KM)

LOCARNO: MADONNA DEL SASSO
This ocher-hued church is an important pilgrimage point in Switzerland.

LOCARNO: CARDADA CIMETTA
Catch the cable car to Locarno's mountaintop, a 7.5-mile (12-km) side trip out of town.

LOCARNO

Pass. This mountain road found fame in 1964, when James Bond film *Goldfinger* saw the suave spy eagerly pursue a villain in his Aston Martin BD5. Whether you're in a sports car or not, driving down this winding track is delightfully fun. Follow in 007's footsteps (or tire marks) and pull up at the Hotel Belvédère. Here, you'll be afforded a spectacular view of the Rhône Glacier.

CINEMATIC STEERING
Showbiz aside, this next stretch is as theatrical as it gets: Gotthard Pass, which connects the towns of Hospental and Airolo, is known as the "King of Mountain Passes." The 17-mile (28 km) long route features eight switchbacks, which snake a trail through the Lepontine Alps. When you reach Airolo, glide through the lush valley toward your final stop, Locarno. Set on the banks of Lake Maggiore, this Swiss town is the country's lowest altitude—which probably has something to do with its Mediterranean microclimate. Wander the colorful old town and visit the Madonna del Sasso church. An important pilgrimage site, it also has the best views across Locarno. Finish with a flurry atop the towering Cardada Cimetta mountain, reached via a modern cable car. You'll be rewarded with views across the very landscape you've just traversed.

RIGHT Inside the majestic Rhône Glacier

BELOW Gotthard Pass and its many switchbacks

OPPOSITE The Reichenbach Falls, reached by funicular

117

GRAND TOUR OF SWITZERLAND

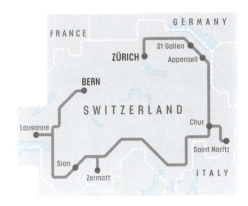

START/END
Zürich/Bern, Switzerland

DISTANCE
500 miles (804 km)

DURATION
2-3 weeks

ROAD CONDITIONS
A mix of smooth highway stretches and winding mountain passes.

THE BEST TIME TO GO
Wintertime, when Switzerland becomes a snow-dusted winter wonderland.

OPPOSITE Aare River, which cuts through Bern's old town

Majestic landscapes unfold at every turn on this tour of Switzerland's most impressive sights and cities. Heritage is proudly cherished here, so take your time to bask in the country's age-old traditions along the way.

It's hard to imagine a destination more densely packed with breathtaking scenery. Nearly two-thirds of the country is covered by mountains and a quarter by forests. That's not to mention the 1,500 lakes. This loop takes in the best that Switzerland has to offer, from towering Alpine peaks to picturesque medieval towns, glittering glaciers to sapphire lakes.

A SWISS SENSATION

Your journey begins in Switzerland's largest and liveliest city, Zürich, which sits on the shore of its namesake lake. Dotted along the shores are traditional open-air bathing clubs, called *Badi*. These swimming spots are a keen staple of local life, and a refreshing dip is a great way to kick off the trip. Once you've dried off, nip into the city's old town, where the cobblestone streets are dotted with small boutiques and cafés, and towered over by the majestic Grossmünster church.

Leaving the city, rooftops are replaced with the rolling hills of Zürich's wine country. Take your time on this stretch, where a patchwork of vine-peppered fields folds out across the landscape. After 53 miles (85 km) on the road, St. Gallen comes into view. The heart of this small city is filled with architectural marvels, such as a grand Baroque cathedral and an ancient Benedictine abbey, which is known for having one of the world's oldest and most beautiful libraries. Walk among the priceless texts, which are housed under frescoed ceilings and wood-paneled interiors.

ZÜRICH

START

ZÜRICH
Look out for the twin towers of the Grossmünster church, which soar above the city's old town.
0 MILES (0 KM)

ST. GALLEN
The abbey library in this small city dates from the 8th century and houses some 160,000 texts.
53 MILES (85 KM)

ROAD TRIPS IN EUROPE

APPENZELL
Explore this picturesque town famed for its colorfully painted houses.

63 MILES (102 KM)

CHUR
This ancient town is the setting-off point for the iconic *Bernina Express* train ride.

111 MILES (179 KM)

ST. MORITZ
Settled 3,000 years ago for its mineral waters, St. Moritz is now a glitzy resort town.

164 MILES (264 KM)

RIGHT St. Moritz in winter, when skiers descend on the town

BELOW The snowcapped Matterhorn mountain

Once you've perused the ancient tomes, graze on regional dishes at Zum Goldenen Schäfli, which is located in the last surviving guild house in town.

From the spoils of St. Gallen, its 10 miles (17 km) through bucolic landscapes filled with wooden farmhouses and lazily grazing cows to Appenzell. Park on the outskirts of this car-free town and take a stroll amid its fairy-tale charm. The central square, Landsgemeindeplatz, is a perfect place for a wander, where you can admire the colorful houses, complete with ornately carved gables.

ON THE RIGHT TRACK
From Appenzell, continue east to the Rhine Valley and follow the river south along Liechtenstein's border. Soon you'll come to Chur, the oldest town in Switzerland, with a settlement history that spans 13,000 years. It's also the starting point for the renowned *Bernina Express* train, which cuts a spectacular route from the Swiss Alps to Italy's Tirano. Keep driving—if you haven't ditched the car for the railroad—until you reach Thusis, where your ascent into the Alps begins. Head southwest to follow a series of winding mountain passes that snake their way upward to St. Moritz, a glitzy resort town that sits 6,000 ft (1,822 m) above sea level. It's been a much-loved destination for the global elite since 1864 and is positioned perfectly

on a beautiful aquamarine lake amid lofty mountain peaks.

From here, wind through the dense green countryside of the Rhône Valley toward Switzerland's most famous mountain, the Matterhorn. Perched beneath its shark-fin-shaped peak is the resort town of Zermatt, a chocolate-box center for skiing and mountaineering in the winter. Hop on the town's Matterhorn Glacier Paradise cable car to reach the Panoramic Platform, which sits at 12,500 ft (3,821 m) above sea level.

A farther 45 miles (75 km) away is Sion, located at the heart of another important wine-growing region. Here, nondrivers can sample a glass of Ferdant, the area's acclaimed white wine, at one of the lively bars. You'll spy not one but two hilltop castles looming over the town. Don't worry, it's not the booze making you see double, these are the medieval fortresses of Tourbillon and Valère. Ascend the steep hiking trail that leads up to their walls, and you'll be rewarded with panoramic views across the valley and snowy peaks beyond.

LET THE GAMES BEGIN
Follow the road from Sion as it veers ever closer to the shores of Lac Léman (Lake Geneva in English), where the route all but touches the watery edge. You'll pass the towns of Montreux and Vevey until, almost halfway around Lac Léman, Lausanne appears. The city cascades down terraced hillsides to the lakeshore, where manicured parks and elegant mansions reside. Aside from its historic charm, it boasts a thriving cultural scene in its Le Flon and Plateforme 10 arts districts. Lausanne is also home to the International Olympic Committee and has a museum dedicated to the games.

It's a sprint of some 60 miles (100 km) to the finish line where Bern, the capital, awaits. It's a warren of covered arcades and alleyways, wrapped within a loop of the Aare River. It seems right to finish this trip of striking scenery with an artistic flourish—and there's nowhere better than Bern's Museum of Fine Arts, one of Switzerland's most important galleries.

LEFT Bern's Zytglogge clock tower

WORDS ON THE STREET

Switzerland is a multilingual country with four official languages: German, spoken by the majority; French, primarily in the west; Italian, in the south; and Romansh, a minority language in certain eastern areas. As you move along this route, you'll notice how the languages shift according to which *canton* (region) you're in.

MATTERHORN GLACIER PARADISE
Spy 14 glaciers and 38 peaks from Zermatt's cable car.
328 MILES (528 KM)

LAUSANNE
This lakeside city has a thriving cultural scene and interesting Olympic heritage.
432 MILES (695 KM)

BERN
The city's Zytglogge clock tower marks the hour with a show by mechanical figures.
500 MILES (804 KM)

BERN
END

GROSSGLOCKNER HIGH ALPINE ROAD

START/END
Fusch an der Grossglocknerstrasse/ Heiligenblut am Grossglockner, Austria

DISTANCE
26 miles (42 km)

DURATION
1 day

ROAD CONDITIONS
Well maintained with lots of twists and turns.

THE BEST TIME TO GO
The road is open from May to November. In winter, the route becomes impassable due to heavy snowfall.

OPPOSITE The winding Fuscher Törl road, overlooked by the Glockner Group peaks

You *could* complete this route in under an hour, but to drive the high-altitude road without stopping would be to miss its very essence. Every turn packs a visual punch, with views across the Alps to Austria's Grossglockner mountain.

Renowned as one of Europe's finest mountain routes, Austria's Grossglockner High Alpine Road was built to impress. The course was constructed in the 1930s when car ownership was increasing and wealthy motorists wanted to take their new set of wheels for a scenic spin. It was designed to offer the best possible views of the Austrian Alps and weaves ribbon-like through the landscape. It's always been a toll road and costs €43 (around $46) to drive the course for the day—but it's worth every cent.

TAKING THE HIGH ROAD

The route takes its name from Austria's tallest mountain, the glacier-topped Grossglockner that towers to your right as you begin your journey. The road leads through a variety of impressive natural landscapes, passing dense woodland and running through lush Alpine pastures and along rugged mountainsides. There are plenty of breathtaking viewpoints on the way, all equipped with information boards that detail the scenery. They're also fitted with picnic benches, where you can pause for a bite to eat. The High Road doesn't just offer stunning scenery—it's a thrilling drive, too, featuring no less than 36 narrow hairpin bends.

Set off from the village of Fusch an der Grossglocknerstrasse, where the road leads south along a narrow, pine-forested mountain valley. After roughly 10 minutes, you'll arrive at the Grosses Wiesbachhorn viewpoint, in Hohe Tauern, Austria's largest national park, which has been UNESCO-protected

FUSCH AN DER GROSSGLOCKNERSTRASSE

FUSCH AN DER GROSSGLOCKNERSTRASSE
This village is surrounded by lush meadows and hiking trails.
0 MILES (0 KM)

HOHE TAUERN NATIONAL PARK
This protected area is home to a variety of species, from bearded vultures to chamois.

WALCHER WASSERFALL
Austria's highest waterfall can be reached via a gentle hike from the Grossglockner road.

5 MILES (8 KM)

FERLEITEN
Fuel up on the Austrian classic *Kaiserschmarren*, shredded pancake with apple, in Ferleiten.

5 MILES (8 KM)

HAUS ALPINE NATURSCHAU
This museum showcases the rich biodiversity of the Hohe Tauern National Park.

12 MILES (19 KM)

since 1992. Stop to take in a particularly stunning view of the surrounding peaks. The Grosses Wiesbachhorn viewpoint is also a great place to stretch your legs. A hiking route—just one of the many that branch off from the road—leads up from here to a series of plunging waterfalls, which cascade dramatically down the steep mountainsides. The most mesmerizing of all is the Walcher Wasserfall. Back at the foot of the trail in Ferleiten, the Tauernhaus inn makes for a good lunch spot, serving hearty Austrian dishes in a cozy interior.

AT ONE WITH NATURE
As you continue on the Alpine road, you'll pass through lush meadows that, come spring, fill with wildflowers. Delicate purple bell flowers, snow-white Alpine marguerites, and dark red nigritella create a stunning technicolor array that adds a vibrant touch to the landscape. But it's not just plant life that drivers should look out for—the Hohe Tauern National Park is among the most species-rich habitats in the Alps. Along with the occasional swooping golden eagle and scurrying marmots, you might also spot an ibex—a long-horned species of goat known as the "King of the Alps." You can learn more about the region's bountiful varieties of flora and fauna at the Haus Alpine Naturschau. This small museum at the foot of the Hochmais mountain is dedicated to the complex ecology of the Hohe Tauern National Park, exploring the region's rich biodiversity and the survival strategies that have been developed by the animals living in these extreme conditions.

With the Hochmais mountain on your right, you'll reach the beginning of a staggeringly steep ascent. The short dead-end road isn't technically part of the Grossglockner High Alpine route—but it would be a shame to miss this dramatic, but thrilling, climb. Branch off from the main road to take the Edelweissstraße, which gains 575 ft

THE PASTERZE PEAK
Just before you reach the journey's end point in Heiligenblut, a side road leads westward toward the Kaiser-Franz-Josefs-Höhe viewpoint. It's named after Emperor Franz-Josef, who is known to have hiked the route in 1856. Expect breathtaking views over the Pasterze Glacier—the biggest in the Eastern Alps—from the glass-domed visitor center.

GROSSGLOCKNER HIGH ALPINE ROAD

14 MILES (22 KM)

EDELWEISSSPITZE
The road's highest drivable point soars 8,435 ft (2,571 m) above sea level.

15 MILES (24 KM)

MITTERTÖRLTUNNEL
This underpass was built in 1934 and runs directly through the mountain.

END

HEILIGENBLUT AM GROSSGLOCKNER

(175 m) in elevation during the 1-mile (1.7 km) track. But it's all worth it as the epic Edelweissspitze summit, the highest drivable point of the route, greets you at the top. Here, sprawling views reach out across 30 mountain peaks and 19 glaciers. There's also a restaurant, the Edelweißhütte, where you can sit out on the terrace and enjoy a warming plate of apple strudel.

SLOW AND SCENIC

Full up on pastries, start the dizzying decent to the main road and continue on the sweeping Fuscher Törl road, passing Fuscher Lacke to Mittertörltunnel, a 380 ft (117 m) long underpass. It may look like an ordinary tunnel from one end, but as you emerge on the other side, you will be rewarded with an unbelievable view of the peaks beyond. From here, the snaking road drops into Heiligenblut am Grossglockner, an idyllic town nestled within a lush mountain valley. Filled with pretty wooden chalets and crowned by the elegant spire of the St. Vincent Pilgrimage Church, it transforms into a ski resort in winter. But the sightseeing trip isn't over yet. There's more to do here—this time on foot. Heiligenblut is home to plenty of walking trails and climbing routes. So, don your hiking boots and set off into the peaceful mountainside.

RIGHT Mittertörltunnel cutting a line through the Alps

BELOW St. Vincent Pilgrimage Church in Heiligenblut town

OPPOSITE A herd of Ibex in the Hohe Tauern National Park

BAROQUE TRAIL

START/END
Vienna, Austria/Prague, Czech Republic

DISTANCE
515 miles (830 km)

DURATION
6-8 days

ROAD CONDITIONS
Expect smooth sailing along easily navigable highways.

THE BEST TIME TO GO
Each season adds its own charm to the route, but the winter months offer plenty of Christmas markets to visit.

OPPOSITE Prague, in all its Baroque beauty

Delve into all that the former Austro-Hungarian Empire has to offer in this epic cross-country trek, which cuts a route through chocolate-box mountain villages, cultural hubs, glistening glacial lakes, and mountain peaks.

This mammoth 500-mile (800 km) road trip runs through a sliver of central Europe that's densely packed with Baroque wonders, which were built between the early 17th and mid-18th century. This route traverses picturesque Austrian centers and weaves into today's Czech Republic. You'll also visit elaborately decorated churches and monasteries along the way.

PICTURE PERFECT

Austria was widely seen as the center for the Baroque movement, and its capital, Vienna, is bedecked with architectural treasures from the era. The city's grand Belvedere Palace is the best place to kick off this resplendent tour. Set among vast Palace of Versailles-style gardens, the sumptuous site—now a museum—is an elegant spot to wander, with opulent frescoed halls home to artworks by the likes of Klimt, Schiele, and Kokoschka. A stroll through the streets, however, will reveal that this gilded city's design goes beyond the Baroque. Stop by Vienna's gargantuan Gothic cathedral, Stephansdom, and neo-Renaissance Staatsoper, before visiting the impressive Museum Quarter.

Say goodbye to Vienna and all its grandeur, and steer toward the Danube River. The road will lead you out into a lush valley and whiz past vine-dotted hills, forested slopes, and traditional Austrian villages. You'll pass the pretty town of Krems an der Donau, which is home to the contemporary art museum, Landesgalerie NÖ, as well as the medieval village of Dürnstein.

VIENNA
START

VIENNA
As well as architectural gems, this city also boasts the world's largest Museum Quarter.

0 MILES (0 KM)

KREMS AN DER DONAU
This traditional village is home to the futuristic Landesgalerie NÖ art museum.

49 MILES (78 KM)

Travel for 23 miles (37 km) to Melk, a town best known for its vast Baroque abbey. From its elevated position on an adjoining hillside, the vivid yellow monastery overlooks the pretty town. Head up the hill for a guided tour of the building and its extravagant Rococo interiors—it's a riot of cherubs, marble, and ornate stucco.

CREATIVE PEAKS

The road continues its gently curving course along the Danube, through the vineyard-blanketed valley to Linz. Austria's third-largest city isn't short on historic charm, but it also prides itself on being a center for contemporary culture. Experience this firsthand at the Ars Electronica Center, where you'll find interactive exhibitions on technology and innovation. At Lentos, one of the country's most important modern art museums, shows from the Austrian avant-garde are held alongside exhibitions by global names, all within a striking glass-and-steel building on the river banks.

The glittering cultural powerhouse of Linz may be behind you, but there's plenty more to discover on the route ahead. The road descends into the scenic Salzkammergut region. The area is particularly popular with hikers, thanks to its postcard-

ABOVE Extravagant Baroque interiors in Melk Abbey

LEFT The Danube Valley, home to vineyards and charming Austrian villages

OPPOSITE The picturesque, lakeside town of Hallstatt

MELK
Explore the town's gilded UNESCO-listed Baroque abbey, which sits high on the hillsides.

72 MILES (115 KM)

LINZ
This city is a dynamic metropolis. Highlights include Lentos and Ars Electronica Center.

146 MILES (235 KM)

193 MILES (311 KM)

SCHLOSS ORT
Stop at the castle's restaurant, which serves delicious local dishes like smoked fish.

224 MILES (360 KM)

HALLSTATT
This pretty lakeside town is a UNESCO World Heritage Site.

DESIGN HISTORY

Baroque originated in early 17th-century Italy and was characterized by dramatic, detailed, and exuberant art and architecture. The style spread across Europe, driven by the Catholic Church's Counter-Reformation efforts, and many of the most extraordinary buildings of the Late Baroque period were constructed in Austria and the Czech Republic to glorify the ruling Habsburg monarchy.

perfect mountainous terrain, which is crisscrossed by a network of 200 miles (340 km) of footpaths. Choose your route, and stretch those legs.

Once you're back on the road, limbs sufficiently exercised, head toward Gmunden am Traunsee. This charming town enjoys an idyllic position at the foot of the Traunsee lake and was the go-to resort for the Viennese aristocracy in the 19th century—which explains the lavish villas that line the shore. Meander along the scenic lakefront promenade to reach Schloss Ort, a pretty medieval castle. It's set on a small island that's connected to the mainland via a wooden bridge and houses a museum and restaurant.

BATHS TO BALLROOMS

Trace the western shore of the lake past Altmünster and Traunkirchen, taking in spectacular views of the emerald waters and snow-tipped peaks of the Dachstein mountains. You'll eventually hit Bad Ischl, a spa town that was once frequented by Emperor Franz Joseph I. The plethora of grand hotels, coffee houses, casinos, and promenades are a reminder of its gilded past—it was a 19th-century playground for the Austrian bourgeoisie who came to bathe in the saline, iodine, and sulfur springs here. There are still thermal baths in the town where visitors indulge in this ancient wellness ritual.

Drive south along the Traun River until you reach the crystalline waters of the Hallstätter See. Cruise along the lake's forest-lined western shore to get to Hallstatt, another fairy-tale town surrounded by steep mountainsides. The UNESCO-listed town is a maze of small cottages, half-timbered houses, and winding streets. For unbeatable views of the town and surrounding lake, jump on one of the funicular's orange railroad cabins to the nail-bitingly high, cantilevered Skywalk observation deck.

Continue your course west from Hallstatt along the Gschütt Pass, cutting through dense pine forests and picturesque wooden chalets toward Salzburg. Best known as composer Mozart's hometown, the city has a long-held reputation as Austria's cultural cradle and there are still plenty of lavishly ornamented concert halls

SALZBURG
Mozart's hometown boasts an immaculately preserved old town on the Salzach River.

277 MILES (446 KM)

ČESKÉ BUDĚJOVICE
Crane your neck to spot the four statues atop the Czech city's town hall.

419 MILES (674 KM)

STATE CHAPEL OF HLUBOKÁ
Take a stroll through the immaculate gardens of this wedding-cake-style chateau.

425 MILES (684 KM)

where visitors can catch classical performances today.

Salzburg's old town is a sight to behold—it perches on the pine-studded banks of the turquoise river Salzach, overlooked by an ancient hilltop fortress and with a swooping mountain backdrop. Standouts from its trove of Baroque treasures include Salzburg Cathedral, with its opulent marble façade, and the heavily frescoed palace named the Alte Residenz, yet another breathtaking example of Austria's gilded splendor, and the last of this trip. Retrace your steps toward Linz, passing lakes Mondsee and Attersee along the way. Both offer well-earned pit stops—their banks are dotted with various public bathing areas with wooden jetties where you can leap into the refreshing waters. Continue past Linz, toward the fortified town of Freistadt. From here, it's only a 10-mile (20 km) drive to the Czech border. *Auf wiedersehen* Austria, it's time to venture north.

CZECHING IN
When your cross the border, head toward České Budějovice, the capital city of the Southern Bohemia Region. In town, make a beeline for the impressive central square, lined with 48 elegant Baroque and Renaissance townhouses and a monumental, blue-fronted town hall. If you're feeling peckish, try regional dishes at Grand Hotel Zvon—it's said to serve the best goulash in the city.

Nip 6 miles (10 km) north to one of the Czech Republic's most significant landmarks: the State Chateau of Hluboká. It's an imposing structure, comprised of chunky towers, lined with thick battlements, and surrounded by manicured gardens. The exterior gives way to immaculate interiors of intricate woodwork, Swiss stained-glass windows, and delicately painted ceilings.

The road north weaves through sprawling plains of farmland studded with pretty villages featuring white-

EXTEND YOUR TRIP
For more Baroque extravagance in the Czech Republic, continue east from Prague for 170 miles (280 km) to the city of Olomouc, which is awash with extraordinary Baroque buildings. Highlights include the ornate Fountains of Olomouc, the city's dramatic cathedral and the Holy Trinity Column.

BAROQUE TRAIL

506 MILES (815 KM)

PARK PRŮHONICE
This UNESCO-listed park is home to more than 8,000 rhododendrons.

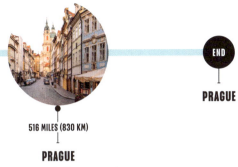

516 MILES (830 KM)

PRAGUE
The Czech capital is a romantic treasure trove of millennia-spanning wonders.

END

PRAGUE

washed, onion-domed churches. Detour to Tabor or Soběslav, to see these typically Southern Bohemian settlements.

TOWER POWER
As the engine roars to life once more, it marks the start of your last leg: the home straight to Prague. Thirty miles (50 km) shy of the Czech capital is the magical Konopiště Castle. The former residence of Archduke Franz Ferdinand is a three-story fusion of medieval and Renaissance architecture with a Baroque palace built on top. Wander freely in the manicured gardens, or join a guided tour to glimpse lavish chandeliers, ornate stucc work, and colorful ceilings inside.

As you drive onward, make a quick detour to Park Průhonice, a densely wooded stretch filled with ponds, streams, and an array of native and exotic trees. It's a final 9 miles (15 km) to the Czech capital from here. On entering the old town, it's instantly clear where Prague's "City of 100 Spires" moniker comes from. At every turn, there's a new architectural marvel to discover, from the statue-lined Charles Bridge to the St. Vitus Cathedral with its soaring towers and intricately carved Gothic façade. Prague is an impressive end point. With more than 500 miles (800 km) under your belt, you've earned a cold beer. Luckily, Prague serves some of the best.

RIGHT The State Chateau of Hluboká's inner courtyard

BELOW Pedestrians crossing Prague's Charles Bridge

OPPOSITE Salzburg's atmospheric old town

131

THE ITALIAN LAKES

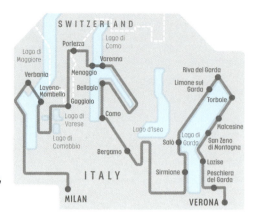

START/END
Verona/Milan, Italy

DISTANCE
363 miles (584 km)

DURATION
7–10 days

ROAD CONDITIONS
Well-maintained paved roads; some are narrow and get congested at busy times.

THE BEST TIME TO GO
Visit in late spring or early fall, to avoid the summer crowds.

OPPOSITE Mountain peaks looming over colorful houses on Lago di Garda's Malcesine

Loop around the lakes of Northern Italy, following shore-hugging roads from one charming village to the next. Each lake has a distinct personality, from outdoorsy Garda and glitzy Como to serene, island-scattered Maggiore.

Lombardy's great lakes are achingly picturesque. Carved by glaciers, their glittering waters and idyllic shoreside villages have been enticing tourists since the 18th century. You could spend a month cruising through this stunning region, but a week is long enough to hit the highlights. Drive the whole of this loop, which takes in lakes Garda, Como, and Maggiore, or alternatively just a section—for now. You'll want to stop often to take in the views, which are nothing short of spectacular.

THE GRANDEUR OF GARDA

The route kicks off with a bang, skirting the shores of Italy's largest (and arguably most beautiful) lake, Lago di Garda. Though perennially popular (it has attracted the likes of Dante and Winston Churchill), it is also spacious, with several quiet spots to be found. Drivers will discover an ensemble of picturesque villages, sandy beaches, and beautiful lakeside villas as they wend their way around the deep blue waters.

Start in the historic (and eternally fair) Verona, and head west for 20 miles (30 km) counter clockwise around the lake. Take your time traversing the narrow roads, though—the turns can be tricky and cyclists can appear out of the blue. Soon, Peschiera del Garda, on the lake's southern tip, appears. The UNESCO-listed town was built on Roman ruins and makes for a beautiful stop. Walk along ancient canals and over stone bridges in the old town. There are shops and museums, as well as trattorias, such as L'Osteria, serving fresh local fare.

VERONA
START

PESCHIERA DEL GARDA: MARKET
Browse this family-friendly town's bustling market, held every Monday.
19 MILES (30 KM)

PESCHIERA DEL GARDA: L'OSTERIA
Sample sardines fresh from the lake at this friendly *trattoria*.
19 MILES (30 KM)

24 MILES (38KM)

LAZISE
Lazise is dotted with beautiful beaches; Spiaggia La Quercia is one of its most picturesque.

53 MILES (85 KM)

MALCESINE
Visit the castle for views across the lake. The town is also home to a natural history museum.

109 MILES (175 KM)

SIRMIONE
Visit Roman ruins in this stunningly located peninsula town.

Continue cruising north, along Garda's shores, passing Lazise, with its sandy, pine-shaded Spiaggia La Quercia beach, and the towns of Bardolino and Torri del Benaco. From here, the road steepens as it funnels you up into the hills of San Zeno di Montagna. The tranquil chestnut-growing village is known as the "balcony overlooking the lake," thanks to its lofty location at 2,230 ft (680 m) above sea level. This hilly area is great for hiking, biking, and climbing in the warmer months and skiing in the winter. Slurp up a bowl of humble chestnut soup before catching the Costabella cable car in nearby Prada for breathtaking mountain views.

Descend from the hills and rejoin the coastal SR249 for 12 miles (20 km) in search of Malcesine, where the streets are lined with terracotta-roofed houses. Its crowning glory, though, is the ancient castle that perches above the town. In summer, the castle is transformed into an open-air theater.

STARS IN THE NORTH
On Garda's northern shores lie the towns of Torbole and Riva del Garda, where the Dolomite mountains propel strong gusts of wind onto the water, making it a super spot for windsurfing and sailing. As you turn onto the western lakeshore, the SS240 takes you through tunnels, past the tumbling Sopino Waterfall and the Ciclopista del Garda pathway that overhangs the lake's rugged cliffs. Pause in Limone sul Garda, a colorful jumble of cobbled streets set beneath spectacular limestone cliffs.

It's now time for one of the most exhilarating roads of the entire trip: drive toward the hilltop hamlet of Vesio where—after a scoop of ice cream at Gelateria Qciari—the SP38, with its hair-raising hairpins, begins. Take your time negotiating the tight turns back down to shore and the bayside town of Salò.

Sirmione, your final stop on Garda, is the lake's most celebrated village, with a delightful castle and waterfront

ABOVE The Ciclopista del Garda pathway

BELOW Cyprus trees lining a scenic road on Garda's shore

THE ITALIAN LAKES

LEFT Bellagio town, on the shores of Lago di Como

blue-tinged mountains in the distance. Start your visit in the city of Como, which is known for its Gothic cathedral—and for its silk. The Museo Didattico della Seta unpicks the textile's production, but to buy silk, head to the historic Mantero Seta factory on the city's outskirts.

From Como, follow the breathtaking SP583 along the shore of the Larian Triangle, which separates the lake's southern branches. Bellagio, at the triangle's tip, is Como's crowning glory. Much visited but still enchanting, it has a collection of coral-pink and sand-colored houses with ornate cast-iron balconies. Stepped side streets, such as Salita Serbelloni, connect the upper and lower parts of town and are lined with restaurants, shops, and galleries.

Tear yourself away from this idyllic spot, if you can, and steer along the shore to Lago di Lecco, Como's southeastern branch. Continue on to Varenna, where you can board a car ferry to the relaxed town of Menaggio on the other side, and from here travel on west to Porlezza to visit another Lombardy lake—Lago di Lugano, on the Swiss border. Drive

EXTEND YOUR TRIP

Serene Lake Orta sits west of Maggiore and is surrounded by forests and Alpine foothills. The scenic SP43A hugs its shore, visiting the charming village of Orta San Giulio. Take a ferry to romantic Isola di San Giulio, splurge on Michelin-starred cuisine at Villa Crespi, or simply relax in the sunny piazza.

restaurants, perched at the end of a slender peninsula.

GRACEFUL ISEO AND GLAMOROUS COMO

Leave the glamour of Garda behind and head west to discover the low-key Lago d'Iseo. This gorgeous spot, flanked by mountains and pretty towns, is a smaller, more serene affair and is home to the SS469, one of the region's loveliest roads.

Continue via Bergamo to Lago di Como, the region's most exclusive destination. Coveted by the jet-set, this lake is generously sprinkled with romantic restaurants, ostentatious villas, and palatial hotels, and activities include waterskiing, seaplane excursions, and luxury speedboat tours, all with

COMO
Visit the imposing cathedral in Como's center, which was built over three centuries.

199 MILES (320 KM)

BELLAGIO: SALITA SERBELLONI
Stepped streets wind down to the lakeside in this lovely town; Salita Serbelloni is the prettiest.

217 MILES (349 KM)

BELLAGIO: VILLA MELZI
The gardens at this waterfront villa are dotted with Neo-Classical sculptures.

218 MILES (351 KM)

135

237 MILES (382 KM)

VILLA FOGAZZARO ROI
Step back in time at the Villa Fogazzaro Roi, the summer residence of an Italian author.

308 MILES (495 KM)

VILLA TARANTO
Visit this elegant *palazzo*'s botanical gardens from spring to fall to see the blooms.

END

MILAN

TREASURE ISLANDS

Maggiore's Borromean Islands comprise of four unique islands: Isola Bella, with its 17th-century Palazzo Borromeo, Isola dei Pescatori, Isola Madre, and Isolino di San Giovanni.

ABOVE Isola Bella on Lago di Maggiore

past Porlezza to Villa Fogazzaro Roi art museum, housed in the lakeside home of author Antonio Fogazzaro.

GILDED RETREATS AND QUIET SHORES

From Villa Fogazzaro, trace Lugano's coastline and cross into Switzerland momentarily before reentering Italy in Gaggiolo. It's a 20-mile (40-km) route through bucolic countryside to Lago di Maggiore. On the way, you will pass a trio of smaller lakes—Varese, Comabbio, and Monate. They each have their unique draws, though all are ringed by meadows, woods, and trails. Varese is favored by hikers and bikers, while Monate boasts the beautiful Monate beach and *spiaggia* (sunbathing and swimming spot). At Lago di Comabbio, you'll find a bit of peace and quiet.

The first town on Lago di Maggiore's shores is the ceramic-producing Laveno-Mombello. It is also home to an amusingly tiny open-air cable car—not advisable for those with a fear of heights—that ascends the Monte Sasso del Ferro and offers spectacular views.

From Laveno-Mombello, take a car ferry to Verbania. Green-fingered travelers should stop at Villa Taranto's botanical garden, before continuing south to Stresa, where palatial villas abound. To explore one of the most impressive, hop on a boat to Isola Bella, the closest of the lake's Borromean Islands, where gilded Palazzo Borromeo awaits. The museum displays priceless art, but it's worth a visit simply to wander the corridors and learn of its regal past: it has hosted Prince Charles and Princess Diana, as well as literary heavyweights including Ernest Hemingway.

It's an appropriately glamorous end to your tour of Italy's great lakes. To bid farewell to Maggiore, return to the mainland and drive south along the water. Hug the coast for as long as you can before tearing yourself away and onto the road in search of another Italian gem—Milan. Wearing silk from Como, you're primed and ready to visit the fashion capital of the world.

LIFE IN THE FAST LANE

No matter where we're going, the human urge is to get there faster. And to sate our need for speed, we've gone to great lengths to design faster vehicles. But that's only half the story. The roads that vehicles travel on are just as important.

Efforts to improve infrastructure started well before automobiles appeared, back when horsepower was measured in actual horses. In 17th-century Britain, roads were rough at best. Their upkeep fell to local governments, which forced residents to do maintenance. As trade grew, the system became untenable. In 1663, officials persuaded Parliament to establish a turnpike on a section of the Great North Road, which linked London with York. Turnpikes were implemented on more than 11,200 miles (18,000 km) over the ensuing century. The funds they raised improved roads and travel times but also boosted economies and encouraged urbanization.

Despite this, it wasn't until 1924 that the modern highway was born when Piero Puricelli's *Autostrada dei Laghi* was completed. Designed when there were just 41,000 cars in Italy, the world's first highway took travelers from the outskirts of Milan to the Italian Lakes. Puricelli was the first to drive the 26.5-mile (42.6-km) *Autostrada*. He was behind the wheel of a Lancia Trikappa, with King Victor Emmanuel III riding shotgun.

Shadows always seem to lurk in this period, though. The *Autostrada* was built under Mussolini's rule, which in turn inspired the Nazis' development of the *Reichsautobahn*. While the Weimar Republic built its first stretch, Hitler greatly expanded it. By 1942, the Nazis had completed some 2,360 miles (3,800 km), creating what was essentially the world's first national expressway.

There's some satisfaction, however, in knowing that later German engineers accomplished far more than the Nazis ever did. Today, the *Bundesautobahn* covers well over 7,200 miles (12,000 km), making it one of the largest national systems in the world. It's also, famously, the closest we've come to satisfying that universal urge to go faster. Although some stretches do, in fact, have speed limits, most of the *Autobahn* does not, leaving you limited only by your car's capabilities...and your own nerves.

ABOVE Germany's fast-moving *Bundesautobahn*

> **Efforts to improve infrastructure started well before automobiles appeared, back when horsepower was measured in actual horses.**

STELVIO PASS

START/END
Prad am Stilfser Joch/ Bormio, Italy

DISTANCE
47 miles (75 km)

DURATION
2–3 hours

ROAD CONDITIONS
Steep and twisting paved roads, which are narrow at times.

THE BEST TIME TO GO
The road is open from May to October, closing for the winter months.

OPPOSITE Switchback turns on the dramatic Stelvio Pass

Famous for its hairpin bends, this twisting mountain road—the highest in the Eastern Alps, and the second-highest drivable route in the entire Alps—offers a thrilling driving experience amid stunning Alpine scenery.

To be immersed in the South Tyrol's Stelvio National Park and Ortler Alps, amid fragrant pines and snowy peaks, is astonishing. But it's the twisting paths that really take your breath away. Regularly dubbed the "Greatest Driving Road in the World," Northern Italy's mighty Strada Statale 38 (known as the Stelvio Pass road, or *Stilfser Joch*) swoops over the mountains near the Italian-Swiss border and features a dizzying sequence of 48 hairpin bends. This is a one-of-a-kind, high-altitude challenge. You can tackle this road in anything from a Vespa or a classic Fiat 500 to a growling and brilliant-red Ferrari, but confidence and technical skill are essential.

FOREST ADVENTURE

The most satisfying direction to drive is northeast to southwest, starting in the German-speaking village of Prad am Stilfser Joch. It's on the edge of Stelvio National Park, where a swath of forests and meadows are dotted with primroses and glacier buttercups. You might glimpse mountain peaks, and the marmots and ibexes that roam them, through the dense trees. Keep your eyes on the road, though, as it's perilously narrow and you may have to dodge lycra-clad cyclists, careering camper vans and even buses on the way.

Soon, you'll round Bend 48, the first of the northeastern hairpins—numbered so you can tally your progress to the road's highest point. The small ski resort of Trafoi, halfway between Prad and the summit in altitude, offers striking views of Ortler, the highest mountain for miles.

PRAD AM STILFSER JOCH — START

STELVIO NATIONAL PARK
The mountain peaks are home to golden eagles, bearded vultures, and ptarmigans.
4 MILES (7 KM)

ORTLER
At 12,800 ft (3,905 m), Ortler is the highest peak in Italy.
12 MILES (20 KM)

24 MILES (38 KM)

TRAFOI
This town's family-run Hotel Bella Vista is a luxury pit stop on the pass.

33 MILES (53 KM)

TIBET-HÜTTE
This is the spot to snap classic photos of the Stelvio Pass hairpin bends.

As you ascend farther into the national park, the trees begin to thin out and the mountain views grow ever more spectacular.

Hotel Bella Vista in Trafoi was the starting point for car races in the 1930s—and makes for a relaxing base today. Weisser Knott, meanwhile, is an excellent spot to sample South Tyrolean cuisine.

As you ascend further into the national park, the trees begin to thin out and the mountain views grow ever more spectacular. Bend 32 marks the start of a rapid strand of hairpin turns that send the road above the tree line into austerely beautiful scenery. A wall separates you from the sheer drops at the road's edge. Four miles (6 km) on and you'll reach the summit in Stilfser Joch, where you'll also find Passo del Stelvio, Italy's only true summer ski resort. Among the town's restaurants and shops, there's a small historical exhibition at Banca Popolare di Sondrio, Europe's highest bank.

TRACES OF THE PAST
Conceived by Emperor Francis I of Austria as a strategic military route, Stelvio Pass was designed by expert mountain-road builder Carlo Donegani. After three years of construction involving more than 2,500 workers, engineers, and geologists, it opened in 1825. Close to the border with Switzerland and just below the Stelvio Pass lies the

19th-century Casa Cantoniera dello Stelvio IV, one of four roadhouses built during the road's construction. The site provided food and shelter for the *rotteri*, the maintenance men who kept the pass clear of snow using plows pulled by hardy horses or mules. The *rotteri* kept the Austrian Empire connected. Even today, the fastest overland route from Vienna to Milan, taking 12 hours or so, is via the Stelvio Pass.

You'll find this southern section of the road less dramatic than the north, but it's easier to drive, with open stretches running through picturesque valleys. The history of the road, though, remains close at hand. A World War I memorial arch and military chapel near the Casa Cantoniera dello Stelvio IV dates from the time when the Stelvio Pass and the Ortler Alps were part of the Italian front. Italy's First Army were positioned here, and Austro-Hungarian forces dug the highest trenches in history on Ortler itself. War relics can still be found on the mountain range today.

BATHTIME IN BORMIO
The road's southwestern hairpins whisk you downhill through yet more awe-inspiring mountain scenery. Make the most of the turnouts to stop and absorb the views—there's a beautiful viewpoint in Spondalunga, next to the Alpenhaus Bar Kiosk Nazionalpark.

Beyond, there's a flurry of tunnels and a few more hairpin bends to conquer before you reach Thermalbad Bormio (Bagni di Bormio), an Alpine spa where you can unwind from the rigors of the road in thermally heated outdoor pools. Your epic drive ends, after a final 3 miles (5 km), in Bormio, an elegant town that has attracted tourists for centuries, thanks to its thermal waters. Stay to explore the historic center and invigorating hiking trails, and enjoy a steaming plate of *pizzocheri* at Vecchia Combo.

ABOVE Bathing in a thermal pool in Bagni di Bormio

OPPOSITE TOP Views from the road include some classic South Tyrolean scenery

OPPOSITE BOTTOM Restaurant Tibet-Hütte in the summit village, Stilfser Joch

CASE CANTONIERA DELLO STELVIO
Look out for the route's four *rotteri* roadhouses.
36 MILES (56 KM)

OSSUARY STELVIO
This arch commemorates the Italian soldiers who lost their lives on the pass in World War I.
37 MILES (60 KM)

BORMIO
Finish the drive with a portion of *pizzocheri* (short noodles) at Vecchia Combo.
47 MILES (75 KM)

BORMIO
END

TUSCAN HILL TOWNS

START/END
Florence, Italy

DISTANCE
305 miles (492 km)

DURATION
5-6 days

ROAD CONDITIONS
Well-maintained paved roads.

THE BEST TIME TO GO
April to May, when the landscape is most vibrant, or August to October, when food festival season hits.

OPPOSITE A misty morning in hilltop Pienza, in Val d'Orcia

Tuscany is one of Italy's most visited regions—and for good reason. Known as the "Cradle of the Renaissance," it features medieval villages, excellent cultural institutions, and a local cuisine that tops the country's gastronomic list.

Tuscany's rolling hills, and the honey-hued towns that lie within them, have become synonymous with the Italian countryside. And a route that cuts across the landscape, driving along winding cypress-tree-lined roads, is up there with the very best. Those who tap into Tuscany's slow, languorous way of life will reap the greatest rewards. So take your time as you wander ancient stone settlements and savor local delicacies—and stop everything to watch the golden sun dip below the horizon.

EXPLORING CASENTINO
The best place to start this circular Tuscan tour is in the utterly enchanting regional capital of Florence, or Firenze. There are plenty of spectacular sights to explore among the atmospheric streets, but, for now, sip an espresso and then sink into the driver's seat. You'll be back to see the sights later.

Leaving Florence, the city rooftops transform into a patchwork of vineyards and wineries, and then the beautiful forests and rolling hillsides of Casentino. But it's not just beautiful swaths of countryside this route has to offer—look into the hills and you'll spot gleaming, fairy-tale towns dotting the horizon. One such settlement is pretty Poppi, with its crowning glory, the Castello dei Conti Guidi, rising majestically above the town. The bell tower was built in the 13th century, and it rewards its visitors with far-reaching views. There are impressive frescoes inside, and a bronze bust of Italian poet Dante outside.

FLORENCE
START

TUSCANY
This region is known for its wines; it produces over 8 million cases of Chianti every year.

POPPI
Say *"ciao"* to the bronze bust of Dante at this town's Castello dei Conti Guidi.

34 MILES (54 KM)

KING OF THE HILL TOWNS

Continue on the scenic SP208, which winds across the Casentino region and joins the SP47 to Anghiari in the Tiber Valley. Here, ancient buildings stack high on the hilltop, teetering above the treetops. Keep venturing into the region's south until you come to Montepulciano. Tuscany's highest hill town, it sits on a limestone ridge that separates Val d'Orcia and Val di Chiana. It's postcard-perfect, with mesmerizing views of the surrounding hills and rolling vineyards. In fact, Montepulciano is one of Italy's finest winemaking regions. After a stroll of the historical streets, which are sprinkled with restaurants, bars, and boutiques, it would be rude not to taste the local tipple, Vino Noble. Luckily, the town is full of hotels to stumble back to.

After a good night's rest, leave magical Montepulciano behind and take the SP146—a scenic road that winds its way through the Val d'Orcia countryside—to Pienza. This tiny UNESCO-listed town was built to impress. Its Renaissance construction was spearheaded by local resident Pope Pius II, who dreamed of a humanistic design for his hometown. The result is an architectural feat and Pienza (which is named after the urban-planning pope) is a delightful place to wander. The tow is also the producer of Pecorino di Pienza, a hard

ABOVE Montepulciano, Tuscany's highest hill town

LEFT A vineyard in Montalcino

OPPOSITE The brick dome of Florence's Duomo

MONTEPULCIANO
Sleep under the frescoed ceilings at the palatial Delcorto Suites hotel in the town center.

113 MILES (182 KM)

PIENZA
This Renaissance town is famed for producing sheep's cheese, Pecorino di Pienza.

122 MILES (197 KM)

221 MILES (355 KM)
MONTALCINO
Stop for a photo at this hilltop spot, which is known for its fairy-tale good looks.

272 MILES (437 KM)
SAN GIMIGNANO
This town of towers once boasted 72 spires. Today only 14 remain.

END
FLORENCE

EXTEND YOUR TRIP

Florence's neighbor Siena makes for an excellent addition to this road trip. The beautiful city features architectural marvels such as the Duomo, Fonte di Fontebranda, and the Basilica of San Domenico.

sheep's cheese. Sample the salty stuff, which rivals siblings Grana Padano and Parmigiano Reggiano, before heading for the hills and the winding roads.

After 50 miles (80 km) cruising up and down the rolling hills, you'll see the dramatic, teetering town of Pitigliano. The village, which seems to burst out of a volcanic rocky spur, has been inhabited since Etruscan times. Its southern district was known as La Piccola Gerusalemme (Little Jerusalem) for the Jewish community who lived there between the 1600s and the 1930s.

TUSCANY'S WINE COUNTRY

From picturesque Pitigliano, whiz along the foliage-fringed roads and head north to Montalcino. Encircled by fortified walls and topped by a medieval fortress, with vineyards and olive groves spooling out around it, this pretty town is a photogenic spot. It is also a gastronomic hub: the locally produced red wine, Brunello di Montalcino, is Tuscany's most famous after Chianti.

About 50 miles (80 km) north is San Gimignano, where ancient towers of the medieval walled town dot the sky. Once a stopover for medieval pilgrims traveling between France and Rome, its churches (and 14 spires) are richly decorated. It is also famous for saffron, and many local dishes are infused with this wonderful spice, making San Gimignano a very tasty place to refuel.

Finally, it's time to say goodbye to the region's rural landscapes and return to its capital. Florence's churches, galleries, and museums contain some of the world's most important paintings and sculptures. The pinnacle, though, is the Santa Maria del Fiore Cathedral, better known as the Duomo. It's topped with the largest brick-and-mortar dome in the world, and its interior is decorated with spectacular frescoes. The art-filled city could keep culture enthusiasts going for weeks; if you've got limited time, head to the Uffizi, Galleria dell'Accademia and Museo dell'Opera del Duomo. Then finish it all off as an Italian would: with an *aperitivo* at sundown.

EMILIA-ROMAGNA

START/END
Bologna/Reggio Emilia, Italy

DISTANCE
157 miles (253 km)

DURATION
4–5 days

ROAD CONDITIONS
Well-maintained, paved roads.

THE BEST TIME TO GO
September to November, when food festivals fill the region's restaurants and town squares.

OPPOSITE A traditional *salumeria* in Emilia-Romagna's historic capital of Bologna

If you're a fan of Italian food, look no further. A full-flavoured affair, this road trip traces the Roman-built Via Emilia from Bologna to Reggio Emilia, taking you straight through Italy's gastronomic heart.

Cast your eyes over a map of Emilia-Romagna, and your mouth is sure to water. Its place names summon the aromas of guarded Italian delicacies: balsamic vinegar from Modena; prosciutto from Parma; Reggio Emilia's Parmigiano Reggiano. But there's more to discover than the tasty big hitters. Tracing the scenic Roman-built SS9, this route dips into historic cities and medieval towns, car-based museums, and a bit of cutting-edge culture, too.

WORK UP AN APPETITE

To whet your appetite, start your Italian tour in the beautiful city of Bologna. The birthplace of *ragù*, the more authentic name for bolognese sauce, Emilia-Romagna's historic capital has quite the foodie legacy—which is perhaps the reason for its nickname, "La Grassa," meaning "The Fat." While you're here, make like the locals and try some of the city's lesser-exported dishes, such as *erbazzone* (a savory pie) and *tigelle* (a type of sandwich). They're best tried at the Quadrilatero, Italy's oldest market.

In between mouthfuls, visit the Basilica di Santo Stefano, Europe's sixth-largest church, and the fascinating Casa di Lucio Dalla, the former home of the Italian singer-songwriter. Before you hit the road, scoop up a world-class gelato at one of the city's exemplary outposts, or visit the modern temple to the craft, the Carpigiani Gelato Museum and University, on the city's fringes.

Bologna isn't just about food, though: a quick detour out of the city will take you to Museo Ferruccio Lamborghini.

BOLOGNA
START

BOLOGNA
The Carpigiani Gelato Museum and University charts the history of gelato and runs workshops.

0 MILES (0 KM)

MUSEO FERRUCCIO LAMBORGHINI
See sports cars and classics at this museum outside Bologna.
12 MILES (19 KM)

33 MILES (53 KM)

MODENA
Feast on local fare at Guisti's Michelin-recommended restaurant.

71 MILES (114 KM)

PARMA
Get your culture fix with a trip to the city's Palazzo della Pilotta complex.

EXTEND YOUR TRIP

East of Bologna, the UNESCO-listed cities of Ferrara and Ravenna each have a lively culinary scene. Ferrara hosts a four-day food festival in November, while Ravenna is a fine place to feast on sardines, shrimp, and clams fresh from the Adriatic.

Here, you can see classics and sports cars up close. If you're particularly car-minded, then you're in luck—another famed manufacturer lies just around the corner. Thirty-two miles (52 km) from Bologna, on the edge of Modena, is the Museo Enzo Ferrari. The museum is located in the car maker's childhood home and features personal trinkets from the Italian's life. There's also a gargantuan canary-yellow showroom.

In Modena itself, you can sample the city's balsamic vinegar at Guisti, one of its oldest producers. Alternatively, pop into its deli and restaurant, which sells Guisti vinegar and serves delicious dishes made with local produce. The best way to experience Modena's cuisine, however, is by sniffing out your own gems. Meander through the backstreets and visit any one of the city's incredible restaurants; whichever you choose, you won't be disappointed. Have a quick glance at the Duomo di Modena and Palazzo Ducale as you hotfoot it back to the car, in search of your next culinary fix.

The upbeat university city of Parma, also the UNESCO Creative City of Gastronomy, awaits 38 miles (61 km) along the SS9. Known for its cured meats—it is the Parma of Parma ham—the city also enjoys an excellent cultural scene with its Baptistery and Palazzo della Pilotta, which houses the grand National Gallery and Teatro Farnese.

A SLICE OF HISTORY

From Parma, delve into the picturesque Italian countryside in search of Soragna, the honey-colored lowland village that is home to the Parmigiano Reggiano museum. Parma and Reggio Emilia, the two provinces that produce the highly sought-after Parmesan, make roughly 4 million wheels a year. But it's not just cheese that's produced here—dine at the local restaurants of Soragna and nearby Busseto, and you'll see a rarer local specialty feature on the menu. *Culatello* is a prized cut of boneless ham that is cured for 24 months to intensify

ABOVE Modena's historic Duomo

the flavor. Thinly sliced, it's delicious with *gnocco fritto*, squares of dough that are fried until crisp and pillowy.

Continue your educational tour of the region's cuisine at Collecchio, home to neighboring museums of pasta and *pomodoro* (tomatoes). They're located on a medieval farm beside the Taro River, within Parco Fluviale Regionale del Taro; you can walk off the many morsels you've consumed on one of the gentle trails that hug the river's banks.

THE HOME OF HAM

If you've got more learning in you, make the 5-mile (8 km) trip to Felino's Museo del Salame. Occupying the cellars of a 15th-century castle, it charts the origins of the local salami. If you're visiting in September, head to nearby Langhirano where the Festival del Prosciutto di Parma, one of Emilia-Romagna's biggest gastronomic events, is held. As well as toasting the area's most celebrated speciality, the festival features tastings, carving demonstrations, music, and exhibitions. If it's any other time of year, sample the goods at a local restaurant or the Museo del Prosciutto di Parma.

Bring your tour of Emilia-Romagna to a close with a fizz of excitement in Reggio Emilia. The town is surrounded by producers of Italy's semi-sparkling wine Lambrusco. This *frizzante* red is designed to be drunk young and is best appreciated in its home region. *Saluti*!

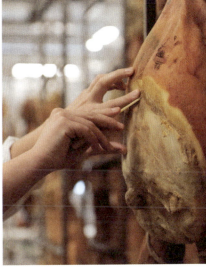

TOP The frescoed dome of Parma's Baptistery

ABOVE Prosciutto di Parma, prepared in Langhirano

LANGHIRANO
The heartland of the Prosciutto Trail features a museum dedicated to air-cured pork.
133 MILES (214 KM)

REGGIO EMILIA
Sip on semi-sparkling Lambrusco, made in vineyards surrounding the town.
157 MILES (253 KM)

REGGIO EMILIA
END

AMALFI COAST

START/END
Sorrento/Salerno, Italy

DISTANCE
72 miles (117 km)

DURATION
1-2 days

ROAD CONDITIONS
Narrow coastal roads, with some steep inclines.

THE BEST TIME TO GO
Early spring or fall; avoid summer, when entry is restricted to help ease congestion.

OPPOSITE The colorful houses of Positano, stacked up high on the Amalfi Coast hills

Whether you purr around the hairpins in a supercar, cruise from bay to bay in a classic Fiat, or nip around on a Vespa, a trip along the edge of Italy's Sorrento Peninsula is one of Europe's finest—and most picturesque—journeys.

The UNESCO-listed scenery south of Naples is as striking as a movie set. Beyond busy Sorrento, pretty fishing villages perch on the shores of the Tyrrhenian Sea, backed by vineyards and steep, scented groves filled with lemon and olive trees. Then there are the charming Amalfi Coast towns, where bougainvillea-draped houses hug the limestone hills. They're connected by the SS163, an exhilarating cliffside road that drops to the sparkling water. For the best views, travel west to east on the outside, sea-facing lane—and hold on tight.

COASTING IT
This tour of the Amalfi Coast starts in the city of Sorrento, with its striking views of the brooding Mount Vesuvius, which famously destroyed the ancient city of Pompeii in 79 CE. Fear not, though, it is one of the world's most monitored volcanoes. All you need to worry about is navigating the twisting turns that await on this road trip.

Rather than heading east out of Sorrento and straight to the Amalfi Coast, delve into the western tip of the Sorrento Peninsula instead. This wild region of twisting lanes and olive groves is dotted with rocky inlets and beaches, which make for perfect pit stops. Bagni Regina Giovanna is a natural swimming hole just 2 miles (3 km) from Sorrento, while Playa de Capitan Cook and Giardino Romantico outside Termini offer more serviced options.

Continue along the bucolic peninsula until you reach San Pietro and join the SS163, which was built in the late 1800s.

SORRENTO
START

SORRENTO
Visit Sorrento's oldest church, Basilica di Sant'Antonino, named after the town's patron saint.
0 MILES (0 KM)

BAGNI REGINA GIOVANNA
Hike to this quaint, sandless swimming hole for unspoiled turquoise waters.
2 MILES (3 KM)

ROAD TRIPS IN EUROPE

POSITANO
Dine at La Tagliata, high in the hills above Positano, for authentic homemade cuisine.

25 MILES (40 KM)

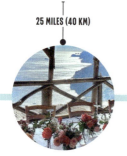

MARISA CUOMO WINERY
This vineyard is perched on the sloping hills overlooking the Gulf of Salerno.

44 MILES (70 KM)

IL SENTIERO DEGLI DEI
Legend has it that this trail was first walked by the gods who came to Earth to save Ulysses.

50 MILES (80 KM)

ABOVE The stone bridge that crosses the Furore gorge

OPPOSITE TOP Amalfi's Byzantine-style cathedral

OPPOSITE BOTTOM Villa Cimbrone in Ravello

In the distance, you'll see Il Gallo Lungo, a rocky, dolphin-shaped island onto which mythological sirens are said to have lured sailors.

From here, picture-perfect Positano is unmissable. The famous Le Sirenuse hotel overlooks a busy beach, while a flight of steps leads to roadside restaurants and cafés with grandstand views of the glittering coast. Pause to take in the views before driving up into the hills to eat at La Tagliata, a restaurant that serves up excellent chargrilled meat and panoramic views.

A TASTE OF AMALFI
As you continue along the SS163, the rocky shores, greenery-covered slopes, and ancient tile-clad churches of Praiano appear. It's attractively sleepy compared to Positano and Amalfi and is a relatively affordable place to stay, with authentic restaurants rustling up delicious seafood dishes.

Farther along the coast, you'll reach another lesser-known beauty spot. Near the village of Furore, the SS163 crosses a dramatically arching stone bridge. At the bottom of the gaping gorge is a pretty beach with crystal waters; park and then follow the stone steps down to the shore for a splash around.

Back in the car, a quick detour into the hills takes you past the Marisa Cuomo winery—oenophiles can pause to enjoy the informative tour—to the starting point of Il Sentiero degli Dei, the Path of Gods. The 4-mile (7 km) trail leads hikers to Positano via a route that sits 2,065 ft (630 m) above sea level. Enjoy the views from this lofty vantage point, even if you don't complete the iconic trek.

A few miles east of Furore, the road winds around the striking Capo di Conca, then curves northeast toward Amalfi, a colorful cluster of historic buildings and narrow streets around the Cattedrale di Sant'Andrea.

55 MILES (89 KM)

AMALFI
Sample the *pastiera*—a sweet ricotta tart—at Pansa, an age-old bakery in Amalfi.

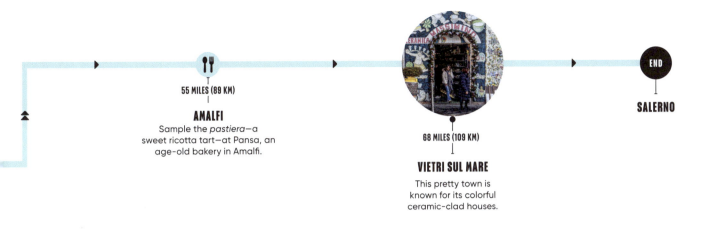

68 MILES (109 KM)

VIETRI SUL MARE
This pretty town is known for its colorful ceramic-clad houses.

END

SALERNO

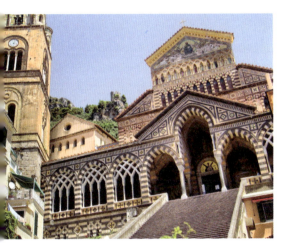

Approached via a broad flight of steps, this grand cathedral features a patterned Byzantine-style façade, an elaborate nave, and, in the crypt, a tomb containing relics of the apostle Saint Andrew. Piazza Duomo, below the cathedral, is a relaxing spot to linger with an *aperitivo* or a sweet treat from Pansa, a *pasticceria* that has been baking pastries in Amalfi since 1830.

Famously, Amalfi is the birthplace of limoncello. For insight into this local liqueur, take a quick detour to the Amalfi Lemon Experience in a valley north of town. The working farm offers tours, cooking classes, and lunches. You can also bag a bottle to enjoy later.

LA DOLCE VITA

As you embark on your final leg, you'll pass a string of beautiful towns on your way to the trip's end point. Atrani is a delightfully uncrowded coastal spot where Netflix series *Ripley* was filmed, while Ravello is a romantic hilltop village with a vibrant cultural scene. For a serene interlude, drift around the formal gardens at Ravello's Villa Cimbrone. Further east, Vietri sul Mare is lifted by the ceramic tilework that decorates its buildings and footpaths. But Salerno is calling. Authentic and charming, this Italian city is a fine way to finish. Glimpse the magnificent cathedral and rustic old town before treating yourself to a gelato from local institution Bar Nettuno Gelateria. A limoncello should quickly follow at sunset to top off the trip, Amalfi-style.

BY THE FEET OF GODS

Il Sentiero degli Dei, the Path of Gods, is the Amalfi Coast's most celebrated hike. Meandering through the herb-scented Latteri Mountains east of Positano, it has several start and end points, including the villages of Praiano, Bomerano, and Nocelle. Even if you have time (and stamina) to tackle only a short section, it's worth it for the superb views of rugged rocks and shimmering sea.

BALTIC CAPITALS

START/END
Vilnius, Lithuania/
Tallinn, Estonia

DISTANCE
649 miles (1,044 km)

DURATION
8–10 days

ROAD CONDITIONS
Well-maintained,
flat roads.

THE BEST TIME TO GO
Midsummer, when the
sun barely sets. Avoid the
winter months when there
is snow and black ice.

OPPOSITE Cobblestoned
backstreet in Tallinn,
Estonia's capital city

This tour of the Baltic capitals is firmly for flat-road enthusiasts. Take the wheel and slowly meander through the medieval towns, quiet islands, and haunting war memorials of this oft-forgotten corner of Europe.

A 600-mile (1,000 km) odyssey, this Baltic tour calls for a serene pace as you journey from Vilnius, with its beautiful Baroque buildings, through Art Nouveau Riga to Tallinn, Estonia's gateway to the Nordics. Quiet landscapes provide hypnotic interludes between the buzz of the big cities, while skyscraper pine trees and big blue skies are a constant.

A SLICE OF THE SOUTH

Lithuania's capital is where your trans-Baltic journey commences. You'd be forgiven for thinking this city, with its Baroque rooftops, hidden courtyards, and cobblestone alleyways, is actually in southern Europe. Saunter around Katedros Aikštė, the old town's dynamic center, and crane your neck to see the top of the 190 ft (57 m) high bell tower and grand cathedral. While strolling this charming area, it's easy to forget the city's tumultuous past. Visitors can learn about Lithuania's darker side with a visit to the important Museum of Occupations and Freedom Fights, housed in former KGB and Gestapo headquarters. For a lighter end to your city tour, follow the winding Vilnia River into the world's smallest republic, Užupis. The bohemian mini-nation, which was formed as an April Fools' Day joke, has its own constitution, government, and currency.

On the road and heading northeast, you'll soon arrive at Lithuania's second city, Kaunas. The former capital is home to a vibrant food scene—so come hungry. Head to the old town and its litany of restaurants to gorge on

VILNIUS

VILNIUS
This Baroque city boasts wide boulevards and spacious parks that are a rarity in the Baltics.
0 MILES (0 KM)

KAUNUS
Latvia's former capital is a tight knit of charming courtyards and cobbled streets.
64 MILES (103 KM)

šaltibarščiai, a cold, bright-pink beet soup, and *cepelinai*, filled potato dumplings. It's not just food on the menu here, though. Visit Pažaislis Monastery, the city's finest example of Baroque architecture, which sits on the banks of the Kaunas Reservoir.

As you embark on the next leg of your journey, circle the city and pause at the 9th fort of the Kaunas Fortress. The chilling 100 ft (32 m) high stone monument stands as a reminder of the country's war-torn past. From here, it's a 120-mile (200 km) drive to another poignant monument: the Hill of Crosses. It's an offbeat pilgrimage site that features 100,000 crucifixes. It was once in danger of destruction by the Soviet regime and stands as a dizzying reminder of hope and resistance today.

Back on the road, there are few notable changes between Lithuania and Latvia. Expect an endless horizon of mystical-looking forests, broken up by the occasional Orthodox church. After 78 miles (125 km), suburban apartment buildings appear on the horizon—you've reached Latvia's cosmopolitan capital of Riga.

ONE CITY NATION

Latvia's size can fool you into believing it has little to offer. On the contrary, its sole city, Riga, is the largest of all the Baltic

ABOVE The grand House of the Blackheads in Riga

LEFT The Hill of Crosses, a Lithuanian pilgrimage site

OPPOSITE The white sands of Latvia's Jūrmala beach

HILL OF CROSSES
Crucifixes started appearing on this hill after an uprising against the Russian regime in 1831.
182 MILES (293 KM)

RIGA: ALBERTA STREET
Latvia's capital features a grand Art Nouveau district around Alberta Street.
260 MILES (418 KM)

BALTIC CAPITALS

262 MILES (422 KM)

RIGA: CENTRAL MARKET
Try some of the city's local cuisine, such as *pelmeņi*, at Riga's Central Market.

JŪRMALA
Riga's seaside resort is a worthy 16-mile (25 km) detour, offering up a bracing dip.

378 MILES (609 KM)

PÄRNU
Estonia's summer capital is known for beach volleyball and affordable spa hotels.

FIT FOR A KING

Estonia's Saaremaa, the largest island in the Muhu archipelago, is steeped in folklore. According to legend, Suur Tõll (the Great Tõll), a local farmer, is the king of the land. You can spot him and his wife Piret in sculpture form in the main town of Kuressaare.

capitals and is a captivating city to explore. Hit the atmospheric old town on foot to best admire the flamboyant architecture. Begin your tour with the Three Brothers, the oldest buildings in Riga, followed by the House of the Blackheads, a guild house built in 1344. At Livu Square, cast your eyes up and you'll glimpse a cat standing atop a spire at the aptly named Cat House. But it's in and around Riga's Alberta Street, known as the "Quiet Center," that you'll find the city's grand Art Nouveau avenues. Top off your visit with lunch at Riga's Central Market. This impressive 1930s-era space attracts 100,000 visitors a day for its mix of fresh produce and street-food options. The industrial arched ceiling makes a fine backdrop for tucking into a *pelmeņi*, filled dumplings.

If you've got time for a detour, hop in the car and whiz across to Riga's neighboring seaside town of Jūrmala. It's an easy side trip and the reward is a postcard-perfect sandy beach. Weather permitting, take a brisk dip—it is the Gulf of Riga after all—and say goodbye to Latvia. Estonia, where the Baltics fizzle out near the Nordics, is the final country on your list.

TO THE FRONTIER

Straight-backed pine trees grow abundantly in Estonia, and they're the first thing that greets you as you cross the border into this northern territory. Hug the coast, taking the densely forested E67 for 40 miles (65 km) to reach the country's summer capital, Pärnu. Known for its brightly painted wooden houses, this laid-back resort town is popular with Balts and Scandinavians for its shallow waters and sandy beaches. Outside the summer months, Pärnu can be ghostly quiet. But that's even more reason to stop and take advantage of its luxury spa hotels, famed for both high-quality treatments and affordability.

The trip's penultimate detour is perhaps its most magical. Estonia's mythical and mystical past opens up on Saaremaa, one of its 2,317 islands.

BELOW The Sõrve lighthouse on Saaremaa Island

Saaremaa Island, accessed by a short ferry ride, was once a hot spot for Viking plunder. The town of Kuressaare, replete with cotton-candy pink buildings, has the highest number of spas per capita in the world and is home to Kuressaare Castle, which is surrounded by a star-shaped fort. Breathe in the fresh air on a scenic drive around the island, taking you past lighthouses (including the majestic Sõrve), pagan tombstones, ruins and the 7,600-year-old Kaali Meteorite Crater.

Hop back on the ferry and drive through Estonia's Matsalu National Park, one of Europe's most important wetlands for birdlife. Keep your eyes on the sky for the endangered white-tailed eagle. The park also has a nature center for those who want to learn more about this wildlife haven.

BALTIC BEAUTY

From Matsalu, cut across the country to the coastal capital of Tallinn, which could be Helsinki's Baltic cousin with its sauna and coffee culture. Colorful wooden houses, influenced by Finnish design, are found across the city—Kalamaja, a former fishing village on the city's fringes, is home to hundreds of vibrant wooden apartments and Scandi-style homes. But Tallinn has its own flavor, most evident in Telliskivi, a former Soviet industrial hub that has been reinvented as the city's cultural center. Here, you can visit the Sõltumatu Tantsu Lava contemporary performing arts venue and dine at one of any number of trendy restaurants.

Finish off your Baltic tour in Tallinn's old town. This stunningly preserved UNESCO World Heritage Site features turret-topped medieval walls and a labyrinth of picturesque alleyways. Climb to the very top of St. Olaf's Church and watch the sun set behind the onion domes of Tallinn's Alexander Nevsky Cathedral, bathing the skyline beyond.

EXTEND YOUR TRIP

Continue your route inland to the Estonian city of Tartu, Europe's City of Culture 2024. The dynamic university city sits on the banks of the Emajõgi River and is home to the fascinating Estonian National Museum. The city is also a great jumping-off point to explore the nearby Lake Peipsi and its collection of villages, which fuse Russian and Estonian traditions.

KURESSAARE
See the fascinating star-shaped fortress on Saaremaa Island.
475 MILES (764 KM)

MATSALU NATIONAL PARK
Climb up one of the birdwatching towers to see the park's myriad birds.
575 MILES (926 KM)

TALLINN
The onion domes of Alexander Nevsky Cathedral dominate the city's skyline.
649 MILES (1,044 KM)

TALLINN
END

TRADING ROUTES

Europe's roads have always been essential for moving goods as well as people. As many as 5,000 years ago, traders were carrying amber out of the Baltics and across the continent on a trade route that became known as the Amber Road. Not so much a fixed route but a regular commercial flow across whatever path made most sense, it was efficient enough to distribute goods across Europe and the Mediterranean. When the ancient Egyptian pharaoh Tutankhamen's tomb was discovered, his breast ornament was found to be decorated with beads from the Baltics.

As the Romans grew their empire, the route became more formalized. Amber, furs, and honey were exported from the Baltics through Poland and Austria to Venice and Rome, with glass and gold heading the other way. Today, drivers in Estonia can follow a section of the old route along highway E67 and 331.

Talk of ancient roads always seems to lead back to the Romans, antiquity's undisputed kings of infrastructure. Though their far-reaching system was built to facilitate troop movements, it became important to commerce. That was true even on the edges of the empire. In Britain, in the 1st century CE, Roman soldiers constructed the Fosse Way to mark the empire's frontier, but merchants soon took advantage of the road to conduct trade among towns between Exeter and Lincoln. Around the same time, the Romans followed a pre-Celtic route to connect Dover with London and St. Albans to Wroxeter, via Watling Street. Today's modern highways in Britain follow more or less the same ground.

Of course, all empires need their roads. The Holy Roman Empire had the Via Regia and Via Imperii. Originally, "via regia" referred to any road under royal protection, but today the term usually refers to the primary road from Spain's Santiago de Compostela to its end points in Lithuania and Ukraine. The empire's corresponding north–south route was the Via Imperii, which linked today's Szczecin in Poland with Italy. Parts of these routes still exist, although merchants and pilgrims have given way to the road-trippers of today.

> **When the ancient Egyptian pharaoh Tutankhamen's tomb was discovered, his breast ornament was found to be decorated with beads from the Baltics.**

ABOVE Amber stones, exported by the Baltic nations

GREAT BIESZCZADY LOOP

START/END
Lesko, Poland

DISTANCE
109 miles (175 km)

DURATION
1-2 days

ROAD CONDITIONS
Well-maintained, flat roads.

THE BEST TIME TO GO
Fall, when the landscape is blanketed in purple, gold, and yellow.

OPPOSITE Winding through Poland's forested Bieszczady National Park

This route passes up Poland's main cities for its southern tip, where the rolling Bieszczady mountains reside. Drive past idyllic meadows and through dramatic countryside, marked with the remnants of a troublesome history.

Not quite a circle, the Great Bieszczady Loop traces the region's theatrical mountain range and draws visitors for its snaking roads, sharp chicanes, and breathtaking scenery. But it's a poignant place with a checkered history: the route was built by the Polish army following Operation Vistula, which saw the deportation of nearly 500,000 Ukrainian people from the Bieszczady region in 1947.

A TOUR OF THE TOWNS

The loop begins—and ends—in Lesko, on the banks of the San Lesko River. This small settlement dates back to the 14th century; it was founded by the Kmita family who built the town's castle.

There is also an attractive market square, and plenty of churches, including Lesko's Gothic Parish Church of Our Lady, which stands pretty and pink in the town's northwest. The Renaissance-style former synagogue is Lesko's most important site, though; it acts as a reminder of the country's once-thriving Jewish community. Take the narrow steps behind the structure to access the Jewish Cemetery, one of the oldest Jewish monuments in Europe with graves dating back to the 16th century.

It's a short 12-mile (20 km) hop to the country village of Baligród. Also built by a family clan, it was once a busy trade site but lost its importance at the turn of the 20th century. The starting point for some great hikes, Baligród has a fine gleaming Greek Catholic church, which features a semicircular chancel, octagonal dome, and screen belfry.

LESKO
START

LESKO
The town's synagogue is one of only five Polish synagogues to survive World War II.
0 MILES (0 KM)

BALIGRÓD
Hike the nature-filled 8-mile (13 km) route to the nearby Chryszczata peak.
12 MILES (20 KM)

24 MILES (38 KM)

CISNA
Siekierezada Bar, the town's mountain refuge, is the perfect spot to sit out bad weather.

40 MILES (65 KM)

BIESZCZADY NATIONAL PARK
This forested region is home to brown bear, lynx, wolf, and bison.

Don't be alarmed if you spot an armored vehicle in the town—the stationary Soviet-era T-34 tank is a monument in the market square.

After another 11 miles (18 km) on the road, this time through dense forest, you'll reach Cisna. In the heart of the mountains, this pretty resort town is easily identified by its picturesque wood-cut houses. This is where hikers congregate before launching into the area's famed treks—making for a lively atmosphere and plenty of good food and drink.

Your first stop should be the cheerful Siekierezada Bar, with its soft mahogany benches and ceilings—and even an art gallery. If you've got time for a longer break, don your hiking boots and try one of Cisna's trails, or head to the train station to catch sight—and sound— of the steam train on Poland's highest narrow-gauge railroad chugging past.

Back on the road, navigate the tight, curving angles on your way to Wetlina, a pretty village known for its mountain views. Here, two hills dominate the village skyline: the magnificent Połonina Wetlińska and Smerek. Both are excellent routes for avid hikers.

BEND TO BEND
With the grassy peaks getting ever smaller as you drive farther down the looping road, you'll enter the Bieszczady National Park. One of the last truly remote, uninhabited corners of Poland, it transforms when fall arrives and the vivid hues spread across the landscape. Turn onto the 896 road and cruise past village after village. This is where the road really comes to life as you tackle the section that drivers travel across Europe for:

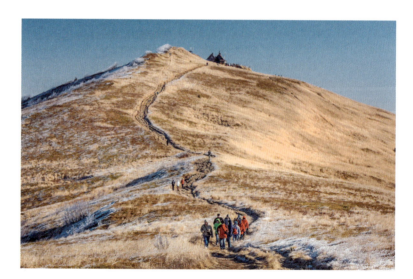

ABOVE The Połonina Wetlińska hike in Wetlina

LEFT The interior of the art-filled Siekierezada Bar

LEFT Lake Solina, Poland's largest reservoir

EXTEND YOUR TRIP

Don't stop in Lesko, keep driving for another 10 miles (15 km) to reach the open-air Muzeum Budownictwa Ludowego—or Museum of Folk Architecture—in Sanok. Constructed in 1958, it comprises 200 traditional buildings relocated from across the Sanok Land. It provides a fascinating glimpse into the area's design history.

around 3 miles (5 km) past Wetlina, the track starts shaping into the adrenaline-pumping snakelike bends it's known for, as you whiz past thick, luscious greenery and finger-thin river arteries.

From here, the road begins its loop back to Lesko and the wilderness begins to subside. Soon, the rooftops, mountain peaks, and ski lifts of Ustrzyki Dolne appear. This chocolate-box village is truly mesmerizing in winter, when the region is blanketed in snow, but it's a perfect pit stop at any time of the year, thanks to its litany of luxury hotels and spa facilities. A guided tour of MŁYN, the Milling and Village Museum, is fun. Set in a historic mill in the center of the village, it is the only museum of its kind in Poland and also houses a restaurant that serves local dishes, including *proziaki*, Polish soda bread, and *kapuśniaki*, a traditional filled pie.

CLOSING THE LOOP

After you've gobbled baked goods fresh from the oven, hit the road for the last leg of the Great Bieszczady Loop, and its most beautiful. You'll cruise past Lake Solina, Poland's largest reservoir, which formed in 1968 when the San River was dammed, and through the resort town of Polańczyk that sits at the tip of one of the lake's peninsulas. Visit the Eko Marina club and take a brisk dip in the tempting swimming pool on the floating harbor, or soak up the sun on one of the lake's beaches.

Backtrack along Solina's shore, admiring the glittering emerald water (or solid ice, if it's winter) until you reach Solina village. Park and then stroll the San Dam for the panoramic views. If you visit during the early hours, you've got a good chance of seeing the sun appear from behind the mountain peaks. Then it's time to tear yourself away to complete your loop to Lesko.

USTRZYKI DOLNE
A ski resort in winter, Ustrzyki Dolne's lifts transport mountain bikers and hikers in the summer.
70 MILES (112 KM)
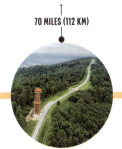

POLAŃCZYK
This resort is a popular spot for trying water sports on Lake Solina.
91 MILES (147 KM)
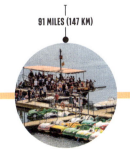

SOLINA
Walk along the Son Dam and take in the far-reaching views across this huge lake.
98 MILES (158 KM)

LESKO
END

HIGH TATRAS

START/END
Štrbské Pleso, Slovakia/ Budapest, Hungary

DISTANCE
215 miles (345 km)

DURATION
5–7 days

ROAD CONDITIONS
Mostly well-maintained roads, some narrow.

THE BEST TIME TO GO
Spring and summer to take advantage of the area's hiking trails. Avoid the snowy conditions over winter.

OPPOSITE Liptovskà Mara lake in the mountainous High Tatras

Traverse the Slovakian Alps, from near the border with Poland to the Hungarian capital. Starting in the High Tatras, this epic route meanders past sapphire lakes, rare flora and fauna, and villages rich in folklore.

The High Tatras is one of Slovakia's most striking natural wonders. With its dramatic craggy peaks and bountiful wildlife, the mountain range is a destination in its own right, offering some of Eastern Europe's best skiing, mountain biking, and hiking. But cruising from the highest heights—the Tatras is home to 25 peaks that top 8,200 ft (2,500 m)—makes for a thrilling drive, too, with some excellent stop offs on the way.

HIGH TIMES

The resort village of Štrbské Pleso sits at 4,400 ft (1,346 m) above sea level, and offers breathtaking views of the magnificent surrounding landscape. It's a picturesque location—and the starting point for this mountainous route. Before you hop in the car, take a hike around the beautiful glacial Popradské Pleso lake. When you're ready to hit the road, do so with care: wildlife encounters are possible in this UNESCO Biosphere Reserve. Make sure you know what to do if you cross paths with a brown bear, Eurasian lynx, or the highly endangered Tatra chamois.

Warnings aside, begin your descent from pretty Štrbské Pleso. Head west on the Ceste Slobody, or "Road to Freedom," where you'll traverse 12 miles (20 km) of forested switchbacks and rocky curves. As you wind your way down the mountain, you'll pass the Tri Studničky nature reserve and the ski resort of Podbanské. Continue down the valley, hugging the Belá Stream until you reach Pribylina, home to the fascinating Liptov Village museum.

ŠTRBSKÉ PLESO
START

ŠTRBSKÉ PLESO
This mountain village is home to the beautiful Popradské lake and stunning hikes.
0 MILES (0 KM)

PRIBYLINA
The Liptov Village museum features buildings from the 18th, 19th, and 20th centuries.
17 MILES (27 KM)

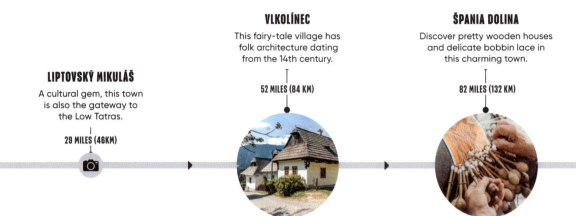

LIPTOVSKÝ MIKULÁŠ
A cultural gem, this town is also the gateway to the Low Tatras.

29 MILES (46KM)

VLKOLÍNEC
This fairy-tale village has folk architecture dating from the 14th century.

52 MILES (84 KM)

ŠPANIA DOLINA
Discover pretty wooden houses and delicate bobbin lace in this charming town.

82 MILES (132 KM)

This pretty town sits at the foot of Kriváň, which is thought to be Slovakia's most beautiful and symbolic mountain.

THE TOWNS OF THE TATRAS
As you venture farther down the mountains, drivers are rewarded with stunning landscapes that are densely packed with forests and trickling streams—and a collection of pretty towns and villages. Liptovský Mikuláš is the craft and cultural center of the mountainous region, home to interesting museums, galleries, and restaurants. It's also a base to explore the area's abundance of thermal pools—Kaďa at Liptovský Ján in the Low Tatras is a natural option.

From Liptovský Mikuláš, hug the shores of Liptovskà Mara, Slovakia's largest reservoir, until you reach the mountain village of Vlkolínec, which is known for its colorful log cabins that date from the 14th century. Soon, you'll come to Špania Dolina, an old copper- and silver-mining community famed for its delicate bobbin lace and now one of the prettiest places in the country. Postcard-perfect, the traditional shingle-roofed houses nestle into the forested valley, a tall church spire cutting into the horizon.

After a little over 60 miles (100 km) on the road, you'll arrive in Banská Bystrica, an important central Slovakian city with beautiful Renaissance and Baroque façades. A climb up its bell tower is rewarded with panoramic views across the city to the peaks beyond. Next up is Banská Štiavnica, a well-preserved medieval town and UNESCO World Heritage Site built in a hollow created by the collapse of a volcano. Founded by Celts in the 3rd century BCE, it's been coveted by many for its reserves of silver ore. The city's mining museum is well worth a stop, too; here, you can take a guided tour of 17th-century underground passageways.

Once you've explored below ground, hike up the Scharffenberg Hill to visit the beautiful and recently restored Calvary pilgrimage site. Visible for miles around,

CITY OF SPAS
Budapest has long been recognized as one of the world's most important cities for thermal bathing. In fact, its spa heritage dates back as far as Ottoman and Habsburg times. If you want a slice of the action, visit Széchenyi or Gellért for an authentic bathing experience.

HIGH TATRAS

153 MILES (246 KM)
TESÁRSKA ROKLINA
See the mysterious rock formations and caves on this woodland walk.

214 MILES (345 KM)
BUDAPEST
Memento Park is a who's who of Socialism, with statues of Stalin, Lenin, and Marx.

END
BUDAPEST

the Baroque church is the pinnacle of the site but, hidden below, is a series of religious "stations"—which includes three churches and 22 chapels.

THE ROUTE TO HUNGARY

The incredible sights of Scharffenberg Hill behind you, it's time to travel toward Hungary. Stretch your legs at Tesárska Roklina with a forested walk through a gorge, then after a further 12 miles (20 km) on the road, you'll wave goodbye to Slovakia. Before you reach Hungary's capital, the thousand-year-old city of Vác offers Baroque delights, including a triangular main square, cathedral, and waterfront promenade.

But perhaps nothing compares to the beauty of Budapest, home to Art Nouveau architecture, ornate public baths, and popular ruin bars. Take a stroll of this majestic city to see the sights, including the Neo-Classical Basilica of St. Stephen, Matthias Church, Parliament, and, on the city's outskirts, Memento Park. A short trip on the Buda Castle funicular delivers travelers at the limestone plateau above the river, where the city's most impressive monuments and museums are found. Gaze out across the Danube, then end your trip as a local would—with a well-earned soak in the restorative thermal pools at a Budapest bathhouse.

ABOVE The church in pretty Špania Dolina

RIGHT Banská Štiavnica's impressive Scharffenberg Hill

OPPOSITE The Kaďa hot spring in Liptovský Ján

167

JULIAN ALPS

START/END
Radovljica/Kobarid, Slovenia

DISTANCE
73 miles (118 km)

DURATION
2–3 days

ROAD CONDITIONS
Paved roads with sections of hairpin bends as you drive through the Alps.

THE BEST TIME TO GO
Early summer, when the rivers and waterfalls are in full flow, or fall, when the leaves start to change color.

OPPOSITE The Church of the Mother of God, overlooking Lake Bled's aquamarine waters

The Julian Alps are a craggy gem in the green heart of Europe. Whether you're looking for adventure, culture, history, or natural beauty—or a mix of all four—a drive through this stirring region of Slovenia will not disappoint.

While the Julian Alps may not be the continent's best-known mountains, their towering jagged peaks, dazzling lakes, and jade rivers offer Alpine charm with a delightful Slovenian twist. As Europe's greenest country is also a fairly small one, traversing Slovenia's major sights makes for an excellent weekend-long road trip. From Radovljica, you'll steer past famed lakes and venture deep into the Soča valley.

THE GREEN GATEWAY

Radovljica, the gateway to Slovenia's mountains, is a medieval town with a bit of a sweet tooth—it's known as a center for honey, chocolate, and even gingerbread. In addition to these tasty morsels, it has quaint alleyways lined with beautifully preserved buildings that date from the 16th century, and a range of unusual museums dedicated to the likes of pharmacy and alchemy. From the town's square, you'll glimpse a striking preview of the road ahead.

Leave Radovljica and its collection of niche museums behind—the Julian Alps are waiting. After only a short drive, you'll arrive at one of Slovenia's most famous locations: Bled. With its mirror lake, mountainous surroundings, and brochure-friendly island, the Green Pearl of Slovenia is recognized the world over. And for good reason—the view is just as breathtaking in real life. Drive toward the lake and skirt the emerald waters. The tiny island at its center is only accessible by boat, but its resident, the Church of the Mother of God, can be admired from the shores, too. If you have

RADOVLJICA
Slovenia's sweetest town sits at the entrance of the epic Julian Alps.

0 MILES (0 KM)

BLED
The Green Pearl of Slovenia, this picture-perfect lake encircles a tiny island.

4 MILES (7 KM)

RADOVLJICA

START

VINTGAR GORGE

Walk the stunning 4-mile (6-km) King of Triglav trail through the Vintgar Gorge.

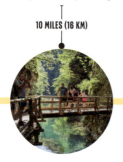

10 MILES (16 KM)

BOHINJ

Much bigger and wilder than Bled, Bohinj is the largest lake in Slovenia.

22 MILES (36 KM)

VOGEL CABLE CAR

Ride this cable car from Lake Bohinj to Brown Rock, some 5,000 ft (1,535 m) high.

22 MILES (36 KM)

RIGHT Bohinj Lake is an adventurer's paradise

BELOW Kayakers attempt the rapids on the Soča River

OPPOSITE Kobarid's Church of St. Anthony, above the town

time, dip into the welcoming waters—the lake is fed by thermal springs and is surprisingly warm. Bled Castle, which clings to a cliff overlooking the lake, is worth a wander, and you can stop by for a drink and slice of local *kremšnita* cake.

Beautiful Bled also provides a perfect base for exploring the striking surroundings. Navigate the rocky Vintgar Gorge, where a rickety wooden walkway crosses the sheltered rapids, or head into Triglav National Park, home to an array of trails and hikes—and the source of Slovenia's peaked national symbol.

LAKE OF THE DAY

Weave your way west past forests, charming villages, and fields filled with traditional Slovenian hayracks, and before long, you'll arrive at another magnificent lake. Much larger and wilder in its proportions than Bled, Lake Bohinj is a hub of activity year round. Expect kayaking, sailing, rock climbing, and paragliding in the summer and snow sports come winter.

Board Bohinj's cable car to reach the heights of Vogel, a popular ski spot with spectacular views. In the summer months, you can hike to the beautiful Savica Waterfall. It is fed by the mighty Sava River, which flows through Slovenia into Croatia and Bosnia and Herzegovina, before meeting the Danube in Serbia.

From Bohinj, navigate 30 miles (50 km) of dense forests and hairpin bends as you snake into the mountains. Stop often to admire the views across the peaks. You'll soon begin your descent into the Soča Valley, where the road winds through leafy glades and past waterfalls.

Continue on to Most na Soči, a small town with a spectacular backdrop on the edge of the Soča and Idrijca rivers. You can take in your surroundings from its picturesque bridge, but the best views are from the water itself: swim (there are beaches dotted along the shore), paddleboard, or hop aboard a paddle-wheeler boat tour. If you'd rather stay on dry land, there's a pleasant footpath at the water's edge with interesting artworks and a couple of atmospheric bar-restaurants.

ON THE RIVER

Back in the car, follow the jewel-like Soča River upstream, cutting through limestone gorges and white stone. Keep your eyes, and ears, out for gushing rapids—this area is famed for its whitewater rafting. Stop to observe the powerful natural phenomenon and, if you're feeling adventurous, dip your toe into this thrilling activity.

Embark on the final stretch of this Alpine adventure, hugging the river's shore for 12 miles (20 km) until you reach the small town of Kobarid, your final destination. An enchanting mix of Alpine and Mediterranean influences, Kobarid is known for its multitude of excellent hiking, biking, and rafting opportunities. It's a fitting end to an outdoorsy adventure. Visit the Church of St. Anthony and Napoleon Bridge, which was originally built in 1750 when Napoleon's troops are said to have marched across it on their way to Predel Pass. And save some time for the Kobarid Museum, which details the arduous and drawn-out battles on the nearby Isonzo Front during World War I. Then finish off this beautiful tour of Slovenia's Julian Alps by feasting on an upmarket take on local Slovenian fare at Hiša Polonka. *Dober tek!*

ALL ABOARD

For a unique transportation experience, and to cut out some of the trip's tricky switchbacks, pick up the car train at Bohinjska Bistrica. Drive onto a flatbed carriage, sit back, and enjoy the wild, rickety ride through the longest tunnel in Slovenia to Most na Soči.

MOST NA SOČI
Cross the picturesque bridge in this stunningly located town, set on the Soči River.
63 MILES (101 KM)

KOBARID: KOBARID MUSEUM
This excellent site reveals the town's complicated and war-torn history.
72 MILES (115 KM)

KOBARID: HIŠA FRANKO
Wind down at this restaurant, which serves refined Slovenian dishes with a modern twist.
73 MILES (118 KM)

KOBARID
END

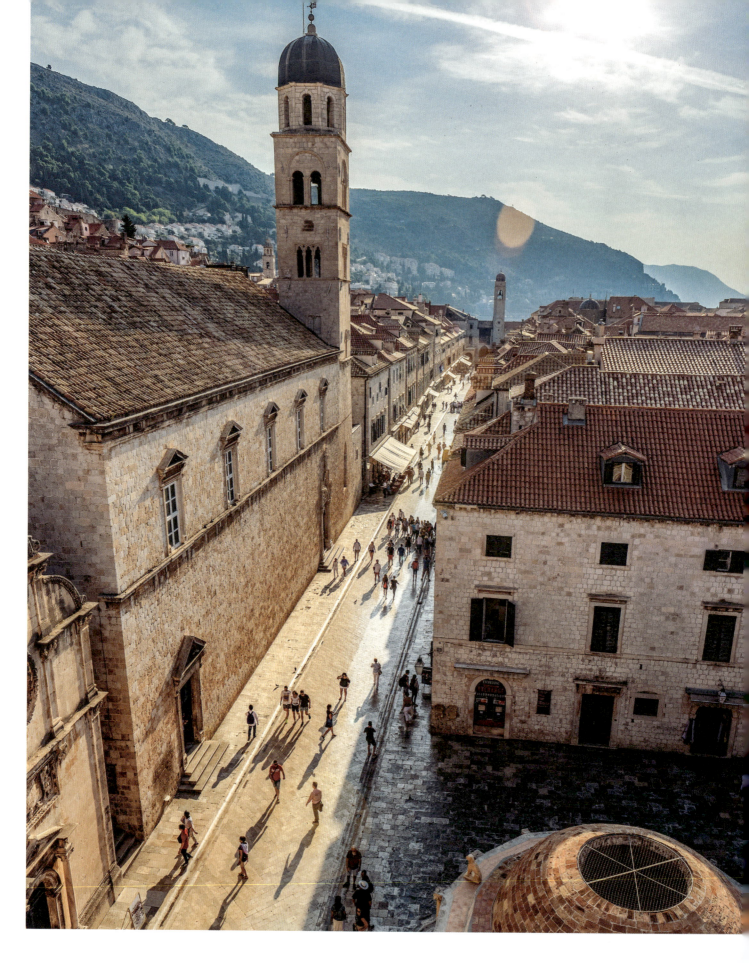

DALMATIAN COAST

START/END
Dubrovnik/Zadar, Croatia

DISTANCE
267 miles (430 km)

DURATION
3-5 days

ROAD CONDITIONS
Paved roads, with some fairly narrow, winding sections.

THE BEST TIME TO GO
September to October, to avoid extreme heat and summer crowds. Beware some roads may be closed in high winds.

OPPOSITE The sun shines on the atmospheric streets of Dubrovnik's old town

This Croatian adventure is not for the fainthearted. Those who take on the challenge will have to navigate narrow coastal roads, but they'll be rewarded with ancient cities, spectacular sea views, and magical sunsets.

The journey from the walled city of Dubrovnik to Zadar's harbor captures the best of the Dalmatian Coast, on a twisting drive that sees you sandwiched between the Adriatic and the brooding Velebit Mountains.

THE CROATIAN COAST

Begin in Dubrovnik, a UNESCO World Heritage Site that dates from the 7th century and Byzantine rule. The old town is a perfectly preserved blend of stone and marble that juts out into the harbor. Inside the fortified walls, you might recognize its Gothic monasteries and Renaissance churches from film and TV: Dubrovnik is a favorite for location scouts and has appeared in *Game of Thrones* and *Star Wars*. From the top of it perimeter walls, there are stunning panoramic views of the sun-baked city, the Adriatic sea, and mountains beyond. Grab a bowl of black risotto in one of Dubrovnik's many restaurants, such as the old town's Proto Fish, before packing up the car and driving north, hugging the coast as you go.

Jadranska Magistrala—also known as the Balkan Route 66 and the Adriatic Highway—is the road this trip takes. It's narrow in parts, and there are many blind, rocky corners, but it's an exciting drive, unsurprisingly popular with drivers who yearn for more than the repetitive humdrum of a highway.

After 45 miles (70 km) on the coastal highway, you'll cross onto the Pelješac peninsula. Quieter than Dubrovnik, it offers natural and historical wonders on a smaller scale. Head for the town

DUBROVNIK

START

DUBROVNIK: ON SCREEN
Game of Thrones and *Star Wars: The Last Jedi* were both filmed within the city's walls.

DUBROVNIK: PROTO FISH
Fuel up on black risotto, a classic Croatian dish, at this restaurant in the old town.

0 MILES (0 KM)

of Ston to view its fortress and walk along the extensive defenses. The stone wall was built in 1333 to protect Dubrovnik and has since been named the "European Great Wall of China," mostly due to its extraordinary length; originally the wall was 23,000 ft (7,000 m) long. Once you've walked the wall—or, at least, some of it—stay in Ston for world-class oysters and wine. Spend as much time as you can spare on this idyllic peninsula, as there are many beaches and hiking trails to explore.

SAND, SEA, AND SUMMITS

When it's time to leave, cross the spectacular Pelješac Bridge, built in 2022 so that travelers rejoining the mainland could bypass Bosnia and Herzegovina, which runs down from the interior in a narrow strip that juts into the Croatian coastline.

On the other side, you'll drive past a series of picturesque towns and sloped, vineyard-dotted hills. The highway is peppered with beaches and rocky inlets, lapped by cool, azure waters, but there's as much to explore inland as there is along the coast. Taking the short detour into Biokovo Nature Park and its Skywalk observation deck offers unbeatable views of the coast.

When you reach the town of Makarska, stop to enjoy its tree-lined promenade

PELJEŠAC BRIDGE
This crossing was built in 2022, allowing drivers to bypass Bosnia and Herzegovina.
51 MILES (82 KM)

MAKARSKA
This beautiful seaside resort offers beaches and mountains to explore.
116 MILES (186 KM)

DALMATIAN COAST

177 MILES (284 KM)

KLIS FORTRESS
Make a quick pit stop at the hilltop castle, which sits 1,260 ft (385 m) above the city.

267 MILES (430 KM)

ZADAR
Watch the sun set in this premium art-filled city with Roman and Venetian history.

END

ZADAR

and fine pebble beaches. Makarska, in the heart of its eponymous riviera, also acts as a gateway to the surrounding mountains, which are popular for hiking, rock climbing, and mountain biking.

SPLIT-TING THE DISTANCE
Originally founded by Greeks in the 2nd or 3rd century BCE, Croatia's second city, Split, became the seat of the Roman Emperor some 500 years later. It's 50 miles (85 km) north of Makarska, but the change is palpable, as you swap a seaside resort for a historical heavyweight. Explore Diocletian's Palace, a city within a city, and its maze of cobbled streets, secret alleyways, and hidden courtyards, which now house shops, restaurants, and museums. Climb the cathedral's bell tower for views across Split's terracotta rooftops. There's so much to see here—if time allows, spend a few days exploring the city, absorbing its dynamic atmosphere and hopping between the picturesque islands just offshore.

Continue north from Split, making a quick detour to Klis Fortress, a castle that sits high in the hilltops above the city. Hop back in the car and breeze 90 miles (145 km) north to Zadar.

A quieter but still cosmopolitan city, Zadar has its fill of historical sites, from an impressive Roman forum and Byzantine church to its monastery.

Zadar's Greeting to the sun art installation comprises tiles that absorb the sun's energy and light up at night as you walk over them.

Come sunset, though, the city reveals its two unique draws. The *Sea Organ*, designed by local architect Nikola Bašić, plays a haunting tune as the waves lap the stone steps, while the *Greeting to the Sun* is an installation comprised of tiles that absorb the sun's energy and light up at night as you walk over them. As the sun sinks behind the islands, and the Sea Organ whistles its melody in the distance, you'll enjoy a memorable end to your trip.

ABOVE Zadar's *Greeting to the Sun* art installation

OPPOSITE TOP Ston village and its 14th-century stone wall

OPPOSITE BOTTOM Biokovo Nature Park's Skywalk deck

SPOMENIK CIRCUIT

START/END
Zagreb, Croatia/
Belgrade, Serbia

DISTANCE
745 miles (1,200 km)

DURATION
5-10 days

ROAD CONDITIONS
Well-maintained roads, with some gravel paths.

THE BEST TIME TO GO
In June, for Croatia's Anti-Fascist Struggle Day.

OPPOSITE Croatia's stainless-steel *Uprising Monument*, by Vojin Bakić

Take the roads less traveled through the Western Balkans on this retro-futurist trip into a country that no longer exists. On the way, you'll discover spomeniks—monuments that reflect the rise and demise of Socialist Yugoslavia.

Some countries put up monuments to the heroes of World War II; Yugoslavia erected *spomeniks*. The difference is more than just linguistic: Marshal Josip Broz Tito, the country's dominant leader from the end of the war until his death in 1980, ordered his architects and artists to create thousands of memorials to the Partisan rebels who ultimately freed Yugoslavia from Nazi occupation. The results—and there are tens of thousands of them—are little short of spectacular.

Spomeniks range in size from humble to humongous. Some are perfectly preserved, while others are dangerously dilapidated—several were victims of the nationalist movements that swept Yugoslavia in the 1990s.

Visiting them all would be an epic challenge. Instead, opt for a route that ties together the most striking, as well as taking in scenic locations and buzzing metropolises on the way.

ZAGREB AND GO

Croatia's capital, Zagreb, and the Dotrščina Memorial Park, is a good place to start. A polished stainless-steel and bronze sculpture, created by sculptor Vojin Bakić, forms the center of the park. It is dedicated to the civilians and resistance fighters murdered and buried in the area by Nazi forces and their Croatian allies, the Ustaše.

From here, make your way west to Mirogoj Cemetery. This quiet Gothic masterpiece on the city's fringes is perhaps one of its most beautiful sites. Explore the abundance of greenery, tiled arcades, and impressive domed

---

ZAGREB

START

SPOMENIKS

It's estimated that up to 40,000 *spomeniks* were erected across the former Yugoslavia.

MIROGOJ CEMETERY
This picturesque cemetery is the final resting place of many Croatian legends.

4 MILES (7 KM)

UPRISING MONUMENT
This eye-catching hilltop structure stretches 120 ft (37 m) high and 130 ft (40 m) wide.

192 MILES (309 KM)

PLITVICE LAKES NATIONAL PARK
Croatia's most famous national park is home to beautiful lakes.

239 MILES (384 KM)

KOZARA
Divert east from Bihać to admire Kozara's *Monument to the Revolution*.

pavilions, and get acquainted with the prominent citizens who permanently reside here. Zagreb's center itself is home to museums, monuments, and the Dolac Market, where you can sample Croatian cuisine and stock up on local produce for the journey ahead.

THE BALKAN WAY
Cruise into the Croatian countryside bound for Podgarić and the *Monument to the Revolution*, which takes the form of a massive winged eye. It honors the Partisan forces who made the surrounding area their base, eventually establishing hospitals, bakeries, schools, and even theaters to service the area's resistance movement. Dušan Džamonja's design was a personal favorite of Tito's, who kept a replica in his Zagreb home.

Leave the (quite possibly) all-seeing eye behind and wind your way through the Croatian countryside. As the pine trees drop away, the gleaming *spomenik* atop Veliki Petrovac hill appears. The *Uprising Monument* is another Vojin Bakić masterpiece. You'd be forgiven for thinking this was a dystopian vision: the monumental stainless-steel, multilevel structure glimmers in the sunlight. Take a closer look, though, and you'll see that many of the mirrored panels are missing or broken. Nevertheless, its undulating exterior—so starkly different from its surroundings—is mesmerizing.

It's not all about industrial wonders in this corner of Croatia, though. The breathtaking UNESCO-listed Plitvice Lakes National Park is home to 16 crystalline lakes, cascading waterfalls, and an abundance of flora and fauna. It's a fitting spot to say your goodbyes to the country, before resuming your drive across the border into Bosnia and Herzegovina.

After a 12-mile (20 km) drive, you'll arrive at the *Garavice Memorial*. The graffiti-covered *spomenik* is in poor condition, but Bihać, the city it calls home, is a perfect stop. From here, a diversion to the *Monument to the Revolution* at Kozara may tempt you.

EXTEND YOUR TRIP
This road trip takes in a tiny proportion of the bewildering number of *spomeniks* all over the former Yugoslavia—now six separate Balkan nations. If this trip has whet your appetite for more, check out the Spomenik Database, which has details on locations, access, and conditions for each site.

SPOMENIK CIRCUIT

449 MILES (722 KM)
SARAJEVO
Sample some of the city's best burek, a filled pastry, at Buregdžinica Sač.

746 MILES (1,200 KM)
BELGRADE
Bed down at the comforting Smokvica Jovanova B&B and explore the Serbian capital.

END
BELGRADE

Otherwise, speed through the mountains to Bosnia's capital, Sarajevo. *Spomenik* spotters should take the city's cable car up to Vraca Memorial Park, although the site is in almost as bad a state as the nearby bobsled track from the 1984 Winter Olympics. Its centerpiece is a mountain-shaped memorial, with steps leading up to an eternal flame.

From here, traverse the hills and valleys to Tjentište, and the *Battle of Sutjeska*, an otherworldly structure comprising two winglike concrete blocks that frame the mountainous scenery behind it. It's an important memorial that remembers 7,000 people who lost their lives here.

SERBO-CHARGED
Cross the border into Serbia and continue on to Belgrade, its capital. It's a lengthy route, but you'll check off some special *spomeniks* along the way. Visit the numerous monuments in Kadinjača Memorial Complex, Popina Memorial Park, Šumarice Memorial Park—a Miodrag Živković spectacular—and Kosmaj Mountain Park, with its spiky, starlike *spomenik*. When you reach Belgrade, let Serbia's warm hospitality wash over you. After a toast to these great, unearthly monuments and all they stand for, there's just one more concrete relic to admire: *Jabuka*, commemorating victims of the Holocaust in Serbia.

ABOVE The *Battle of Sutjeska,* in Tjentište

RIGHT The *spomenik* in Serbia's Kosmaj Mountain Park

OPPOSITE Dušan Džamonja's *Monument to the Revolution*

TRANSFĂGĂRĂȘAN HIGHWAY

START/END
Curtea de Argeș/ Cârțișoara, Romania

DISTANCE
80 miles (128 km)

DURATION
1 day

ROAD CONDITIONS
Tarmac road with twisting hairpins, swooping curves, and unguarded drops.

THE BEST TIME TO GO
The summer months; avoid November to mid-June, when the road is usually impassable.

OPPOSITE Lake Bâlea, crowning the high point of the Transfăgărășan Highway

To some, it's a dictator's folly. To others, it's the most beautiful road in the world. Either way, Romania's Transfăgărășan Highway makes for a spectacular journey into the country's stretch of the Carpathian Mountains.

The official designation gives nothing away. "DN7C" could mean anything from a chess move to a set of map coordinates. But, for those in the know, it points to one of the most remarkable routes in Europe: the Transfăgărășan Highway. Drivers, cyclists, and motorcyclists all make the pilgrimage to central Romania for this wild ride across the southern section of the Carpathians.

Don't be fooled by the name. This is not a six-lane expressway, but a single roadway with few obvious opportunities for overtaking. The road is narrow and by no means straight. Viewed from above, it seems like an Expressionist artist has been busy at work across the hilly landscape. It's a delightful and continuous squiggle that swoops up and down, taking an apparently whimsical tarmac path around the area's rocky formations. The Transfăgărășan may be paved, but, in every other respect, it remains untamed.

SHOW ON THE ROAD
Start your journey in Curtea de Argeș. The town's monastery dates back to the 16th century, and for generations Romanian royals were laid to rest here—right up to the funeral of the country's last king, Michael I, which was held in 2017. It is also the source of one of Romania's most cherished, and somber, folk tales: according to legend, the cathedral's macabre master mason, Manole, entombed his wife alive inside its walls to ensure the structure's integrity. Take a stroll around the grand ocher

CURTEA DE ARGEȘ — START

CARPATHIAN MOUNTAINS
The Carpathian Mountains stretch from the Czech Republic to Romania.

CURTEA DE ARGEȘ
This small town is home to a monastery with a royal history and grisly myth.
0 MILES (0 KM)

17 MILES (27 KM)

POENARI CITADEL

Hike up to Vlad the Impaler's home, thought to have inspired Bram Stoker's *Dracula*.

22 MILES (36 KM)

LAKE VIDRARU

Popular with canoers, this lake was formed when a dam was erected in the 1960s.

TOP The tumbledown walls of the now-ruined Poenari Citadel

ABOVE Brown bears abound in the Carpathian Mountains

exterior and make sure to pop your head inside to gaze at the interior's dark and dramatic frescoes.

Further tales from the dark side lie 17 miles (27 km) north along the first fairly straight section of the highway: Poenari Citadel is the former residence of a 15th-century warlord known as Vlad the Impaler. It is thought that the castle's violent owner served as the inspiration for Bram Stoker's blood-sucking Count Dracula. The castle itself is still suitably intimidating. Hidden within lush greenery, the ruin's tumbledown walls are reached by climbing 1,500 rickety steps.

A BALKAN BATTLE

Breath caught and legs stretched, it's time to brace yourself for the fun part of the Transfăgărășan, as it hugs the perimeter of Lake Vidraru. Pause at the gigantic dam for a vertiginous totter along the top of the 540 ft (166 m) high structure (bungee jump optional), before proceeding along the road as it traces the water's edge. Wildlife abounds here, so watch out for bears, foxes, and deer.

Drive north from the top of Lake Vidraru, where the road starts its steep climb and you'll start to get a sense of the scale of Romanian dictator Nicolae Ceaușescu's ambition when he ordered the highway's construction. The 1968 Soviet invasion of Czechoslovakia had made him nervous. The Transfăgărășan would ensure his forces could move quickly in the event of an invasion—with a route across the Făgăraș Mountains that divide northwestern and southern Romania. Construction lasted for more than a decade from its start in 1970, although the road officially opened for traffic in 1974. The human cost of Ceaușescu's project was considerable. Officially, 40 people died, but there's evidence from workers—most of them untrained junior military personnel—that puts casualties in the hundreds. Many accidents were thought to have been caused during the detonations of some 6,600 tons (6,000,000 kg) of dynamite.

Take care as you climb up the steep section, as cyclists like to descend the sweeping curves at high speed and you might meet two-wheeled traffic coming the other way.

A MOMENT ON THE MOUNTAIN

Soon, you'll pass the roaring Capra Waterfall. Pause to take a closer look at this tumbling natural beauty, before a tunnel takes you to the road's peak at the glacial Lake Bâlea. Here, the wooden terrace of the Bâlea Lake Cabin makes for a perfect pit stop. The peaks remain snow-topped, even in the summer months, and their lower slopes are a peaceful place for a stroll. Walks lead across rickety wooden bridges over bubbling streams, where you can watch the water flowing over rocks and into the lake.

The descent from Bâlea is the most challenging part of the drive, as the road twists tightly through the verdant forest. The bends at the top are broader, with fine views across the mountains; Bâlea Waterfall, with its 200 ft (60 m) drop, is a beautiful spot to stop and drink them in. Take it easy from here until the end of the drive—average speeds are around 25 mph (40 km/h) and potential hazards include flocks of slow-moving sheep bleating their away along the road.

The switchbacks continue right down to the village of Cârțișoara, where the Highway comes to an end. It's a quiet village with only its natural surroundings to entertain you, but after a day on the thrilling Transfăgărășan, that's the only entertainment you'll need.

> **The descent from Lake Bâlea makes for the most challenging part of the drive, as the road twists tightly through the verdant forest.**

ABOVE The elegant Capra Waterfall

BÂLEA LAKE CABIN
Stop at the Tiroliana Bâlea Lac viewpoint for a photo of the cabin across the lake.
60 MILES (97 KM)

BÂLEA WATERFALL
This pretty cascade features a mighty 200 ft (60 m) drop, which roars loudest in spring.
65 MILES (105 KM)

CÂRȚIȘOARA
This small town offers cozy hotels and B&Bs to relax in after your thrilling drive.
80 MILES (128 KM)

CÂRȚIȘOARA
END

CENTRAL MOUNTAINS

START/END
Plovdiv/Veliko Târnovo, Bulgaria

DISTANCE
158 miles (255 km)

DURATION
2–3 days

ROAD CONDITIONS
Single roadways with limited overtaking opportunities.

THE BEST TIME TO GO
An early June trip will coincide with Kazanlak's renowned Rose Festival.

OPPOSITE Inside the abandoned Buzludzha Monument

This winding drive up and over the mountain range that gives the Balkan peninsula its name takes in some of Europe's most ancient settlements, as well as monuments to history-altering battles and vibrant folklore.

The mountain range that cuts a line across Bulgaria's middle has many names. Locals call it Stara Planina, the "Old Mountain," while visitors refer to it as the Central Mountains. It is also known simply as Balkan, a word that derives from Turkish and means "a chain of wooded mountains." It's a fitting moniker for a route that traverses impenetrable forests and sweeping valleys. But the route also explores the country's tumultuous history, weaving between Roman ruins, hidden Thracian tombs and Communist-era monuments.

PLOVDING ALONG

Bulgaria's second city, Plovdiv, is where your journey starts. Like Rome, it was built on seven hills (though, thanks to one being quarried, there are now only six). One of the city's oldest sights is its hilltop amphitheater, the Ancient Theatre of Philippopolis. Don't be fooled by its appearance—the 6,000-seat venue is now a modern hub that hosts everything from opera and heavy metal to music festivals.

The two hills in Plovdiv's old town reveal fascinating historical structures at their summits: Nebet Tepe is home to Thracian ruins from 5000 BCE, while Bunardzhik Tepe is topped with a towering statue that depicts a Russian soldier. It's Bulgaria's answer to Rio de Janeiro's *Christ the Redeemer*. Back down to earth, whiz around Plovdiv's creative arm for galleries, shops, and restaurants, where you can buy folkloric art and fuel up on *banitsa*, a cheese-filled phyllo pastry pie.

PLOVDIV
START

CENTRAL MOUNTAINS
This mountain range is known as Balkan, Turkish for "a chain of wooded mountains."

PLOVDIV
Plovdiv is said to be the oldest continuously inhabited city in Europe.
0 MILES (0 KM)

STARA ZAGORA
Explore Roman ruins and pretty parks and visit the Zagorka Brewery Museum.

64 MILES (103 KM)

SHIPKA MEMORIAL CHURCH
This beautiful church is dedicated to soldiers killed in the Russo-Turkish War.

93 MILES (150 KM)

MOUNT STOLETOV
This peak sits at 4,360 ft (1,329 m) above sea level.

103 MILES (165 KM)

ABOVE The unique frescoes inside the Thracian tomb of Aleksandrovo.

OPPOSITE ABOVE Kazanlak's Buzludzha Monument exterior

OPPOSITE BELOW Veliko Tărnovo from inside the Tsarevets Fortress walls

CONCRETE JUNGLE

When you're ready, hit Bulgaria's answer to Route 66, bound for Stara Zagora. Set in the southern foothills of the Sredna Mountains, the city was decimated during the Russo-Turkish War in 1877, when around 14,000 civilians died. The Samara Flag monument commemorates the city's doomed defenders, who fought until they ran out of ammunition. Unveiled in 1977, the huge Brutalist memorial comprises a 50 ft (15 m) high monolith alongside seven stone columns featuring encased soldiers. It's an epic concrete compilation.

Driving on through the mountainous scenery, tranquil greenery gives way to dense forests, and a towering stone Roman bridge cuts dramatically across the highway. Soon, Rose Valley appears.

The name is literal: the region, which produces half of the world's rose oil, is dedicated to cultivating the sweetly scented blooms. Head for Kazanlak, the valley's central point and the host town of the annual Rose Festival. During the region's celebrations in early June, visitors are invited to take part in the traditional rose-picking rituals. If you're there in the offseason, the Museum of Roses is an informative alternative stop.

Like the Central Mountains, this whole area has another name: the Valley of Thracian Kings, for its concentration of ancient tombs. Highlights include the Kazanlak Tomb and the Tomb of Seuthes III, with an imposing bust of the king himself, although the best-preserved example is the UNESCO-listed 4th-century Thracian Tomb of Aleksandrovo, 37 miles (60 km) south of Stara Zagora but worth the detour, thanks to its unique frescoes.

North of Kazanlak, stop by the Muscovite-style Shipka Memorial Church, with its golden onion domes and Russian

CENTRAL MOUNTAINS

131 MILES (210 KM)

GABROVO
Brush up on your one-liners at Gabrovo's House of Humor and Satire.

158 MILES (255 KM)

TSAREVETS FORTRESS
Veliko Tărnovo hilltop fortress is home to Ascension Cathedral and its secular frescoes.

END

VELIKO TĂRNOVO

Orthodox crosses. From here, the road twists and turns as it climbs to Mount Stoletov, where a turnoff leads to the Buzludzha Monument. This hulking concrete building, accompanied by a tower topped with a huge red star, could be mistaken for a grounded spaceship. In reality, it's a former Socialist assembly hall fallen into disrepair—but a work of architectural mastery nonetheless.

SHIPKA SHAPE
Back on the E85, the serpentine bends of the Shipka Pass reward drivers with 26 monuments that commemorate the area's past battles. On the other side lies Gabrovo, best known for its House of Humor and Satire. It's more than just a laugh, though; the locals take their jokes seriously and host a witty carnival each May.

As you keep descending, the road straightens out and Veliko Tărnovo and the imposing Tsarevets Fortress take shape. Within the hilltop settlement—the remains of the Second Bulgarian Kingdom's capital—is the Ascension Cathedral museum. Rebuilt in 1981, the site's nonreligious frescoes have since prevented it from being reconsecrated. In town, kick back at a café on Gurko Street for a view of the Interhotel Veliko Tărnovo—a decaying yet fascinating example of Brutalist design—and the serene Yantra River below. Behind, the 5th-century Tsarevets Fortress looms large, a fittingly architectural finale to a route steeped in contrasting wonders.

STRATEGIC SHIPKA

Between 1877 and 1878, the four battles that took place on and around the Shipka Pass ultimately helped secure Bulgaria's freedom after more than 500 years of Ottoman control. The *opalchentsi* (volunteer soldiers) who fought with the Russians at the Battle of Shipka Pass went on to form the Bulgarian Army.

187

ALBANIAN RIVIERA

START/END
Durrës/Ksamil, Albania

DISTANCE
168 miles (269 km)

DURATION
5-7 days

ROAD CONDITIONS
Paved roads, with some in need of repair. Mountain passes have narrow sections and blind corners.

THE BEST TIME TO GO
Late spring to early fall, for the clearest views and best road conditions.

OPPOSITE The water-lapped shores of Butrint National Park

Albania's Riviera is one of Europe's last remaining secrets. On a drive along this underappreciated coast, you'll discover a Roman amphitheater, Cold War–era bunkers, and a string of sandy beaches. Hit the Riviera road before word gets out.

The Albanian Riveria, which runs south of Tirana as far as Greece and faces the heel of Italy's boot, is a wild and beautiful coastline. This journey delivers pristine beaches—lapped by the crystal-clear Ionian sea—in spades, not to mention mountains, lagoons, and forests. There are human-made treasures, too, with building that have witnessed immense historical shifts, from the rule of the Ottoman Empire right up to Albania's ill-fated Communist regime.

UNDER DURRËS

Albania's second city, coastal Durrës, makes for an excellent starting point. It was founded by the Corinthians in 627 BCE and still bears the influence of past empires. Among them are Hadrian's Roman amphitheater, once the largest ancient arena in the Balkans, and Durrës Castle, a walled fortress that counts Byzantines, Romans, and Ottomans among its past occupiers. But it's not all ancient history here. While the Communist era has left its mark on the city's skyline by way of old Soviet-style housing blocks, there's a burgeoning creative scene in Dürres, with art galleries and live-music venues cropping up on nearly every street.

Swing by the golden 6-mile (10 km) long beach on your way out of town. One of the only vacation options under Communist rule, it is still a hub of activity today. The promenade is a beautiful place for an evening walk or *xhiro*, while the modern concrete embankment, the *Sfinksi* (the Sphinx of Durrës), is a popular place to watch the sun go down.

DURRËS

START

XHIRO
An evening *xhiro*, which translates as "walk," is a key element of Albanian culture.

DURRËS
Watch the sunset from the *Sfinksi* steps—part art installation, part sea defense.
0 MILES (0 KM)
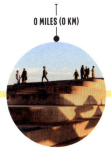

33 MILES (53 KM)

DIVJAKA-KARAVASTA NATIONAL PARK

Tour this vast wetland to spot more than 200 species of birds.

76 MILES (123 KM)

VLORË

The National Independence Museum charts Albania's complex history.

South of Durrës is a site of unusual natural beauty and significance—Divjaka-Karavasta National Park, a vast wetlands home to more than 200 species of birds, including the endangered Dalmatian pelican and greater flamingo. Continuing on the road leads shortly to another park, this time for history buffs. Greek colonists founded the resort town of Apollonia in the 6th century, and today its Greek and Roman ruins are a fascinating place to visit. Philosopher Cicero called it "a great and important city."

With archaeology under your belt, continue south to Vlorë, the former capital of Albania. This coastal town, set in a natural harbor opposite Italy's Brindisi where the Ionian and Adriatic meet, has a distinctly Mediterranean feel, with local restaurants serving Neapolitan pizza, fresh seafood, and gelato beside the glittering seashore. It was in Vlorë that Albania declared independence from the Ottoman Empire in 1912; the National Independence Monument and museum are well worth a stop.

TUNNEL VISION

Hug the coast until you reach the bobbing boats in Orikum marina, where the road cuts inland toward the Dukat Valley. You'll pass the alpine meadows, rocky cliffs, and dense forests of Llogara National Park, as the imposing peaks of the Ceraunian Mountains appear ahead of you.

From here, you can take the quick route to Llogara through Albania's longest tunnel, which runs beneath the rocky peaks, or plump for an exhilarating mountain pass that snakes upward to more than 3,300 ft (1,000 m) above sea level and offers

LEFT National Independence Monument in Vlorë

BELOW The white-sand beaches of Ksamil

ALBANIAN RIVIERA

LEFT The Roman amphitheater ruins in Butrint National Park

DAFT BUNK

Bunkers are ubiquitous in Albania. They were dictator Enver Hoxha's response to his fears of being invaded. Thousands of these dome-shaped concrete shelters were built, ranging from two-person huts to multiroomed lairs, and Hoxha impoverished the country by spending vast amounts on their construction. Many have crumbled, while others have been repurposed as museums, barns, food stalls, and changing rooms.

stunning vistas at every hairpin bend. If you opt for the spine-tingling ascent, pause at one of the roadside restaurants at the top to savor the views of Mount Çika, at 6,706 ft (2,044 m), the Ceraunian ountains' highest peak—and a taste of Albanian fare.

SOUTHERN SUN

On your descent from the pass, keep an eye out for Cold War–era bunkers, which are often half obscured by the trees. When you reach the other side of the mountain, the first beaches you'll hit are in Himarë, a fishing village with a small castle with views across to Corfu. Stop for a quick dip before continuing on to Porto Palermo, a giant triangular fortress perched dramatically on a peninsula and looking out over the sea. The Albanian ruler Ali Pasha, who served the Ottoman Empire, built the castle in the early 19th century. It was used as a prison during World War II, and a Soviet submarine base during the Communist regime.

Continue motoring south, tracing the coastline as you go. The farther south you travel, the better the beaches and the more turquoise the waters, and there are any number of tempting coves and little bays along this stretch. After 40 miles (60 km), you'll arrive in Ksamil, nicknamed the "Maldives of Albania" for its white sand and crystalline sea. It's an enchanting end point to your trip and the perfect base to explore the surrounding area—there's more than enough in and around Ksamil to extend your stay in Albania. Sporty types can rent a boat or kayak to visit the islands just off the coast, while the nearby UNESCO-listed Butrint National Park is home to marshes, forests, sandy beaches, a bounty of wildlife, and, most spectacularly of all, concealed Greek and Roman ruins. As with the rest of the country, you will want to take your time uncovering its hidden treasures.

MOUNT ÇIKA
Stretch your legs on a hike to the Ceraunian Mountains' highest peak.

103 MILES (165 KM)

HIMARË
This quiet fishing village is a great base to explore the area's beautiful beaches.

129 MILES (208 KM)

KSAMIL
Visit the nearby Butrint National Park to see ancient ruins and abundant wildlife.

167 MILES (269 KM)

KSAMIL

END

PELOPONNESE PENINSULA

START/END
Porto Cheli/Ancient Olympia, Greece

DISTANCE
372 miles (599 km)

DURATION
7–10 days

ROAD CONDITIONS
Highways are smooth and easily navigable, but some of the rural, mountainous roads are less well maintained.

THE BEST TIME TO GO
Beaches and cultural sites are quieter in fall.

OPPOSITE Epidauros's 4th-century BCE amphitheater

Follow in the footsteps of the ancients with this tour of the rural Peloponnese peninsula, a rugged region famed for its quintessential Greek charm. Among its pristine natural beauty, a variety of intriguing ruins await.

Many vacationers to Greece head straight for its idyllic islands. Stick to the Peloponnese peninsula, on the mainland's southernmost tip, however, and you'll be signing up for an epic, and ancient, cross-country road trip. Spend a week or so cruising by Mycenaean palaces, Byzantine cities, and Venetian fortresses, all against a backdrop of turquoise seas and mythic mountains.

THE GATEWAY TO GREECE
The Mycenaeans ruled from 1600 to 1100 BCE, and traces of their mighty dominion still lie scattered across Greece's eastern region, Argolis. Porto Cheli, a jet-setter's beach town, is where your journey starts. With a large port popular with wealthy yacht owners, the glitzy seaside resort has become known as the "Riviera of the Peloponnese" for its buzzy, cosmopolitan atmosphere. The glut of lovely local restaurants makes it a great base for exploring the surrounding vineyards, while the plentiful pine and cyprus groves on either side of town conceal a warren of unspoiled coves and beaches that are just a scenic hike away.

It's tempting to linger in this tranquil spot, but this is just a taster. Hop in the car and head north past the rolling green hills toward Epidauros. Once famed for the healing qualities of its waters, this ancient town attracts modern crowds for a different reason today: its impeccable 14,000-seater limestone amphitheater. Dating from the 4th century BCE, the site is one of the best-conserved ancient Greek

PORTO CHELI

PORTO CHELI
Before you hit the road, take advantage of Porto Cheli's beautiful beaches.

0 MILES (0 KM)

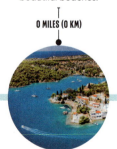

EPIDAUROS
Not only is this amphitheater still standing, it's still in use. Greek plays are staged every summer.

34 MILES (55 KM)

51 MILES (82 KM)

NAFPLIO
Bourtzi Castle is accessible by boat and has striking views of the Nafplio and Argolic Gulf.

150 MILES (242 KM)

SPARTA
Greet the late King Leonidas I's statue and stroll ancient ruins in this once-significant city.

structures in existence. Test out the fine acoustics—a whispered word on stage can supposedly be heard on the top row—before heading into the hinterland.

Drive west on the vibrant oleander-flanked roads to the pretty coastal town of Nafplio, the first capital of modern Greece. The romantic city boasts resplendent Neo-Classical architecture, such as the Fortress of Palamidi, which was built by the Venetians in the 17th century. The 15th-century fortified islet in the harbor, known as Bourtzi, is accessible only by boat and is a magical place to visit—especially at sunset. Handily, Nafplio has an abundance of smart hotels, boutiques, and tavernas, tucked away down narrow alleys, if you want to stay the night.

Well rested and raring to go, cut across the sprawling plains filled with dense olive groves to the modern village of Mykines. Here, you will find the UNESCO-listed archaeological site of Mycenae. Set against a majestic mountain backdrop, the complex of ruins was once the fortified capital of the Mycenaean civilization, and was discovered by amateur archaeologist Heinrich Schliemann in the 1870s. The Lion Gate entrance and vast beehive-shaped tombs mark the site where rulers, including famed King Agamemnon, are said to be buried.

Set against a majestic mountain backdrop, the complex of ruins was once the fortified capital of the Mycenaean civilization.

THIS IS SPARTA
Cruise through the rugged, sun-scorched hills of Arcadia to Tripoli, continuing south to Sparta. Little remains in this modern city to point to its mythic significance, but in ancient times the kingdom was famed for its fearless warriors, and rivaled Athens in size. Its last "remaining soldier" is King Leonidas I, who stands defiantly (in statue form) beside the

BELOW The ancient ruins of UNESCO-listed Mycenae

LEFT The seaside village of Kardamyli

ANCIENT GREECE

Reportedly founded in the 9th century BCE, Sparta was an important military city in ancient Greece. According to legend, the city was always ruled by two kings at the same time, who were both directly descended from Hercules, the son of Zeus.

city's soccer stadium. Glimpse further into Sparta's period of antiquity at the Archaeological Museum or the ruins of the Agora and Temple of Artemis on the Acropolis Hill.

DIGGING DEEP IN MANI

From Sparta, continue south along the E961 with the snowcapped peaks of the Taÿgetos—the peninsula's highest mountain range—towering to your right. When the hills begin to close in, you've entered the Mani peninsula, a region famed for its wild beauty. For centuries, the area was beset by pirates, forcing inhabitants to build their homes in small mountain settlements. Traverse the rugged terrain to reach the peninsula's western coast, which is made up of rocky, secluded coves hemmed in by pristine forests and small fishing villages. From here, you can drop south into the lesser-visited Inner or "Deep" Mani. A thistle-flanked main road (there is only one) transports you into the barely populated region. It is used by few, though you may spot an occasional sheep roaming the dusty lanes. From the main town of Areopoli, head to Gerolimenas for its deserted pebble beaches, before climbing the hills to the ancient, and eerie, abandoned village of Vathia. If you're mythically minded, delve deeper in search of the so-called Cave of Hades and Cape Tainaron lighthouse, set at the alleged entrance to the Underworld, before retracing your steps out of Mani.

Back on the main highway, where folklore feels once again fictitious, an oasis awaits. The seaside village of Kardamyli boasts a fortified complex at its center, crowned by the stocky stone spire of St. Spyridon church. The village, with its nearby Mount Taÿgetos, makes a great base for hikers. Continue along the coast, where scenic, olive-

TAŸGETOS
This mountain range is crisscrossed with scenic hikes that lead to stone villages.

157 MILES (252 KM)

GEROLIMENAS
Recharge at one of the boutique hotels in this tranquil town in Deep Mani.

193 MILES (310 KM)

MANI PENINSULA
The Cape Tainaron lighthouse sits on the southernmost tip of this rugged promontory.

203 MILES (327 KM)

300 MILES (482 KM)
POLYLIMNIO WATERFALLS
Take a dip beneath the cascading waters at this natural beauty spot.

313 MILES (503 KM)
GIALOVA LAGOON
This coastal wetland is a birdwatcher's paradise, home to more than 270 species.

END — OLYMPIA

ABOVE Doric columns stand tall in ancient Olympia

EXTEND YOUR TRIP

Ready to flop on a Greek island? From Olympia, it's a two-hour drive north to Patras, at the top of the Peloponnese peninsula. Regular ferry services run from here to the Ionian islands of Zakynthos and Kefalonia.

tree-lined beaches such as Ritsa and Kalamitsi are lapped by the warm waters of the Messenian Gulf.

Soon, you'll enter Messenia itself, a region loved by locals for its cruise-ship-free coastline. As you travel deeper, you'll pass acre upon acre of sprawling olive groves. Beyond the inland town of Kazarma, you'll reach a spectacular natural formation: the Polylimnio waterfalls. A hike into the densely forested gorge here takes you to this paradisiacal series of cascades for a cooling dip in the turquoise rock pools.

As the sea appears once more, the picturesque town of Pylos lies dead ahead, across two hills facing the bay of Navarino. Historic monuments dot the landscape, including two castles; one built by the Turks in 1573, the other dating from the 13th century.

From here, the final leg takes you north past the Gialova Lagoon, a stretch of coastal wetland populated by rare species of birds such as flamingos, ospreys, and herons. Nearby is Voidokilia beach, a perfect white-sand crescent with brilliant azure waters. After 40 miles (70 km) on the road—and lots of potential beachy pit stops along the way—Lake Kaiafas, a serene thermal pool, takes shape on the horizon. According to ancient Greek mythology, this is where nymphs bathed and centaurs came to heal.

LET THE GAMES BEGIN

Leave the coast behind and steer through the pine-forested hills to reach the trip's pinnacle: ancient Olympia. This iconic UNESCO World Heritage Site was the birthplace of the Olympic Games, which were founded in the 8th century BCE and took place every four years for over a millennium. While the Games are now held around the world, the Olympic flame is still lit here before each new Games begins. Today, the olive-tree-shaded ruins, with their towering Doric columns, point to the site's former glory.

THE GRAND TOUR

The Grand Tour started with aristocratic young Englishmen in the 17th and 18th centuries. They would bid farewell to their family, cross the Channel, and set off in search of adventure and edification on the Continent. It became a rite of passage.

The "Tour"—a term coined by Catholic priest and travel writer Richard Lassels in 1670—existed somewhere between a term abroad and a gap year. The wealthy men, and later women, who embarked on these journeys had been educated in the Classics. The Tour was deemed an opportunity to further their education, by studying Italian art or Greek architecture at their source. Of course, being young people, studying wasn't all they did. They also took advantage of their independence to indulge in drinking, carousing, and gambling in locales such as Venice.

Grand Tourists traveled primarily by carriage and frequently spent a year or more on the Continent. The Tour didn't have a defined route, but a stop in Paris was de rigueur, and nearly all routes culminated, or spent significant time, in Italy—Rome in particular.

There were few museums in Europe, so most art was encountered in situ or in private collections, and these intimate experiences often had a lasting impact. Many travelers bought art to take home. Giovanni Battista Piranesi's prints of Rome and Canaletto's Venetian scenes were popular in the 1700s. Others returned with architectural inspiration. Inigo Jones, whose 1613 to 1614 jaunt around Italy made him one of the earliest Grand Tourists, went on to design the first classical building in England, the Queen's House in Greenwich. Two centuries later, Sir Charles Monck based his designs for Belsay Hall on the Athenian Temple of Hephaestus.

The Grand Tour eventually fell victim to geopolitical events, coming to an end around the turn of the 19th century, as the French Revolutionary War and Napoleonic Wars hindered travel to France and Italy. By then, Europe had fully caught the tourism bug. Today the spirit of the Tour lives on in the Erasmus+ program, Eurail passes, and, of course, the great European road trip.

> The "Tour"— a term coined by Catholic priest and travel writer Richard Lassels in 1670—existed somewhere between a term abroad and a gap year.

ABOVE An Englishman leaving for the Grand Tour

PINDUS MOUNTAINS

START/END
Athens/Zagori, Greece

DISTANCE
433 miles (698 km)

DURATION
7-10 days

ROAD CONDITIONS
The mountain roads are well maintained but a little precarious at times. Highways are smooth and safe but operate using a toll-paying system.

THE BEST TIME TO GO
Spring or summer, to avoid snowy road closures in the winter.

OPPOSITE Meteora's natural rock formations, topped with ancient monasteries

Greece's rugged beauty is at its most dramatic on this spellbinding route, which runs the length of the country. On the way, you'll discover the untamed wilds of the Pindus mountains, with high peaks, lush forests, and deep valleys.

Greece's photogenic coastline might hog the limelight, but visitors who stray from the seashore to travel inland will be rewarded by an unspoiled, wild beauty and sense of tranquility that feels far from the madding crowds. Traversing the Pindus mountains, the backbone of mainland Greece, is the pinnacle of such a drive, as you make your way from the Greek capital to the border with Albania.

THE CITY OF THE VIOLET CROWN
There's no better place to start than the vibrant metropolis of Athens. The ruin-strewn Greek capital is towered over by perhaps its most famed site, the Acropolis. Soak up nearly 2,500 years of history—plus sprawling views across the city—before descending into the trendy Koukaki neighborhood. Tucked away in the shadows of the ancient citadel, this atmospheric spot offers a slice of true Athenian life. It's filled with lively restaurants and bakeries and is just the place to grab a bite to eat before hitting the road.

Head west from Athens on the A8, following the shoreline across the northern edge of the Saronic Gulf, where you'll cross the Corinth Canal. The steep-sided tidal waterway is a real engineering marvel, cutting a line through the solid rock of the Isthmus of Corinth and joining two bodies of water on either side. It was finished in the late 19th century, but the idea was first proposed in the 7th century BCE. Stop to peer down into the channel to glimpse the boats squeezing through.

ATHENS
START

ATHENS
Fuel up for your journey at Koukaki's Pandora bakery with a traditional Greek pie.
0 MILES (0 KM)

CORINTH CANAL
Admire this 19th-century waterway, which connects the gulfs on either side.
48 MILES (77 KM)

RIO-ANTIRRIO BRIDGE
The world's longest cable-stayed bridge transports drivers over the Gulf of Corinth.

130 MILES (209 KM)

PANTA VRECHEI
Falls provide a constant showerlike stream of water in this ethereal gorge.

195 MILES (313 KM)

METEORA
Visit the ancient monasteries atop natural sky-high rocks in this dramatic region.

330 MILES (531 KM)

Continue along the A8, tracing the northern shore of the Peloponnese. Just before you hit Patras, you'll take the Rio-Antirrio Bridge to cross back into mainland Greece. Your journey into the foothills of the Pindus mountains soon begins, with a winding route that leads through thick greenery to reach Ano Chora, a picturesque mountain village of traditional stone dwellings.

Head eastward toward Trichonida, Greece's largest lake. It's a serene spot surrounded by forests and dotted with small pebble beaches—which are perfect for a swimming pit stop. From here, the road starts to wind along paths that are carved dramatically into the steep mountainsides. After 45 miles (75 km), you'll reach the village of Roska, where you can hike through Panta Vrechei, a canyon lined with hundreds of small waterfalls that form rocky pools for more swimming. It's a natural phenomenon with fairy-tale appeal. On clear days, the magic intensifies when the sun's rays refract in the mist to create miniature rainbows.

IN THE HEAVENS
Continue snaking along the high-altitude roads before dropping down into the sprawling plain of Thessaly. Cruise north through this vast stretch of flat, agricultural land to one of Greece's most striking heritage sites. The Meteora region is home to dozens of extraordinary sandstone formations that jut sharply out of the forested valley floor. If that wasn't impressive enough, ancient monasteries perch perilously atop the rocky pillars. A visit to one of these religious houses—which were somehow fixed into place from the 11th century—is worth it for the views alone: epic vistas down over plains, up to the mountains, and across to the other tower-top structures nearby. If you visit only one of the six active sites, make it Moni Agias Varvaras Rousanou, so you can meet its welcoming nuns and admire the chapel's stunning stained-

EXTEND YOUR TRIP
The northern region of Epirus boasts a stretch of idyllic coastline along its western edge. The colorful seaside town of Parga is just over an hour's drive from Ioannina and has regular ferry services to the nearby island of Paxos.

394 MILES (634 KM)

IOANNINA
Greece's third-largest city has plentiful cultural sights, such as its Silversmithing Museum.

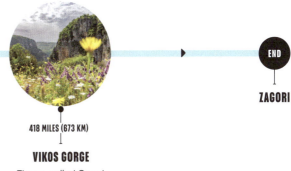

418 MILES (673 KM)

VIKOS GORGE
The so-called Grand Canyon of Greece is rife with adventurous hiking trails.

END

ZAGORI

glass windows. Better yet, stay the night to experience the incredible—and photo-worthy—sunrises and sunsets.

GORGE-OUS ZAGORI
Return to the Pindus mountains and wind westward through dense pine forests and craggy peaks to Metsovo, a pretty mountain town renowned for its traditional stone architecture. Continue to Ioannina, the lakeside capital of the Epirus region. While it might be Greece's third-largest city, it's far from a modern metropolis—the city is brimming with immaculately preserved cultural heritage sites. Most are found in the fortified old town, which occupies a rocky promontory in the lake. Visit the Silversmithing Museum and hop across the water by boat to Ioannina Island to see the fascinating frescoes of Moni Filanthropinon monastery.

Ioannina is a worthy end point to this trip, but drive a little further to the undiscovered northern region of Zagori and you'll be rewarded with plunging gorges, glacial rivers, and ancient stone villages. This enchanting region, where you'll encounter more wildlife than fellow travelers, is known for its hiking routes that lead to sites of real natural beauty. Pocket your car keys and soothe away the journey in the hot-spring-fed rock pools at Papingo and lush Vikos Gorge.

RIGHT The mountain town of Metsovo

BELOW Zagori's Papingo rock pools, fed by hot springs

OPPOSITE The waterfall-lined Panta Vrechei gorge

ANATOLIA

START/END
Ankara, Turkey

DISTANCE
612 miles (985 km)

DURATION
5-7 days

ROAD CONDITIONS
The highways are long, straight, and flat—perfect for cruise control.

THE BEST TIME TO GO
Late spring and early fall, when temperatures cool and there are fewer tourists to contend with at major sights.

OPPOSITE Hot-air balloons floating above Göreme in Cappadocia

This circular route winds around Turkey's Anatolia region, taking in the extraordinary ruins of some of the country's earliest civilizations and crossing unearthly landscapes to balloon-strewn Cappadocia.

This central sweep of Turkey sees you traversing one of the great crossroads of ancient civilizations. In its rich history, Anatolia has been ruled by the Hittites, Romans, and Byzantines. It has survived a string of invasions by the Arabs and Mongols and was conquered by the Ottomans in the 15th century, who made Istanbul (then known as Constantinople) the center of their territories. When their empire crumbled in 1922, Kemal Atatürk set up government in the Anatolian city of Ankara, which is the capital today.

DROPPING IN TO ANKARA

The bustling streets of Ankara mark the starting point of this Turkish sojourn. The youthful city houses the fascinating Museum of Anatolian Civilizations, where you can give yourself a good grounding in the history of the region, and the well-preserved 9th-century citadel, which serves as a reminder of the city's Byzantine roots. Trace the thick walls that circle the capital before setting off.

Travel east through the vast open plains to reach Hattuşa, the capital of the ancient Hittite kingdom. This mountainous, isolated spot was discovered by archaeologists in 1834, and certain parts are still under excavation. Visitors can wander among the enchanting ruins and admire the impressive ornamental structures, such as Lions Gate. Around 1 mile (2 km) away is the open-air temple and gallery of Yazılıkaya, which means "Inscribed Rock." Aptly, it is filled with figurative depictions of gods and goddesses, which have been carved into stone.

ANKARA
Turkey's cosmopolitan capital also boasts a Byzantine hilltop citadel.
0 MILES (0 KM)

HATTUŞA
The ancient Hittite capital was built in the 14th century BCE and is rife with carved ruins.
124 MILES (200 KM)

ANKARA
START

ABOVE The majestic snow-capped Hasandağı volcano

LEFT The Dark Church, in Göreme Open-Air Museum

OPPOSITE Konya's Mevlâna Museum, an important pilgrimage site

THE CITY THAT ROCKS

From Yazılıkaya, the road dips south into sun-baked Cappadocia. The rugged plateau north of the Taurus Mountains is known for its extraordinary geological formations, which were created some 25 million years ago out of the lava and ash from the surrounding volcanoes. These otherworldly landscapes are particularly pronounced in Göreme National Park, an epic stretch of sweeping valleys that are spiked with uncannily shaped rock chimneys. It's customary to view them from the sky: ride a hot-air balloon at sunrise when the landscape below is bathed in the golden light of dawn.

It's not all hot air, though. The park is awash with impressive archaeological wonders, the most famous at the UNESCO-listed Göreme Open-Air Museum. Here, a cluster of churches, originally believed to be a Byzantine monastic settlement, are chiseled into the rising cliff-face. The most spectacular is the Dark Church (so-called for its lack of windows), which is filled with a stunning array of colorful frescoes depicting biblical scenes. You can get a feel for this unusual settlement with an overnight stay at one of Göreme's cave hotels, which have been carved out of the soft volcanic rock.

CAPPADOCIA
Known for hot-air balloon rides and rocky churches, this region is also a hiker's paradise.

244 MILES (393 KM)

GÖREME
Spend a night in an ancient cave dwelling—with a few modern amenities, of course.

246 MILES (396 KM)

ANATOLIA

411 MILES (661 KM)

KONYA
Visit one of Turkey's biggest pilgrimage sites, before browsing Bedesten Bazaar.

529 MILES (851 KM)

LAKE TUZ
This sprawling salt lake offers stunning crimson hues and unique birdlife in the summer.

END

ANKARA

EXTEND YOUR TRIP

A few hours northwest of Ankara lies the lush province of Bolu, a region renowned for its tranquil lakes, dense forests, and pretty Ottoman towns. It feels a world away from the sprawling moonscapes of Cappadocia. In summer, this is a great spot for hiking, and when snow falls in winter, you can head to the resorts in the Köroğlu Mountains for skiing.

DOWN UNDER

You've seen a city built into the rocks, but what about a subterranean settlement? Derinkuyu Underground City, 20 miles (35 km) south of Göreme, lies some 280 ft (85 m) below ground, and comprises 18 levels of tunnels. It's thought the Hittites constructed the site to provide protection against invading forces, and its vast network of chambers continued to grow for millennia. During the Byzantine period, up to 20,000 people made their home here, with the sunken city remaining occupied until the last inhabitants left in the 1920s.

From here, the road sweeps through pink- and yellow-hued hillsides, past the soaring, snowcapped peak of Hasandağı volcano, and through Bozdağ National Park. When you reach the buzzy university city of Konya, you'll see its ancient mosques and a maze-like market district at its core. Within the Islamic world, Konya has serious religious significance; it's the home of Sufism, a practice in which believers seek to obtain direct personal experience of God through a variety of mystical practices. The best known is the deeply spiritual whirling dervish dance. The city's Mevlâna Museum is dedicated to Sufism and its 13th-century leader, Mevlâna Celaleddin Rumi, and the center has become one of Turkey's biggest pilgrimage sites. The museum, housed in the elegant mosque in which Mevlâna is buried, stages performances of this dynamic, spinning ritual that visitors can experience free of charge.

Leave Konya and all its spinning glory behind, and start the straight run through sparsely populated plains and large green fields to the village of Bozan on the banks of Lake Tuz. This enormous salt flat produces 60 percent of Turkey's salt and is a spectacle year-round. In winter, its waters are a glassy shade of ice blue; while it mostly dries up in summer, what's left turns a dramatic shade of crimson as the algae blooms.

This final stretch ends in the city where your trip began: magnificent Ankara. If you arrive early, gorge on a traditional Turkish breakfast complete with sesame-seed encrusted bread, briny olives, fresh tomatoes, fried eggs, and spiced *sucuk* sausage. *Günaydın!*

ATLANTIC ROAD

START/END
Kvernes/Bud, Norway

DISTANCE
33 miles (53 km)

DURATION
3-6 hours

ROAD CONDITIONS
Well-maintained, paved roads.

THE BEST TIME TO GO
Spring, when the wildflowers bloom.

OPPOSITE An island-hopping stretch of Norway's scenic Atlantic Road

An exquisite expression of what happens when engineering genius meets show-stopping natural beauty, the Atlantic Road is an unforgettable drive through a dramatic archipelago on Norway's windswept northern coast.

What do you and James Bond have in common? A thirst for adventure, snappy dress sense, and a clever way with words, sure. Hit Norway's Atlantic Road and you'll be able to add another one. This sweep of tarmac, which connects a chain of islands in the country's far northern Hustadvika and Averøy regions, is so spectacular that 007 raced down it in *No Time to Die*, taking in—as you will—historical churches, relics of war, and the rusting hulks of shipwrecks.

CROSSING THE ARCHIPELAGO

The Atlantic Road's eastern edge is awash with silvery fjords bound by soaring mountains, and bejeweled with forested islands. It's also home to the village of Kvernes and its stave church, which is where this theatrical expedition begins. These traditional spiky structures were some of the most advanced wooden buildings constructed across the Nordics in the Middle Ages. In their heyday, there were around 1,000 stave churches; today, Kvernes is one of only 28 still standing.

Trace the scenic coastal road north from here, curving inland to pass the town of Bruhagen and Storvatnet Lake, with its air of stillness and mystery, especially when a curtain of mist hangs over the forested shores. From the lake, the road returns to the coast on the outskirts of Kårvåg, where the land begins to break into fractured islands and the route is propped up on long bridges. Stop at the Eldhusøya Turistvegprosjekt, a contemporary walkway that hovers above protected

KVERNES
START

ATLANTIC ROAD
This remarkable road featured in the 2021 James Bond film, *No Time to Die*.

KVERNES
See one of Norway's 28 historical stave churches in this small village.

0 MILES (0 KM)

207

LYNGHOLMEN
Stop on this island for coffee and cakes at Eldhuset, then hike the coastal walkway.

14 MILES (23 KM)

MYRBÆRHOLMBRUA BRIDGE
This bridge has a secret feature: a pedestrianized section specifically for fishing.

15 MILES (24 KM)

ABOVE The Atlantic Road, linked by eight bridges

RIGHT A waterfall in the eerie Troll Church

OPPOSITE The fishing village of Bud, the route's end point

marshland. The steel structure loops around the western end of the island, offering jaw-dropping vistas along its 2,300 ft (700 m) length.

AN ENGINEERING MARVEL
Of the eight bridges that make up the Atlantic Road, the longest and most impressive is the Storseisundet, which curves for 850 ft (260 m) between the islands of Lyngholmen and Skipsholmen. It's this section that film buffs might recognize from the car chase from *No Time to Die*. The scenery is suitably cinematic: blue sea on either side studded with gemlike green islets. It's best viewed, however, outside of the car. Stop at one of the viewpoints to truly appreciate the extraordinary landscape, with the sea breeze blowing and the sound of the Atlantic lapping at the rocks.

Skipsholmen is one of the prettiest islands, offering a glimpse of the arching Myrbærholmbrua Bridge. Along the route, rusting shipwrecks—some shorn in two on the sharp rocks—serve as a reminder that danger lurks beneath the beauty, but exploring this stretch of coastline on foot reveals its perilous nature even further—look out for the tower of the Kvitholmen Lighthouse, about 1 mile (1.5 km) off the coast. The ground beneath your feet becomes pockmarked with rock pools, and it's not clear where land ends and sea begins.

This unique topography is harnessed to artistic effect at Vevang, where a series of small sculptures, known as *Columna Transatlantica*, hide among the rocky coastal pools. The twisting white-marble columns resemble squirming sticks of the Spanish street food, *churros*. And the village houses a darker relic: Vevang Battery, a German World War II gun emplacement. It's a reminder that this was once a place of war, which is hard to comprehend in such a peaceful corner of the world.

MYTHS AND MOUNTAINS

As the road whisks you once again inland, rugged rocks give way to towering pines. Make for the summit of Stemshesten, a modest mountain that promises unbeatable views over the islets and rocky coastline you've just driven. The landscape in these parts has long inspired folklore. Beyond Hostadvatnet Lake lies Troll Church. While its name may lead you to believe there's a host of religious iconography within, instead you'll find a warren of marble and limestone caves. Explore the natural waterfalls and pools (some of which you can dip into) to your heart's content, but just be wary of the site's mythical residents.

Backtrack through the municipality of Hustadvika to Farstadsanden. Stark and beautiful, this sandy beach is popular with windsurfers, thanks to its ferocious winds. The water is shallow enough for a swim—if you're brave enough to endure the chilly temperature, that is.

Revitalized after a bracing dip—or from watching others submerge into the icy Atlantic—return to the road, where you'll pass quaint fishing settlements on your way to the trip's final destination: Bud. When you reach this colorful fishing village, with its red clapboard houses, gently bobbing boats, and cozy restaurants serving warming bowls of fish soup, it feels like this is the end of all roads, everywhere. And it almost is. Walk along Bud's rocky harbor wall, which juts out into the water; only the frosty, Norwegian Sea lies west from here.

EXTEND YOUR TRIP

Tag on a detour at the start of your trip to the charming city of Kristiansund, a 20-minute drive or so from Kvernes. Spread across four islands, this maritime city is famous for its salted cod, traditionally dried in the sun on ocean rocks.

STEMSHESTEN
Stretch your legs with a hike up the gentle Stemshesten summit.
23 MILES (37 KM)

BUD
Finish with a warming fish soup in this town. Bryggjen i Bud serves its with epic sea views.
33 MILES (53 KM)

BUD
END

NORWEGIAN FJORDS

START/END
Bergen/Trondheim, Norway

DISTANCE
528 miles (850 km)

DURATION
7–10 days

ROAD CONDITIONS
Paved roads; some steep and winding routes.

THE BEST TIME TO GO
Between spring and fall, when the roads are free of ice and snow.

OPPOSITE Snow-dusted houses on the fjordshore in Bergen

The Norwegian fjords are a universe of their own. The vast coastline has been carved out by glaciers into long inlets, which ripple inland, creating a world of green valleys, still blue waters, and soaring mountain passes.

With more than 60,000 miles (100,000 km) of dramatic coastline, Norway's rugged fjord country requires a heroic undertaking—but it's well worth the mileage. In fact, exploring this vast, beautiful landscape by car will allow you to venture away from the crowds and take in pretty towns, glaciers, and waterfalls along the way. You might even spot the aurora borealis, too.

ENTERING THE FJORDS

Where better to kick off this Nordic affair than the "Capital of the Fjords"? Bergen is an impossibly charming city complete with a bustling waterfront that's famed for its colorfully painted historic wooden houses. This was Norway's capital in the days when seafaring reigned supreme. Make the most of its urban charms—this is as big as cities get around these parts.

Civilization recedes quickly on the drive north. Pine forests crowd the hills, and winding roads conspire with tall rocky mountains to block the horizon. Eventually, the view opens up to sublime effect as the road reaches Sognefjord. Nicknamed the "King of the Fjords," this is the longest and deepest of Norway's inlets. It's not just the fjord itself that is astounding, the surrounding landscape is supremely vast, and the unmoving water and height of the mountains create an eerie calmness—a sense that everything here stands still. But time moves on and a car ferry is on hand to whisk you and your wheels across the water. As you travel farther north, the tourist crowds begin to recede and fjordside villages give way to the

BERGEN
START

BERGEN
The "Capital of the Fjords" is surrounded by no less than seven inlets.

0 MILES (0 KM)

SOGNEFJORD
The reflective waters of Norway's longest fjord make a glorious setting for a cruise.
71 MILES (114 KM)

mountains of Naustdal-Gjengedal nature reserve. You're more likely to spot a herd of reindeer here than fellow travelers, and there'll be a wealth of avian activity happening just above you, too. Gannets, gulls, and white-tailed eagles soar and squawk in the wide open skies, enjoying their spectacular bird's-eye view. For a similar outlook, visit the Geiranger Skywalk atop Dalsnibba mountain. The road up to it features a winding network of 11 hairpin bends. At the top, the platform is both terrifying and mesmerizing in equal measure, with views of the Blåbreen glacier and Geirangerfjord itself below.

THE TROLL PATH

It may be difficult to believe, but the best is yet to come: Trollstigen, one of the world's most spectacular roads, awaits. On the way there, you'll pass a roaring waterfall in Geiranger, navigate the twists and turns up to Ørnesvingen viewpoint, and board another ferryboat in Eidsdal. It's an epic roll call of wonders. As you near the Romsdalen valley, the road begins to climb with every hairpin bend. When an angular, glass-clad structure appears, you've reached the visitor's center at the summit. You'd be forgiven for taking your eyes off the road on this scenic stretch, but you mustn't—

GEIRANGER SKYWALK
Spot gannets, gulls, and white-tailed eagles from this cantilevered viewpoint.

227 MILES (366 KM)

TROLLSTIGEN
Stop at the road's highest point to visit the café and contemporary visitor center.

269 MILES (433 KM)

NORWEGIAN FJORDS

MOLDE
This creative city hosts the annual festival, Moldejazz, every July.

528 MILES (850 KM)

TRONDHEIM
A hub for New Nordic cuisine, Trondheim also boasts wooden wharfs and buzzing nightlife.

END

TRONDHEIM

vigilance is key when it comes to maneuvering your car through Trollstigen's serpentine switchbacks.

BACK TO CIVILIZATION

Descend from the mountain pass, and, slowly but surely, civilization returns. There are many pretty towns to explore, each with a unique pull. Ålesund, a port town 75 miles (120 km) west, was ravaged by fire in 1904 and rebuilt in technicolor Art Nouveau–style; the village's pharmacy-turned-museum, Senteret, depicts Ålesund's aesthetic rebirth. Open-air Sunnmøre Museum, meanwhile, provides a glimpse into traditional rural life, with old fishing boats and reconstructed turf-roofed buildings on display. Around 50 miles (80 km) up the coast lies another creative city, Molde. This time it's music rather than architecture that grabs the attention. Every July, the city plays host to Moldejazz, the world's oldest jazz festival. It was initiated by local venue Storyville Jazz Club, which attracts leading acts year-round.

After the boutique charms of Ålesund and Molde, pulling into Trondheim feels like entering a mighty metropolis, with its looming Gothic cathedral (Europe's most northerly) and the modern Rockheim Museum, the country's monument to popular music. This is something of a foodie destination, too,

> You'd be forgiven for taking your eyes off the road, but you mustn't—vigilance is key when it comes to maneuvering Trollstigen's serpentine switchbacks.

so head out in search of Norwegian cuisine at places like Troll Restaurant, known for traditional dishes like cod tongue, reindeer, and brown cheese, then hit one of the city's many live-music venues, a grand way to readjust to urban life. After you've bounced to some of Trondheim's best beats, finish your journey with a stroll along the waterfront, gazing at the colorful wooden houses. It's a fitting reflection of the trip's beginning in Bergen.

ABOVE Trondheim's colorful waterfront

OPPOSITE TOP A boat cruising along Geirangerfjord

OPPOSITE BOTTOM Trollstigen road in the Romsdalen valley

WEST COAST SWEDEN

START/END
Gothenburg, Sweden

DISTANCE
201 miles (324 km)

DURATION
5–7 days

ROAD CONDITIONS
Well maintained year-round. Expect dry conditions in summer and snow in winter.

THE BEST TIME TO GO
During the summer, when there are clear blue skies; a coastal breeze; and bright, long evenings.

OPPOSITE Swimming in the crystal-clear waters off Tjörn, Sweden's sixth-largest island

Sweden's west coast is famed for its cute fishing villages, rocky islands, granite cliffs, and fresh seafood. And this relaxed road trip through the Bohuslän region serves up a smorgasbord of coastal highlights.

Two-thirds of Sweden—a skinny, snakelike landmass squeezed between its two Nordic neighbors—is covered in dense, impenetrable forest. The final third is home to its archipelagos, chains of craggy islands surrounded by the deep blue waters of the Gulf of Bothnia, and the Baltic and North seas. Bohuslän, stretching from the city of Gothenburg to the Norwegian border, is one of the most picturesque, its smooth, granite coastline dotted with more than 8,000 islands. The region is known for its pretty fishing villages, complete with red boathouses and a vibrant cultural heritage. And a road trip—aided by a few ferries here and there—is the best way to see it all.

THE BEST OF THE WEST

The west coast of Sweden is known by locals as the "best coast," and the region's city, Gothenburg, certainly fits the bill. Once a center of fishing and shipbuilding, the country's pocket-sized second metropolis, where this journey begins, is now a trendy cultural hub, bested only by Stockholm. Gothenburg is delightfully walkable, so there's no need to hop in the car just yet. Set out to admire the city's beautiful Renaissance architecture, making use of the quaint tram system to get around. The city has some of the country's best seafood restaurants. For a quick culinary introduction, head to Feskekörka, the striking church-shaped fish market, whose counters display some of the region's famed shellfish and where restaurants cook up your seafood shopping there and then.

GOTHENBURG
START

GOTHENBURG
The city is regularly ranked as the most sustainable in the world.

GOTHENBURG
The city's Jubilee Park features three harbor pools, a skate ramp, and a public sauna.
0 MILES (0 KM)

FIKA
An important part of local culture, *fika* is about enjoying a hot drink, a snack, and a chat.

ÅSTOL
Take a ferry to this volcanic-rock island to see the charming whitewashed houses.

67 MILES (107 KM)

PATER NOSTER LIGHTHOUSE
Set on a private island, this isolated lighthouse is a destination hotel like no other.

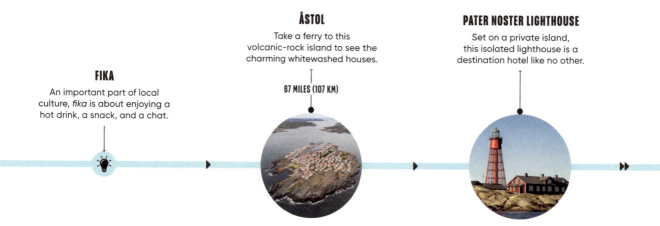

HOP TO IT

You can reach many islands directly from Gothenburg, but choose idyllic Marstrand, one of the most beautiful. It's around 30 miles (50 km) across grassy plains, via a short (and free) passenger-only ferry from Köön. Marstrand is known for its impressive Carlsten Fort: head to the top for sensational panoramic views of boats bobbing in the harbor and the many uninhabited tiny islands out into the sea. While you're here, take a pause for the keenly observed Swedish tradition of *fika*, a midafternoon coffee break with a sweet treat, before exploring the island's various walking paths.

Retrace your steps to the mainland—possibly stopping at Köön, where more hiking routes run along the coastline—and journey 60 miles (100 km) north to Tjörn. This much bigger island (the sixth largest in Sweden) has become a hub for kayakers and hikers—Bohuslän's Kuststigen coastal path, which begins in Gothenburg and snakes its way up to the Norwegian capital of Oslo, can be joined here. With easy access to nearby islands, there's enough to see and do on and around Tjörn for a weeklong stay. To cover the best parts, start in the village of Rönnäng, on the island's southwestern tip, from where you can catch a passenger ferry and hop between the vehicle-free islands of Dyrön and Åstol. Åstol, the smaller of the two, is a volcanic rock island that's almost entirely covered with quaint whitewashed houses. Dyrön is best known for the boardwalk trail that traces the island's coast, offering views of the Pater Noster lighthouse, as well as Risön, Hättan, and Hake fjord to the east. Keep an eye out for unusual flora and fauna as you trek; the island is home to blue anemone and viper grass, marsh tits and hawfinches, and wild mouflon sheep. Before you leave, make sure you visit Dyröns Bastu sauna, perched on the island's craggy southern tip, and watch the boats go by as you work up a sweat.

On your return to Rönnäng, hop back in the car and drive along Tjörn's coastline to Skärhamn. On the very

EXTEND YOUR TRIP
From Lysekil, travel farther along the west coast to Kosterhavet, Sweden's first marine national park. Here, divers can get up close with one of the largest coastal coral reefs in the Atlantic Ocean.

WEST COAST SWEDEN

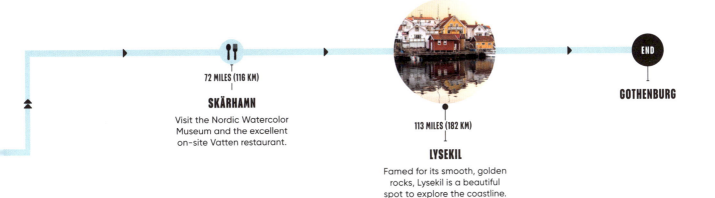

72 MILES (116 KM)
SKÄRHAMN
Visit the Nordic Watercolor Museum and the excellent on-site Vatten restaurant.

113 MILES (182 KM)
LYSEKIL
Famed for its smooth, golden rocks, Lysekil is a beautiful spot to explore the coastline.

END
GOTHENBURG

edge of town is the waterside Nordic Watercolor Museum, an artistic masterpiece itself. The wooden-clad structure, which blends into the craggy coastline it cuts into, isn't your average museum. As well as viewing the artworks here, visitors are encouraged to swim in the sea, paint in the open studio, and dine on locally sourced, organic produce at the on-site Vatten restaurant.

CATCH OF THE DAY

Skärhamn is a tough place to wave goodbye to, but the harbor town of Lysekil, with its charming wooden houses and winding streets, is waiting. Here, the terracotta hue of the rocks, where the Gullmarsfjord meets the deep sea of Skagerrak, deepens in the sunlight. Take a foraging trip for oysters and mussels, where you'll learn about the coastline and the industry and catch your lunch at the same time. Then walk off your meal on the 3,600 ft (1,100 m) Västerhavspromenade, which traces the golden coastline.

The return leg to Gothenburg may seem long, so pause in Ljungskile for a bite to eat. Musselbaren, the Mussel Bar, serves the shellfish and even allows patrons to harvest their own (you'll surely be a dab hand by now). Belly full, and lungs filled with sea air, you're ready to complete your loop back to Gothenburg.

RIGHT A snowy Nordic Watercolor Museum

BELOW Catching oysters and mussels in Lysekil

OPPOSITE Hiking the Kuststigen coastal path

FINNISH LAKELAND

START/END
Savonlinna/Kuopio, Finland

DISTANCE
290 miles (467 km)

DURATION
5–7 days

ROAD CONDITIONS
Roads are impeccable; make sure you have the correct tires in winter.

THE BEST TIME TO GO
Around the summer solstice, when the sun barely sets at night.

OPPOSITE Taking in the view in Finnish Lakeland

Despite its moniker, Finland's Land of a Thousand Lakes makes for a fine road trip. Expect charming villages, thick emerald forests, and cute log cabins in the country's water-filled Lakeland region.

Nature, and indeed lakes, is a huge part of Finnish life. Even in the country's big cities, a hike into the wilderness or a bracing dip in the sea is never far away. In summer, Finns routinely leave behind the stresses of modern-day life behind to relax by a lake, a practice staunchly observed by everyone, from students to CEOs. Finnish Lakeland, the biggest pool-pocked district in Europe, is the best place to experience the country's authentic pastime. In the warmer months, lake-goers board historic steamboats, paddleboard on crystalline waters, canoe, kayak, or swim; in winter, when the lakes freeze over, skating, Nordic skiing, and ice fishing are on the menu. And where there's a lake, there's a lakeside cabin, or *mökki*, to retreat to. Although it might feel like there's more water here than there is *terra firma*, this easterly region serves up an exceptional road trip. Just expect to get out on the water—and most probably in it—during the course of your journey.

LAY OF THE LAKELAND
The Karelian town of Savonlinna is your starting point, home to Olavinlinna Castle, the area's best-known site. Built on a small island in Saimaa, Finland's largest lake, the picturesquely placed 15th-century fortification has a fascinating history. The castle was constructed on this specific lake, thanks to its strong currents, which stopped the water from freezing in the winter and therefore prevented unwanted visitors from crossing the ice and easily raiding

SAVONLINNA

FINNISH LAKELAND
This area is home to roughly 188,000 lakes, including Saimaa, the country's largest.

SAVONLINNA
Visit the impressive Olavinlinna Castle and gastronomic Linnankatu street.

0 MILES (0 KM)

17 MILES (28 KM)

LUSTO

The Finnish Forest Museum's main building is designed to resemble the rings of a tree trunk.

19 MILES (30 KM)

PUNKAHARJU

Stay to explore this pretty region's Ice Age ridges. Hotel Punkaharju is a homely option.

ABOVE The tree-lined, Ice Age ridges of Punkaharju

RIGHT Admiring the ancient Astuvansalmi rock paintings

it. Wander the town's small avenues, with their quaint wooden houses, and visit Linnankatu, named by locals as "Parisian Street" due to its pretty cobblestones and excellent restaurants and cafés.

TOP OF THE TREES

Head east out of Savonlinna toward Punkaharju, a stretch that cuts a spectacular line through jewel-green forests on roads that skirt the water's edge. Soon, you'll pass Lusto, the Finnish Forest Museum, set in a wonderful wooded lakeside location and offering a fascinating insight into how forest culture has shaped the country. Grab a bite at the museum's restaurant, which serves award-winning local fare with beautiful views of the landscape. Lusto's serene surroundings are also worth exploring: there are stunning hiking trails that delve deep into the forest, and smart, locally run hotels to retreat to at end of day.

When you eventually move on, the road is mesmerizing—Punkaharju's ancient ridges, formed by retreating glaciers, are one of Finland's most famous natural wonders, and the 4792 road to Punkaharjun Harjutie is particularly picturesque. The route sweeps across a long, narrow ridge between Lake Puruvesi and Lake Pihlajavesi. It's only a few miles long but affords drivers dazzling, far-reaching views. Continue to Imatra where, if you're visiting at the right time of year, the deafening sound of the Imatrankoski rapids—some of Europe's biggest—fill the air. Formed 5,000 years ago, the waters of this powerful phenomenon are now regulated by a dam; on select days in June, August, October, and December, the floodgates are opened and 14,000 cubic ft (400 cubic m) of raging water surges out.

Make your way from the rapids to Lappeenranta, a small city that blends Finnish, Russian, and Swedish cultures. Despite its size, it's home to 11 churches, including Finland's oldest Orthodox church, and the futuristic Lauritsala. Make sure you sample a Karelian pastry, a comforting filled pie, before you leave.

TO THE FINNISH LINE

Sufficiently sated, continue to the ancient site of Astuvansalmi. Set on the banks of Yövesi lake, the rock face features prehistoric paintings that depict elk, people, and boats, and date from around 4000 to 2200 BCE. Rejoin the highway and soon you'll reach Mikkeli, known for its hilltop observation tower and historic manor houses. Nature excursions from Mikkeli include moonlit snowshoeing in winter and kayaking in summer. Meander through forested landscapes to Puumala and Route 62,

> **Punkaharju's ancient ridges, formed by retreating Ice Age glaciers, are one of Finland's most famous natural wonders.**

one of the Nordics' most beautiful routes. This serpentine stretch follows the shores of Lake Saimaa, which makes for a perfect spot to hunker down at a lakeside cottage. For an off-grid experience, hail one of the lake's water taxis to explore the unspoiled beaches of Rokansaari island, where you can rent a cabin, visit one of the rustic saunas, and kayak on clear waters.

Finish your adventure with a final flurry in Kuopio, the "Capital of Lakeland." The small shore-side city has both beautiful natural surroundings and a cosmopolitan buzz. Scale the 250 ft (75 m) tall Puijo Tower for views across Kallavesi lake, stopping for a black Finnish coffee at the very top, and learn about the city's history at the Kuopio Museum. There's no better way to end a trip to Finland than in a sauna. So much more than a simple sweat, a visit to one of these heated cabins is a real insight into local culture, and Kuopio's lakeside Saana spa is the perfect place to Finnish.

ABOVE A lakeside Finnish sauna

LAPPEENRANTA
Fuel up on the city's comforting Karelian pies, rice-porridge pastries baked until golden.
99 MILES (160 KM)

ASTUVANSALMI
These prehistoric rock paintings date back to around 4000 BCE.
167 MILES (268 KM)

KUOPIO
Sweat it out at the city's Saana, an apt end to your journey.
290 MILES (467 KM)

KUOPIO
END

VIKING TRAIL

START/END
Copenhagen, Denmark

DISTANCE
237 miles (382 km)

DURATION
4–5 days

ROAD CONDITIONS
Well-maintained, paved roads.

THE BEST TIME TO GO
July, for long days (and nights) and Trelleborg's Viking Festival.

OPPOSITE Cycling along the Nyhavn waterfront in Copenhagen

The age of the Vikings lives on in this historic tour of Danish museums and archaeological sites, offset by a dash of cosmopolitan cool courtesy of Copenhagen, the country's artsy, cerebral capital.

The seafaring Vikings presided over Denmark from around 800 to 1050 CE, when the first kings ruled ferociously over the region. Today, history buffs can step back in time by visiting the remnants this ruthless people left behind—but with all the modern attractions that the country has come to offer.

MODERN ART AND ANCIENT CRAFTS

The best place to start your journey is in Denmark's cool capital, Copenhagen. A center of New Nordic cuisine and Scandi design, it's also known for its leading environmental policies and quality of life. Denmark often nears the top of the World Happiness Report, and as you stroll (or cycle) the city's streets, it's easy to see why. There's a laid-back bustle to Copenhagen, far removed from the fraught Viking times it once lived through. Wander Nyhavn, the city's colorful harborfront, and visit the Meatpacking District, where you can watch the well-dressed locals go by.

You've experienced modern Denmark, now it's time to delve back in time. Set off for Roskilde, Denmark's Viking capital, a lively fjord-side city that was once a jumping-off point for the fearsome seafarers. Today, the fantastic Viking Ship Museum is on hand to teach you all about their iconic sailing vessels. In the working boatyard, you can learn about these majestic watercraft, and how the Vikings built them with overlapping planks and carved prows topped with terrifying dragon heads. The exhibits are just as interesting and tell the story of how these ships were

COPENHAGEN
START

COPENHAGEN
Visit the city's Meatpacking District, a trendy cultural hub with restaurants and galleries.
0 MILES (0 KM)

ROSKILDE
The Viking capital's Danish rock museum, Ragnarock, reveals another key period for the city.
22 MILES (36 KM)

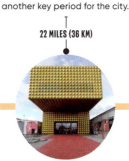

EGESKOV SLOT

This 16th-century castle is a worthy detour on the way to Odense.

104 MILES (167 KM)

FUNEN

In the waters south of Funen is the South Funen Archipelago. It comprises 96 tiny islands.

ABOVE Trelleborg's Viking Festival in full swing

OPPOSITE TOP A traditional ship at Ladby Viking Museum

OPPOSITE BOTTOM Christiania, Copenhagen's artsy district

used to terrorize northern Europe. Come summer, you can get out on the water yourself, as the museum launches traditional wooden ships into the fjord, crewed by willing members of the public.

A BRUSH WITH THE PAST

Believe it or not, the Vikings weren't all bad. Their sophisticated culture also included ornate artwork, a rich body of folklore, and well-designed fortresses—like the one in Trelleborg. All that's left of the 10th-century structure is a ring-shaped mound of earth, but the past has been helpfully brought to life here with a reconstructed Viking village, complete with basic houses topped with turf roofs—Viking insulation. The site also exhibits the artifacts found in the area, including a remarkable millennium-old shield and a burial ground containing pottery, jewelry, and ax heads. Most fun of all, though, is the groundbreaking digital technology on display—fitting, given that the fortress was built by the Viking king Harald Bluetooth. An augmented-reality app transports you into the midst of a white-knuckle battle between two Viking warriors, while a virtual-reality headset helps you relive the Battle of Trelleborg, which took place here some time in the 10th century.

After all that excitement, the island of Funen—pronounced "Foon"—will feel all the more peaceful. If you've time for a quick detour, take National Road 9 south to Egeskov Slot, an impressive Renaissance castle with attractive gardens; otherwise, take National Road 9 north to the country's third city, Odense. The birthplace of fairy-tale author Hans Christian Andersen—who penned such classics as *The Little Mermaid* and *Thumbelina*—is filled with references to its famed writer. You'll spot statues, a painted mural, and two museums dedicated to him. Visit the Kengo

124 MILES (200 KM)

ODENSE
The home of author Hans Christian Andersen, the city is awash with literary references.

139 MILES (224 KM)

LADBY VIKING MUSEUM
Fully immerse yourself in Viking life at this museum, where you can literally walk in their shoes.

237 MILES (382 KM)

COPENHAGEN
Smørrebrød is so much more than a sandwich. Try a plate at award-winning Schønnemann.

END

COPENHAGEN

Kuma-designed H. C. Andersens Hus museum, which features a mazelike garden and underground exhibition space in dreamlike hues, as well as the writer's childhood home. For a slice of something in the real world, hit Storms Pakhus street-food market.

Retracing your steps toward the capital, Funen serves up one more hit on the Viking trail. The Ladby Viking Museum occupies the site where a king was buried a thousand years ago, laid inside his ship beside his beloved horses, dogs, and weaponry. You can try on Viking attire and step out to admire a reconstruction of the original ship bobbing in the fjord, perhaps the closest you'll get to walking in the shoes of a Norse warrior.

A VIKING HOMECOMING
Finish up in Copenhagen with the rides of Tivoli Gardens. The spectacular theme park is one of the world's oldest and is said to have inspired Walt Disney. Before you leave, sample the capital's world-renowned cuisine, or try *Smørrebrød*, a traditional open sandwich that is all about the toppings, which come piled high and range from smoked salmon to caviar. The Vikings aren't forgotten in this modern city, though. Christiania, a former military base, is a place of free-spiritedness, vibrant street art, and political activism. As you stroll the district, boomboxes blare out the Danish flower-power anthem "You Cannot Kill Us." It's a slogan fit for a Viking.

LIVING THE LIFE
Visit Trelleborg in July, when hundreds of people descend on the museum in traditional Viking dress. Market stalls sell traditional food and drink, while workshops showcase Viking crafts such as blacksmithing, wood-working, and Old Norse storytelling. The pinnacle is a full-scale reenactment of the Battle of Trelleborg, when 250 costumed warriors (safely) go to war.

ICELAND'S RING ROAD

START/END
Reykjavík, Iceland

DISTANCE
1,088 miles (1,751 km)

DURATION
7–10 days

ROAD CONDITIONS
Well-maintained roads; in winter, tire chains are essential.

THE BEST TIME TO GO
Fall and early winter afford icy scenery but few hours of sunlight; if you want to cover more ground, opt for summer's midnight sun.

OPPOSITE A route off the Ring Road cutting through volcanic landscape near Mývatn

There aren't many countries that you can loop around on just one laneway. The Ring Road would be mesmerizing enough for its fjords, peaks, and valleys, but the sense of completion by circling back to Reykjavík is half the reward.

Sigur Rós, the experimental Icelandic band and one of the country's most hallowed music exports, are famous fans of Iceland's Route 1—as the Ring Road is officially known. So great is their appreciation that in 2016 the band filmed themselves driving the entire length of the circular route nonstop for 24 hours during the summer solstice, when at latitudes near the Arctic Circle the sun barely sets. It's an enchanting watch.

In theory, the average road tripper can follow in their wake, rolling along the tarmac for the road's gorgeous looping entirety without ever branching off. But to drive this mammoth stretch in one go would mean missing the roaring waterfalls, diminutive villages, and exquisite fjords that require you to deviate. The delight here is in the detours.

THE ARCTIC ADVENTURE
For virtually all visitors to Iceland, the journey begins in Reykjavík, a compact, cheery capital that warrants exploring on foot. Pop into its quirky museums, visit its working harbor, and ride the elevator to the top of the futuristic Hallgrimskirkja church. After a quick wander—it's a very small city—fire up the engine, get the heat on, and hit the road.

Head north out of the city until the beltway turns into the famous Ring Road. The boxy homes of Reykjavík soon dissipate and the landscape opens into wide valleys, guarded by mighty peaks that have been smoothed over by centuries of heavy snowfall. This elemental landscape is

REYKJAVÍK
START

THE RING ROAD
The construction of Iceland's Route 1, as it is otherwise known, was completed in 1974.

REYKJAVÍK
Take a boat trip from Iceland's capital to spot puffins on the islands in Faxaflói bay.

0 MILES (0 KM)

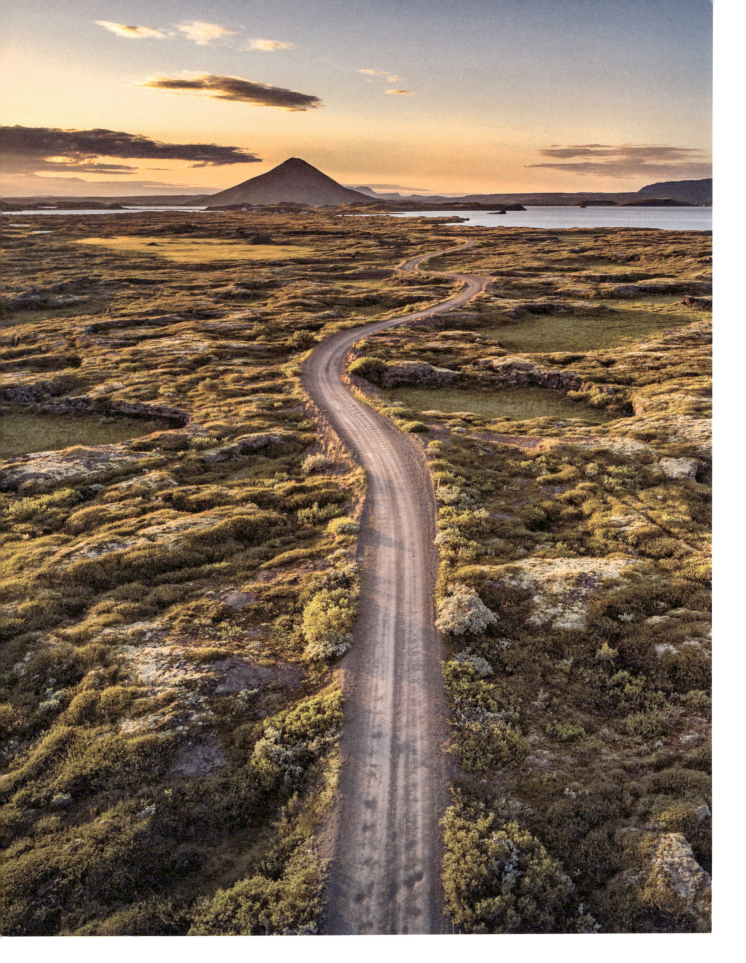

HVAMMSVÍK
Submerge in the area's steaming hot tubs before braving a dip in the fjord.

35 MILES (57 KM)

HÓTEL BÚDIR
After peeking inside the nearby Búðakirkja, relax for the night at this charming spot.

112 MILES (180 KM)

DJÚPALÓNSSANDUR BEACH
Also known as the Black Lava Pearl, this beach's rocky shore makes for impressive photos.

129 MILES (207 KM)

what this journey is all about. Trees are few and far between; instead, the horizon reveals only rocks, moss, and grass, and the occasional herd of steadfast long-haired ponies. Tune in to the environment's subtle changes, and you'll never tire of the view.

There might be a lack of vegetation, but the land here is alive with geological activity—and nowhere is this more palpable than in the country's thermal baths. Akin to a national pastime, soaking in a hot spring is an integral part of the Icelandic way of life. As you drive north of Reykjavík, a quick detour around the resplendent Hvalfjördur fjord will bring you to Hvammsvík. This natural complex of serenely quiet hot springs sits just off the beach and is surrounded by golden reeds that sway in the wind. Dip into the searing waters, and let the warmth reach all the way to your bones.

INTO THE WILD

Though the Ring Road officially skirts the "rabbit ears" of the Westfjords, a jaunt into and around the rugged Snæfellsness peninsula is a quick way to sample the country's craggier landscapes. Seemingly a world away from the hot springs at Hvammsvík, the tiny wooden church of Búðakirkja makes a fitting introduction to this quirky peninsula. All that remains of Búdir village, it occupies a stark but beautiful spot, its black silhouette a dramatic contrast to the surroundings. At the promontory's very tip is the magnificent Djúpalónssandur beach, where black lava sands and pointy rock formations meet the white foam of the Atlantic Ocean. Close the loop along the peninsula's northern coast, passing Snæfellsjökull volcano and the ice-white, almost glacier-like form of the striking Stykkishólmskirkja church.

By the time you reach the turf houses at Glaumbær Museum—a 150-mile (250 km) traverse across wide-open and sparsely populated hinterlands—you may wonder how the country's past peoples coped in such remote

HIDDEN PEOPLE

Folklore is very important to Icelanders. Estimates suggest over half of the population secretly believe in elves, and there is a cautious ambivalence about traditional folktales due to the risk of upsetting magical beings. *Huldufólk*, or hidden people, are considered particularly peevish and prone to anger if their natural living space is impinged on. So much so that roads have been diverted to avoid crossing over contested terrain.

ICELAND'S RING ROAD

230 MILES (370KM)

TRÖLLASKAGI PENINSULA
As well as its imposing peaks, the Tröllaskagi is known for its wild Icelandic horses.

467 MILES (751 KM)

AKUREYRI
Iceland's second city is dominated by the imposing Art Deco Akureyrarkirkja church.

and inhospitable terrain. Turf houses, or *torfbæi*, are one of the oldest examples of architecture in Iceland, and the curious grass-roofed residences at places like Glaumbær hint at how previous generations of Icelanders tried to temper their harsh surroundings. The buildings are typically half encased in earth, with roofs covered by a tufty lawn carpet, and were in use from 930 CE right up until the the late 20th century. As well as the informative Glaumbær Museum, you can find these almost-mythical houses (and churches) at several places along the Ring Road: the turf church of Hofskirkja is a wonderful sunken example, while Keldur is one of the oldest turf houses in the country.

NORTHEN DE-LIGHTS
From Glaumbær, swing by Tröllaskagi peninsula for another hot swim in the waterfront pool at Hofsós, and for the chance to spy glacial rivers and wild Icelandic horses. Trace the coast to Akureyri, the diminutive capital of the north. Built into a steep slope on a fjord's edges, this tiny city of less than 20,000 residents packs a punch. Dominating the skyline is the city's Akureyrarkirkja church, which was designed by Icelandic architect Guðjón Samúelsson in the 1940s. Its two basalt columns rise into the sky in an imposing Art Deco fashion.

ABOVE Hofskirkja, a traditional turf church

RIGHT Akureyri, North Iceland's answer to Reykjavík

OPPOSITE The craggy Snæfellsness peninsula

514 MILES (827 KM)

HÚSAVÍK

Join a whale-watching tour or visit the insightful museum in this northerly town.

570 MILES (918 KM)

DETTIFOSS WATERFALL

Europe's second-most powerful waterfall is a noisy, impressive sight to behold.

TOP Lake Mývatn and its volcanic landscape

ABOVE The elegant, and epic, Goðafoss waterfall

The direction you take next depends on the time of year. If it's summer, travel north to see majestic whales off the coast of Húsavík—though the town's Whale Museum provides an illuminating out-of-season stop. The geothermal glories of volcanic Lake Mývatn, east of Akureyri, can be enjoyed year-round, but it's a special sight when plumes of steam rise from its mud pots amid a blindingly white carpet of snow.

FALLS AND FJORDS

Iceland has no end of impressive waterfalls, and there are plenty to spot on your journey along the Ring Road. Some you can see from behind the wheel—Goðafoss, which you'll pass en route to Mývatn from Akureyri, lies virtually beside the road—while others require a detour. Thundering Dettifoss, Europe's second-most powerful waterfall, is a 12-mile (20 km) drive off the main road east of Mývatn but well worth the extra mileage.

Hitting the east coast of Iceland, the scenery alters dramatically, as the route snakes along the edges of spectacular fjords that are so unbelievably still they mirror whatever lies in the skies above. A short wiggle off the main road just after East Iceland's regional hub of Egilsstaðir takes you to Seydisfjörður, a pretty chocolate-box fishing village that sits on the edge of its namesake fjord. Here, tucking into a pizza topped with Arctic langoustines will make you wonder how far gastronomic and cultural exchanges can reach, even in a village as tiny and remote as this.

Stop by the impressive Gufufoss waterfall on your return to the Ring Road. From here, the route seems to trace every nook and cranny on the east coast as it snakes its way for 200 miles (310 km) toward Vatnajökull glacier. There's plenty to see and do on this lengthy stretch: learn how French fishermen once hunted whales in the Eastfjords at Fáskrúðsfjörður; walk along the inky black sands of Fauskasandur beach, beneath the rocky monolith that stands tall and lonely on its shores; and hike to the magnificent velvet-green Múlagljúfur Canyon.

Nothing can quite prepare you for the vast expanse of ice that is Vatnajökull, though. Don crampons for a guided hike to one of its translucent ice caves or just sit back and spot the azure icebergs that float surreally across Jökulsárlón lagoon from the comfy confines of your car. It's a perfect compromise for the kind of day that's crisp and clear but windy and bitterly cold. Icelanders call it "window weather"—and by this point in the trip, you will have learned to love its collateral comforts.

> The route seems to trace every nook and cranny on the east coast as it snakes its way for 200 miles (310 km) toward Vatnajökull glacier.

HOMEWARD BOUND

It's tough to wave goodbye to the wilderness that has accompanied you for much of the route until now. But there's still plenty to see in South Iceland. The road takes you past Reynisfjara beach, whose basalt columns resemble the climbing piano keys of a natural organ, and through Hveragerði, where bananas grow in greenhouses warmed by geothermal heat and the steaming Reykjadalur river makes an enchanting place for a final soak.

Take one last detour and follow the longer route back to Reyjavík that runs inland past Geysir. Although the Great Geysir itself is no longer active—its last eruptions were in 2016 and 2000—Strokkur is a fine alternative. There's something almost Disneyland-esque about this mighty jet of water that surges skyward every few minutes. As you drive the last 30 miles (50 km) from here back to Reykjavík, you'll feel like you've come anything but full circle.

TOP An ice cave within Vatnajökull glacier

ABOVE Reykjavík, Iceland's bijou capital city

FAUSKASANDUR BEACH
Walk along this black-sand beach on Iceland's eastern coast.
636 MILES (1,024 KM)

JÖKULSÁRLÓN LAGOON
Vatnajökull is astounding, whether seen from the shore, a kayak, or even inside the car.
830 MILES (1,335 KM)

STROKKUR GEYSER
Where else can you marvel at such a reliable (and impressive) natural phenomenon?
1,022 MILES (1,645 KM)

REYKJAVÍK
END

INDEX

A
A Coruña (Spain) 65
Abbaye Notre-Dame de Sénanque (France) 56
Abd-al Rahman III, Caliph 74
Adelsköld, Claes 53
Agamemnon, King 194
Akureyri (Iceland) 229
Albanian Riviera 189–91
Alcohol limits 9
Alentejo, the (Portugal) 80–3
Ålesund (Norway) 213
Alfonso XIII, King of Spain 73
Algodonales (Spain) 70
Ali Pasha 191
Amalfi (Italy) 152–3
Amalfi Coast (Italy) 150–4
Amber Road 7, 159
Amboise (France) 47
Anatolia (Turkey) 202–5
Andalusia (Spain) 70–4
Andersen, Hans Christian 224, 225
Angers (France) 44
Anglesey (Wales) 29
Ankara (Turkey) 202, 205
Antibes (France) 60–1, 75
Apollonia (Albania) 190
Appenzell (Switzerland) 120
Appledore (England) 31
Ardennes, the (Belgium) 85–7
Arran Islands (Ireland) 37
Arromanches-les-Bains (France) 42–3
Arthur, King 32–3
As Catedrais (Spain) 65
Åstol (Sweden) 216
Astuvansalmi (Finland) 221
Atatürk, Kemal 202
Athens (Greece) 199
Atlantic Highway (England) 31–3
Atlantic Road (Norway) 207–9
Augsburg (Germany) 98–9
Austria
  Baroque Trail 127–31
  Grossglockner High Alpine Road 122–5
Aveiro (Portugal) 78
Avignon (France) 54
Ávila (Spain) 67–8
Azay-le-Rideau (France) 46
Azulejo tiles (Portugal) 77–8

B
Bad Ischl (Austria) 129
Bad Reichenhall (Germany) 113
Baden-Baden (Germany) 101
Bagni Regina Giovanna (Italy) 150
Bakić, Vojin 176, 178
Bâlea Lake Cabin (Romania) 183
Bâlea waterfall (Romania) 183
Baligród (Poland) 160–2
Ballycastle (Northern Ireland) 20
Baltic capitals (Lithuania/Estonia) 155–8
Bannau Brycheiniog (Wales) 26
Banska Bystrica (Slovakia) 166
Banska Štiavnica (Slovakia) 166
Barcelonnette (France) 52
Barnstaple (England) 31
Baroque Trail (Austria/Czech Republic) 127–31
Bašić, Nikola 175
Bastogne (Belgium) 86
Battle of Sutjeska (Bosnia) 179
Bavaria (Germany) 96–9
Bayeux (France) 42
Bealach na Bà (Scotland) 15
Beaumaris Castle (Wales) 29
Bedruthan Steps (England) 33
Belfast (Northern Ireland) 18
Belgium
  The Ardennes 85–7
Belgrade (Serbia) 179
Bellagio (Italy) 135
Benz, Karl 7, 109
Berchtesgaden (Germany) 113
Bergen (Norway) 210
Bern (Switzerland) 121
Betws-y-Coed (Wales) 29
Bieszczady National Park (Poland) 162
Bilbao (Spain) 62
Black Forest Road (Germany) 101–3
Black Isle (Scotland) 17
Blaenau Ffestiniog (Wales) 29
Bled (Slovenia) 168–70
Blennerville Windmill (Ireland) 38
Blois (France) 47
Bodnant Garden (Wales) 29
Bohinj, Lake (Slovenia) 170
Bohuslän (Sweden) 215
Bologna (Italy) 147–8
Bonneval-sur-Arc (France) 51
Bormio (Italy) 141
Borromean Islands (Italy) 136
Boscastle (England) 32
Bosnia and Herzegovina
  Spomenik Circuit 176–9
Bouillon (Belgium) 86
Briançon (France) 51, 52
Britain see England; Northern Ireland; Scotland; Wales
Brow Head (Ireland) 39
Buck's Mills (England) 31
Bud (Norway) 209
Budapest (Hungary) 166, 167
Bude (England) 32
Builth Wells (Wales) 28
Bulgaria
  Central Mountains 184–7
Bunkers (Albania) 191
Burg Querfurt (Germany) 107
Burgos (Spain) 68–9
Busseto (Italy) 148
Búðakirkja (Iceland) 228
Butrint National Park (Albania) 191
Buxton (England) 25
Buzludzha Monument (Bulgaria) 187

C
Caen (France) 43
El Caminito del Rey (Spain) 73
Canaletto 197
Cannes (France) 61
Cappadocia (Turkey) 204
Capra waterfalls (Romania) 183
Caravanserai 75
Cardada Cimetta (Switzerland) 117
Cardiff (Wales) 26
Carpathian Mountains (Romania) 181, 183
Carrick-a-Rede (Northern Ireland) 20
Carrickfergus Castle (Northern Ireland) 18
Cars 7, 109, 137
  renting 8
  rules of the road 9
Cârţişoara (Romania) 183
Casa Cantoniera Dello Stelvio IV (Italy) 141
Casse Déserte (France) 52
Castell Coch (Wales) 26
Castell Dolwyddelan (Wales) 29
Castile and Léon (Spain) 67–9
Castleton (England) 24
Catholic Church 129
Causeway Coast (Northern Ireland) 18–21
Ceaucescu, Nicolae 182–3
Central Mountains (Bulgaria) 184–7
České Budejovice (Czech Republic) 130
Chagall, Marc 59, 60
Chälrütirank viewing point (Switzerland) 116
Chambord, Château de (France) 47
Chartreuse du Reposoir (France) 49
Chenonceau, Château de (France) 47
Chiemsee (Germany) 113
Chinon (France) 46
Chur (Switzerland) 120
Churchill, Winston 59, 132
Cid, El 69
Cisna (Poland) 162
Cliffs of Moher (Ireland) 37
Clovelly (England) 31–2
Clywedog Reservoir (Wales) 28
Coimbra (Portugal) 78–9

232

INDEX

Col de l'Iseran (France) 50–1, 53
Colleville-sur-Mer (France) 42
Comillas (Spain) 64
Como (Italy) 135
Como, Lake (Italy) 116
Copenhagen (Denmark) 53, 75, 223, 225
Córdoba (Spain) 74
Corinth Canal (Greece) 199
Cornwall at War Museum (England) 33
Cospudener See (Germany) 108
Costa da Morte (Spain) 64
Costa Norte (Spain) 62–5
Côte d'Azur (France) 59–61
Counter-Reformation 129
Coustellet (France) 54
Covadonga, Lakes of (Spain) 64
Covarrubias (Spain) 69
Croagh Patrick (Ireland) 36
Croatia
    Dalmatian Coast 173–5
    Spomenik Circuit 176–9
Currencies 8
Curtea de Arges (Romania) 181–2
Cushendun (Northern Ireland) 20
Czech Republic
    Baroque Trail 127–31

D

D-Day beaches (France) 41–3
D-Day Experience (France) 41
Dalmatian Coast (Croatia) 173–5
Dante Alighieri 132, 142
Dark Sky Alqueva (Portugal) 83
Deauville (France) 42
Delta Works, Zeeland (Netherlands) 88–91
Denmark
    Viking Trail 223–5
Derigimlagh Bog (Ireland) 36–7
Derinkuyu Underground City (Turkey) 205
Derry (Northern Ireland) 21
Dettifoss waterfall (Iceland) 230
Deutsches Kinderwagenmuseum (Germany) 108
Digne-les-Bains (France) 57
Dingle (Ireland) 38
Dion, Mark 94
Disney, Walt 67, 99, 225
Divjaka-Karavasta National Park (Albania) 190
Djúpalónssandur Beach (Iceland) 228
Dokkum (Netherlands) 95
Donegal (Ireland) 34–6
Doyle, Arthur Conan 116
Driver's licences 8
Drombeg Stone Circle (Ireland) 39
Dubrovnik (Croatia) 173–4
Duncansby Head (Scotland) 17
Dunluce Castle (Northern Ireland) 21
Dunnet Head (Scotland) 17
Dunrobin Castle (Scotland) 17
Durrës (Albania) 189
Dyrön (Sweden) 216

E

Echelsbach Bridge (Germany) 112
Edelweissspitze (Austria) 125
Egeskov Slot (Denmark) 224–5
Elan Valley (Wales) 28
Elizabeth of Thuringia, St 107
Emissions rules 9
England
    Atlantic Highway 31–3
    Peak District 23–5
Entlebuch Biosphere (Switzerland) 114
Epidavros (Greece) 192–4
Ericeira (Portugal) 79
Eryri and the Bannau (Wales) 26–9
Estonia
    Baltic capitals 155–8
Évora (Portugal) 82
Èze (France) 59

F

Faroe Islands (Denmark) 53
Farstadsanden (Norway) 209
Fastnet Rock (Ireland) 39
Fauskasandur Beach (Iceland) 231
Ferleiten (Austria) 124
Ferrari, Enzo 148
Fika (Sweden) 216
Finn McCool 18, 20
Finnish Lakeland 218–21
Fitzgerald, Ella 61
Florence (Italy) 142, 145
Fogazzaro, Antonio 136
Fort Victor-Emmanuel (France) 51
France
    D-Day beaches 41–3
    French Riviera 59–61
    Lavender Route 54–7
    Loire Valley 44–7
    Route des Grandes Alpes 49–52
France, Anatole 61
Francis I, Emperor of Austria 140
Francorchamps (Belgium) 85–6
Franeker (Netherlands) 95
Franz Ferdinand, Archduke 131
Franz-Josef, Emperor of Austria 124, 129
Frederick I, Duke of Württemberg 103
Frederick the Great, King of Prussia 107
Freiburg (Germany) 75
French Riviera 59–61
Freudenstadt (Germany) 103
Fuente Azul (Spain) 69
Funen (Denmark) 224
Furka Pass (Switzerland) 117
Fusch an der Glocknerstrasse (Austria) 122
Füssen (Germany) 99

G

Gabrovo (Bulgaria) 187
Galway (Ireland) 37
Garavice Memorial (Croatia) 178
Garda, Lago di (Italy) 132–5
Garmisch-Partenkirchen (Germany) 112
Gasthaus Jennerwein (Germany) 112
Gaudí, Antoni 64
Gehry, Frank 62
Geiranger Skywalk (Norway) 212
Germany
    Black Forest Road 101–3
    German Alpine Road 111–13
    Romanesque Road 104–8
    Romantic Road 96–9
Geroldsauer waterfall (Germany) 101–2
Gerolimenas (Greece) 195
Giant's Causeway (Northern Ireland) 18, 20
Giardini di Villa Melzi, Il (Italy) 135
Glaumboer Museum (Iceland) 228–9
Glossop (England) 23
Gmunden am Traunsee (Austria) 129
Gobbins, the (Northern Ireland) 18
Gold Beach (France) 42–3
Gordes (France) 54–6
Göreme (Turkey) 204
Gorges du Pont du Diable (France) 49
Gothenberg (Sweden) 215, 216, 217
Gotthard Pass (Switzerland) 117
Granada (Spain) 73–4, 75

233

Grand Hotel Svon (Czech Republic) 130
Grand Tour 7, 197
Great Bieszczady Loop (Poland) 160–3
Greece
　Peloponnese Peninsula 192–6
　Pindus Mountains 199–201
Grevelingen (Netherlands) 90
Grossglockner High Alpine Road (Austria) 122–5
Gufufoss waterfall 231
Guinguettes (France) 47

H

Habsburg monarchy 129
Halberstadt (Germany) 106
Hallstatt (Austria) 129
Hamilton, Lewis 86
Han-sur-Lesse (Belgium) 87
Hannibal 51
Harald Bluetooth 224
Harburg Castle (Germany) 98
Haringvlietdam (Netherlands) 91
Hartland Peninsula (England) 32
Hattuşa (Turkey) 202
Haus Alpine Naturschau (Austria) 124
Heiligenblut am Grossglockne (Austria) 125
Herdade do Freixo winery (Portugal) 82
Herzegovina see Bosnia and Herzegovina
High Passes of the Swiss Alps (Switzerland) 114–17
High Tatras (Slovakia/Hungary) 165–7
Hill of Crosses (Lithuania) 156
Himarë (Albania) 191
Hitler, Adolf 137
Hluboká, State Chateau of (Czech Republic) 130
Hohe Tauern National Park (Austria) 122–4
Holmes, Sherlock 116
Holy Roman Empire 104, 159
Honfleur (France) 42
Hope (England) 24
Hospitality 75
Hótel Búdir (Iceland) 228
Hotel Hof und Post (Switzerland) 116
hotels 75
Hoxsa, Enver 191
Huisman, Jopie 95
Huldufólk (Iceland) 228
Hungary
　High Tatras 165–7
Húsavík (Iceland) 230
Hvammsvik (Iceland) 228

I

Iceland's Ring Road 226–31
Igreja Matriz de Santa Maria de Válega (Portugal) 78
IJlst (Netherlands) 94
Île d'Or (France) 61
Imatra (Finland) 221
Imatrankoski rapids (Finland) 221
Insurance 8
Inverewe Garden (Scotland) 16
Inverness (Scotland) 15, 17
Ioannina (Greece) 201
Ireland
　Wild Atlantic Way 34–9
　see also Northern Ireland
Iseo, Lago d' (Italy) 135
Isola Bella (Italy) 136
Italy
　Amalfi Coast 150–4
　Emilia-Romagna 147–9
　The Italian Lakes 132–6
　Stelvio Pass 139–41
　Tuscan Hill Towns 142–5

J

James Bond films 114, 117, 207, 208
Jardins de Roquelin (France) 47
Jerichow (Germany) 104
John, Elton 59
Jökulsárlón Lagoon (Iceland) 231
Jones, Inigo 197
Julian Alps (Slovenia) 168–71
Juno Beach (France) 42–3
Jürmala (Latvia) 157

K

Kaiser-Franz-Josefs-Höhe viewpoint (Austria) 124
Kardamyli (Greece) 195
Kaunus (Lithuania) 155–6
Kazaniak (Bulgaria) 186
Kinbane Castle (Northern Ireland) 20
Kinder Scout (England) 23
Kinsale (Ireland) 39
Klis Fortress (Croatia) 175
Kobarid (Slovenia) 171
Kobarid Museum (Slovenia) 171
Konopiště Castle (Czech Republic) 131
Konya (Turkey) 205
Kosterhavet (Sweden) 216
Kozara (Croatia) 178
Krems an der Donau (Austria) 127
Kristiansund (Norway) 209
Ksamil (Albania) 191
Kuopio (Finland) 221
Kuressaare Castle (Estonia) 158
Kvernes (Norway) 207
Kylemore Abbey (Ireland) 37

L

La Roche-en-Ardenne (Belgium) 86
Lacoste (France) 56
Ladby Viking Museum (Denmark) 225
Lady of Stavoren (Netherlands) 94
Ladybower Reservoir (England) 24
Lærdal Tunnel (Norway) 53
Lagunas de Villafáfila Nature Reserve (Spain) 68
Lambrusco wine (Italy) 149
Langhirano (Italy) 149
Languages, Switzerland 121
Lappeenranta (Finland) 221
Las Alpujarras (Spain) 73
Lassels, Richard 197
Latvia
　Baltic capitals 155–8
Lausanne (Switzerland) 121
Lavender Route (France) 54–7
Laveno-Mombello (Italy) 136
Lazise (Italy) 134
Lebrun, Albert 53
Leeuwarden (Netherlands) 93
Leipzig (Germany) 108
Léman, Lake (Switzerland) 121
Léon and Castile (Spain) 67–9
Leonardo da Vinci 47
Leonidas I, King of Sparta 194–5
Lesko (Poland) 160, 163
Lewis, C S 21
Liège (Belgium) 85, 87
Limerick (Ireland) 38
Lindau (Germany) 111
Linderhof Palace (Germany) 112
Linnankatu (Finland) 220
Linz (Austria) 128
Liptov Village (Slovakia) 165–6
Liptovský Mikuláš (Slovakia) 166
Lisbon (Portugal) 79, 80
Lithuania
　Baltic capitals 155–8
Llandudno (Wales) 29
Llanidloes (Wales) 28
Llogara (Albania) 190–1
Llywelyn ap Gruffydd 28
Locarno (Switzerland) 117
Loire Valley (France) 44–7
Londonderry (Northern Ireland) 21
L'Osteria (Italy) 132
Louis XIV, King of France 51, 52
Lucerne (Switzerland) 114
Ludwig II, King of Bavaria 99, 112
Lugano (Switzerland) 116
Lugano, Lago di (Italy) 135–6
Lusto (Finland) 220
Lyngholmen (Norway) 208
Lysekil (Sweden) 217

M

Macclesfield (England) 25
Madonna del Sasso (Switzerland) 117
Magdeburg (Germany) 104–6
Makarska (Croatia) 174–5
Málaga (Spain) 73
Malcesine (Italy) 134
Malin Head (Ireland) 34
Malmö (Sweden) 53
Mani peninsula (Greece) 195
Marconi, Guglielmo 37
Marie Antoinette, Queen of France 60
Marisa Cuomo winery (Italy) 152
Marstrand (Sweden) 216
Matisse, Henri 60
Matsalu National Park (Estonia) 158
Matterhorn Glacier Paradise cable car (Switzerland) 121
Maximilian II, King of Bavaria 111
Medina Azahara (Spain) 74
Meiringen (Switzerland) 116
Melk (Austria) 128
Memento Park (Hungary) 167
Memleben (Germany) 107
Menton (France) 52
Merseburg (Germany) 106
Meteora (Greece) 200
Middelburg (Netherlands) 90
Mikkeli (Finland) 221
Milan (Italy) 116, 136
Miller, Hugh 17
Mirogoj Cemetery (Croatia) 176–8
Mittertörtltunnel (Austria) 125
Mizen Head (Ireland) 39
Modena (Italy) 148
Molde (Norway) 213
Monaco 59
Monasteries 75
Monck, Sir Charles 197
Money 8
Moni Agias Varvaras Rousanou (Greece) 200–1
Mont-Dauphin (France) 52
Montalcino (Italy) 145

Montemor-o-Novo Castle (Portugal) 82
Montepulciano (Italy) 144
Monument to the Revolution (Croatia) 178
Most na Soči (Slovenia) 171
Motorways 137, 159
Mount Çika (Albania) 191
Mount Stoletov (Bulgaria) 186–7
Mouro Island (Spain) 64
Mozart, Wolfgang Amadeus 113, 129, 130
Muff (Ireland) 34
Mullaghmore Head (Ireland) 36
Mummelsee Hotel (Germany) 102–3
Musée du Débarquement Utah Beach (France) 41
Museo Ferruccio Lamborghini (Italy) 147–8
Mussenden Temple (Northern Ireland) 21
Mussolini, Benito 137
Muzeum Budownictwa Ludowego (Poland) 163
Mycenaeans (Greece) 192, 194
Myrbœrholmbrua Bridge (Norway) 208

N

Nafplio (Greece) 194
Napoleon I, Emperor 171
National parks
  Bieszczady National Park (Poland) 162
  Butrint National Park (Albania) 191
  Divjaka-Karavasta National Park (Albania) 190
  Hohe Tauern National Park (Austria) 122–4
  Matsalu National Park (Estonia) 158
  Parc national du Mercantour (France) 52
  Plitvice Lakes National Park (Croatia) 178

National parks (cont.)
  Stelvio National Park (Italy) 139
Nationalparzentrum Ruhestein (Germany) 103
Naumburg (Germany) 107
Naustdal-Gjengedal nature reserve (Norway) 212
Nazis 137, 176
Netherlands
  The Elfstedentocht 93–5
  Zeeland's Delta Works 88–91
Neumann, Balthasar 96
Neuschwanstein Castle (Germany) 67, 99, 112
Newquay (England) 33
Nice (France) 60
Nördlingen (Germany) 98
Normandy beaches (France) 41–3
North Sea Flood (1953) 88, 91
North Wales Way 29
Northern Ireland
Causeway Coast 18–21
  see also Ireland
Norway
  Atlantic Road 207–9
  Norwegian Fjords 210–13

O

Oberammergau (Germany) 112
Odeceixe (Portugal) 83
Odeceixe Beach (Portugal) 83
Odense (Denmark) 225
Olavinlinna Castle (Finland) 218
Olomouc (Czech Republic) 130
Olvera (Spain) 73
Olympia (Greece) 196
Omaha Beach (France) 42
Oosterscheldekering (Netherlands) 90–1
Operation Overlord 41–3
Øresund Bridge (Sweden/Denmark) 53
Orléans (France) 47
Orta, Lake (Italy) 135
Ortler (Italy) 139
Ossuary Stelvio (Italy) 141

Otto the Great, Emperor 104, 107
Oviedo (Spain) 64–5
Owain Glyndŵr 28

P

Padstow (England) 33
Panta Vrechei (Greece) 200
Parador de Segovia (Spain) 67
Parc national du Mercantour (France) 52
Parc Naturel Régional du Verdon (France) 56
Parga (Greece) 200
Park Průhonice (Czech Republic) 131
Parma (Italy) 148
Pärnu (Estonia) 157
Parque Natural da Arrábida (Portugal) 80
Passo del Stelvio (Italy) 140
Pater Noster Lighthouse (Sweden) 216
Patrick, St 18, 20, 36
Patursson, Tróndur 53
Peak District (England) 23–5
Pelješac Bridge (Croatia) 174
Peloponnese Peninsula (Greece) 192–6
Pen y Fan (Wales) 26
Peschiera del Garda (Italy) 132
Pfaffenwinkel (Germany) 99
Philipsdam (Netherlands) 88, 90
Piano, Renzo 64
Picasso, Pablo 59, 60
Picos de Europa (Spain) 64
Pienza (Italy) 144–5
Pilgrimage Church of Wies (Germany) 99
Pindus Mountains (Greece) 199–201
Piranesi, Giovanni Battista 197
Pitigliano (Italy) 145
Pius II, Pope 144
Planning road trips 8
Pliny the Elder 86
Plitvice Lakes National Park (Croatia) 178

Plovdiv (Bulgaria) 184
Podkarpacie (Poland) 163
Poenari Citadel (Romania) 182
Poland
   Great Bieszczady Loop 160–3
Polylimnio waterfalls (Greece) 196
Ponds of Villepey (France) 61
Poolewe (Scotland) 15–16
Poppi (Italy) 142
Popradské Pleso Lake (Slovakia) 165
Port Isaac (England) 33
Port Zélande (Netherlands) 91
Porto (Portugal) 77
Porto Cheli (Greece) 192
Porto Palermo (Albania) 191
Portstewart (Northern Ireland) 21
Portugal
   The Alentejo 80–3
   Route 1 77–9
Positano (Italy) 152
Potsdam (Germany) 107
Prad am Stilfser Joch (Italy) 139
Prague (Czech Republic) 131
Praiano (Italy) 152, 153
Predrigstuhl (Germany) 113
Punkaharju (Finland) 220
Puumala (Finland) 221
Pylos (Greece) 196

Q

Quinta da Regaleira (Portugal) 79

R

Radovljica (Slovenia) 168
Rainier III, Prince of Monaco 59
Ravello (Italy) 153
Reggio Emilia (Italy) 149
Regulations 9
Renoir, Pierre-Auguste 60
Reykjavík (Iceland) 226, 231
Reynisfjara (Iceland) 231
Rhayader (Wales) 28

Riga (Latvia) 156–7
Ring Road (Iceland) 226–31
Rio-Antirrio Bridge (Greece) 200
Riviera (Albania) 189–91
Riviera (France) 59–61
Roads 53, 137
Roe Valley (Northern Ireland) 20
Rogie Falls (Scotland) 15
Rokansaari island (Finland) 221
Romanesque Road (Germany) 104–8
Romania
   Transfăgărășan Highway 181–3
Romans 25, 53, 75, 77, 82, 159, 189
Romantic Road (Germany) 96–9
Ronda (Spain) 72
Roselend Lake (France) 50
Roskilde (Denmark) 223–4
Rothenburg ob der Tauber (Germany) 96–8
Rothschild, Baroness Béatrice Ephrussi de 59–60
Rotterdam (Netherlands) 91
Roussillon (France) 56
Route 1 (Portugal) 77–9
Route des Grandes Alpes (France) 49–52
Royal Alcázar of Seville (Spain) 70
Rules of the road 9

S

Saaremaa island (Estonia) 158
Sade, Marquis de 56
Safety 8
Sagres (Portugal) 83
Saimaa, Lake (Finland) 221
St. Gallen (Switzerland) 119–20
Saint-Jean-Cap-Ferrat (France) 59–60
Sainte-Marie-du-Mont (France) 41
St. Moritz (Switzerland) 120–1

Saint-Raphaël (France) 61
Saint-Tropez (France) 61
Salamanca (Spain) 68
Salerno (Italy) 153
Salzburg (Austria) 113, 129–30
Samara Flag monument (Bulgaria) 186
Samúelsson, Guðjón 229
San Gimignano (Italy) 145
San Sebastián (Spain) 62
Sand (Germany) 102
Sandwood Bay (Scotland) 17
Sango Bay (Scotland) 16–17
Santander (Spain) 62–4
Santiago de Compostela (Spain) 65, 75, 159
Santo André e da Sancha Nature Reserve (Portugal) 83
São Bento Railway Station (Portugal) 77
Sarajevo (Bosnia) 179
Sault (France) 57
Saumur (France) 44–6
Savica waterfall (Slovenia) 170
Savonlinna (Finland) 218–20
Scharffenberg Hill (Slovakia) 166–7
Scheidegger Wasserfälle (Germany) 111
Schickardt, Heinrich 103
Schliemann, Heinrich 194
Schloss Hohenschwangau (Germany) 99, 112
Schloss Neuenburg (Germany) 107
Schloss Ort (Austria) 129
Schloss Sanssouci (Germany) 107
Schlosshotel Bühlerhöhe (Germany) 102
Schrattenfluh (Switzerland) 114
Scotland
   Scottish Highlands 15–17
Scottish Highlands (Scotland) 15–17
Segovia (Spain) 67–8
Senna, Ayrton 86
Il Sentiero Degli Dei (Italy) 152
Serbia
   Spomenik Circuit 176–9

Setenil de las Bodegas (Spain) 72
Seville (Spain) 70
Seydisfjördur (Iceland) 230–1
Shipka (Bulgaria) 187
Shipka Memorial Church (Bulgaria) 186, 187
Siena (Italy) 145
Silk Road 7
Sintra (Portugal) 79
Sion (Switzerland) 121
Sirmione (Italy) 134–5
Sisteron (France) 57
Skärhamn (Sweden) 216–17
Skelligs (Ireland) 38
Skipsholmen (Norway) 208
Slieve League (Ireland) 34
Sloten (Netherlands) 94
Slovakia
   High Tatras 165–7
Slovenia
   Julian Alps 168–71
Snake Pass Summit (England) 23–4
Sneek (Netherlands) 93
Snowdonia (Wales) 26–9
Soča River 171
Sognefjord (Norway) 210
Solina, Lake (Poland) 163
Soragna (Italy) 148
Sorrento (Italy) 150
Sospel (France) 52
South West Coast Path (England) 31
Spa (Belgium) 85, 86
Spain
   Andalusia 70–4
   Castile and Léon 67–9
   Costa Norte 62–5
Špania Dolina (Slovakia) 166
Sparta (Greece) 194–5
Speed limits 9
Split (Croatia) 175
Spomenik Circuit (Croatia/Serbia) 176–9
Stara Zagora (Bulgaria) 186
Stavoren (Netherlands) 94
Stelvio National Park (Italy) 139
Stelvio Pass (Italy) 139–41
Stemshesten (Norway) 209

INDEX

Stoker, Bram 182
Ston (Croatia) 174
Storseisundet (Norway) 208
Strasbourg (France) 103
Štrbské Pleso (Slovakia) 165
Strokkur Geyser (Iceland) 231
Sufism 205
Suilven (Scotland) 16
Sweden
    West Coast Sweden 215–17
Switzerland
    Grand Tour of Switzerland 119–21
    High Passes of the Swiss Alps 114–17
Sword Beach (France) 43

T

Tallinn (Estonia) 158
Tarifa (Spain) 74
Tartu (Estonia) 157
Taÿgetos (Greece) 195
Taylor, Elizabeth 61
Tesárska Roklina (Slovakia) 167
Thonon-les-Bains (France) 49
Thurso (Scotland) 17
Tibet-Hütte (Italy) 140
Tintagel (England) 32–3
Tito, Marshal Josip Broz 176, 178
Tjörn (Sweden) 216
Tolls, motorways 9
Torcal de Antequera (Spain) 73
Torr Head (Northern Ireland) 20
Tours (France) 46–7
Trabant cars 109
Trading routes 159
Trafoi (Italy) 140
Transfăgărășan Highway (Romania) 181–3
Trelleborg (Denmark) 224, 225
Trichonida (Greece) 200
Troll Church (Norway) 209
Tröllaskagi peninsula (Iceland) 229
Trollstigen (Norway) 212
Trondheim (Norway) 213
Trouville (France) 42

Tsaravets Fortress (Bulgaria) 187
Tunnels 53
Turf houses (Iceland) 229
Turkey
    Anatolia 202–5
Tuscan Hill Towns (Italy) 142–5
Tuz, Lake (Turkey) 205

U

UNESCO 52, 67, 69, 186
    Amalfi Coast (Italy) 150–4
    Banska Štiavnica (Slovakia) 166
    Bayeux (France) 42
    Burgos (Spain) 69
    Butrint National Park (Albania) 191
    Córdoba (Spain) 74
    Dubrovnik (Croatia) 173
    Entlebuch Biosphere (Switzerland) 114
    Franeker (Netherlands) 95
    Göreme Open-Air Museum (Turkey) 204
    Hallstatt (Austria) 129
    Hohe Tauern National Park (Austria) 122–4
    Loire Valley (France) 44–7
    Mycenae (Greece) 194
    Naumburg Dom (Germany) 107
    Olympia (Greece) 196
    Park Průhonice (Czech Republic) 131
    Parma (Italy) 148
    Peschiera del Garda (Italy) 132
    Pienza (Italy) 144–5
    Plitvice Lakes National Park (Croatia) 178
    Popradské Pleso Lake (Slovakia) 165
    Segovia (Spain) 67
    Tallinn (Estonia) 158
    Würzburg (Germany) 96
Unterstmatt (Germany) 102
Uprising Monument (Croatia) 178

Ustrzyki Dolne (Poland) 163
Utah Beach (France) 41–2

V

Valensole (France) 56
Valentia Island (Ireland) 38
Valley of Thracian Kings (Bulgaria) 186
Vatnajökull (Iceland) 231
Vauban, Sébastien Le Prestre, Marquis of 51, 52
Veliko Târnovo (Bulgaria) 187
Verdon Gorge (France) 56
Verona (Italy) 132
Vevang (Norway) 209
Vidraru, Lake (Romania) 182, 183
Vienna (Austria) 127
Vietri sul Mare (Italy) 153
Viking Trail (Denmark) 223–5
Vikos Gorge (Greece) 201
Villa Ephrussi de Rothschild (France) 59–60
Villa Fogazzaro Roi (Italy) 136
Villa Melzi (Italy) 135
Villa Taranto (Italy) 136
Village des Bories (France) 54
Villepey, Ponds of (France) 61
Vilnius (Lithuania) 155
Vintgar Gorge (Slovenia) 170
Vista Alegre Porcelain Museum (Portugal) 78
Vlad the Impaler 182
Vlkolínec (Slovakia) 166
Vlorë (Albania) 190
Vogel cable car (Slovenia) 170
Volkerakdam (Netherlands) 88

W

Walcher Wasserfall (Austria) 124
Wales
    Eryri and the Bannau 26–9
Weather 8
Websites 9
West Coast Sweden 215–17
Wetlina (Poland) 162
Wies Pilgrimage Church (Germany) 99

Wild Atlantic Way (Ireland) 34–9
Winnats Pass (England) 25
Wonneberger, Christoph 108
Workum (Netherlands) 95
World War I
    Kobarid Museum (Slovenia) 171
    Ossuary Stelvio (Italy) 141
World War II
    Battle of the Bulge (Belgium) 86
    Cornwall at War Museum (England) 33
    D-Day beaches (France) 41–3
    Spomeniks (Croatia/Serbia) 176
Vevang (Norway) 209
Würzburg (Germany) 96

X

Xhiro (Albania) 189

Y

Yeats, W B 36

Z

Zadar (Croatia) 175
Zagori (Greece) 201
Zagreb (Croatia) 176–8
Zahara de la Sierra (Spain) 70–2
Zamora (Spain) 68
Zeeland Bridge (Netherlands) 91
Zeeland's Delta Works (Netherlands) 88–91
Zeitz (Germany) 108
Zermatt (Switzerland) 121
Zimmermann, Dominikus 99
Zur Grossen Tanne (Germany) 102
Zurich (Switzerland) 119
Zwickau (Germany) 109

ACKNOWLEDGMENTS

The publisher would like to thank the following for their kind permission to reproduce their photographs:

(Key: a-above; b-below/bottom; c-centre; f-far; l-left; r-right; t-top)

123RF.com: rokastenys 175cr, wirestock 124tc.

4Corners: Pietro Canali 32br; Olimpio Fantuz 19c; Reinhard Schmid 33br.

Alamy Stock Photo: 107tl, 107bl, 206c, 215br; aerialphotos.com 52bl; Andia 49bl; Ange 207br; Artexplorer 4fbr; 197cra; blickwinkel 101br; Angela to Roxel / imageBROKER 57tl; ClickAlps 51tr; Eddie Cloud 22c; Sorin Colac 113br; Roberto Colino 64tl; Colouria Media 102cl; David Cordner 20tl; Marco Cristofori 225tl; David Crossland 43tr; Luis Dafos 4bl, 75cra; Ian Dagnall 16cla, 39br, 147br; dinosmichail 196tl; Piotr Domarecki 212bc; dpa picture alliance 103tl, 108bl; dragoncello 178bl; Egeris 129tlr; Sina Ettmer 104bl, 106tl, 120tl; Greg Balfour Evans 59br; Frank Fichtmueller 208bc; Gestur Gíslason 191bl; Manfred Gottschalk 43cr; Tim Graham 81c; Robbert Frank Hagens 89c; Robert Harding 28tl, 216tc; Nick Hatton 25br; Hemis 95cr, 119br, 122bc; Esa Hiltula 220bc; Image Professionals GmbH 106bl, 136tl, 209tr; ImageBROKER.com GmbH & Co. KG 140tl; imageimage 199br; Mattis Kaminer 107tr; Andrey Khrobostov 65br; Stephan Langhans 17tr; Hervé Lenain 45c, 47tr; Life Collection Photography 78bl; David Lyons 37cra, 156tl; manfredrf 98tr; Stefano Politi Markovina 56tc; Iain Masterton 16br; Lorenzo Mattei 51bl; Rene Mattes 51tl; Michael Matthews 83tl; Mauritius Images GmbH 106cl, 108br, 112br, 124tr, 125cr, 140clb, 141tr, 163bl, 225cl; Hercules Milas 167tc; Ania Molodynska / Stockimo 160bl; Jaroslav Moravcik 166cl; multimaps360 110c; Pedro Ferrão Patrício 70br; Bombaert Patrick 87tl, Pattarawut In-udom 116tl; Kim Petersen 224cl; eye35.pix 25cra; PjrTravel 130tc; Rory Prior 23br; Prisma by Dukas Presseagentur GmbH 112tl; Giovanni Raucci 141br; robertharding 103cl; William Robinson 24bl; Ed Rooney 37br; Henryk Sadura 161c; Daniel Schoenen 46c; Karl F. Schöfmann 60tr; jozef sedmak 167br; Ragnar Th Sigurdsson 227c; Ievgen Skrypko 182cl; John Stuij 94tl; Dmytro Surkov 140bl; Geoffrey Taunton 116tc; Nik Taylor 32tr; Martin Thomas Photography 82tl; travelbildgermany 98cl; Valeohoh / Stockimo 138c; Steve Vidler 29tr; volkerpreusser 128br; Walter 64 190tl; Sebastian Wasek 33tl; bastiaan wesseling 92c; Fred van Wijk 50br; David Williams 26bl; Wirestock 177c; Jan Woitas / dpa picture alliance archive 108tl; Xinhua 85br; Zoonar GmbH 106br.

AWL Images: Peter Adams 214c; Jon Arnold 105c, 168bl; Marco Bottigelli 2c, 20tc, 134bc; ClickAlps 6c, 35c, 139bl; Alan Copson 16cl; Kav Dadfar 17br; Cornelia Doer Photodesign 61bl; Guy Edwardes 56tr; Hans Georg Eiben 47bl; Jeremy Flint 97c; Hemis 41bl, 46bl, 56bl, 178tc; ImageBroker 6c; Karol Kozlowski 154c; Susanne Kremer 60bl, 76c; Francesco Iacobelli 148bl; Francesco Ricardo Iacomino 146c, 152cl; Nick Ledger 77bc; Tom Mackie 24cl, 34bc; Stefano Politi Markovina 128cl, 133c; Christian Mueringer 102tl; Doug Pearson 136cl; Ian Trower 96bc; Bridgeman Images: Patrice Cartier 4fbl, 53cra.

Dreamstime.com: Kari Ahlers 86tr; Charalambos Andronos 195br; Artmim 225tr; Frank Bach 190crb; Cristim77 39tl; Simon Dannhauer 134cr; Devy 91bc; Dpvue 150br; Alena Dudaeva 153br; Dziewul 162crb; Sergey Dzyuba 148tr; Maria Luisa Lopez Estivill 50cl; Fotokon 162bc, 179tl; Sven Hansche 192bc; Irakite 167crb; Jojjik 195tl; Marcin Jucha 179cr; Miroslav Liska 228tc; Zdeněk Matyás 188c; Milosk50 166tc; Minnystock 99br; Marketa Novakova 178tr; Olgavisavi 175tl; Olga Peshkova 166tr; Pytyczech 170tr; Roibul 185c; Aleksandar Todorovic 191tl; Larysa Uhryn 169c; Hilda Weges 90tc; Sara Winter 90bl; Wirestock 86tl, 163br; Xalanx 182tr; Xantana 117tl; Xbrchx 174tl.

Finnish Forest Museum Lusto: 220tl.

Getty Images: Peter Adams 65cr; Walter Bibikow / DigitalVision 20bl; Michael Blann / Stone 48c; Marco Bottigelli / Moment 21tr, 135bc; Rachel Carbonell 69cl; Catherine Falls Commercial 7crb; David Clapp 33bc; Matteo Colombo / Stone 135tl; Comezora / Moment 120bl; Sergiu Cozorici 38tr; Sven Creutzmann / Mambo Photo / Hulton Archive 4bc, 109cra; Luis Dafos / Moment 62br; Edoardo Fornaciari / Hulton Archive 149cra; Phil Haber Photography 57cr; John Harper 58c; John Harper / Stone 79cr; imageBROKER / Norbert Neetz 98bl; George W Johnson 25bl; Jacek Kadaj / Moment 125br; Carmen Martínez Torrón / Moment 42tr; José Mendes 83bl; Eric Meola / Stone 128tl; mlsfotografia 69tl; Roberto Moola / Sysaworld 208cl; Jonathan NACKSTRAND / AFP 216tr; Andreas Neuburger / Moment 123c; Rick Neves 111bl; Jean-Philippe Tournut / Moment 46tr; Andrea Pistolesi / Photodisc 40c, 42cl; Andrea Pistolesi / Stone 21cr; Michael Roberts 27c; Davide Seddio 68tc; Martin Siepmann / imageBROKER 113bl; David Sones Photography 37bl; Alexander Spatari / Moment 61cra, 131tc; Rory Trappe Photography 29br; Santiago Urquijo / Moment Open 84c; Leo Vilner / 500px 100c; Westend61 4br, 29cl, 117br, 124bl, 137cr.

Getty Images / iStock: ABBPhoto 7cra; AJ Watt 37tl; AlbertPego 120tc; alexeys 230tl; anatoliy_gleb 183bc; Frank Anschuetz 73tl; Antagain 121bl; AzmanJaka 170c; Filippo Bacci 145br, 149br; Baloncici 179br; BanarTABS 99cr; Enrico

ACKNOWLEDGMENTS

Baroni 164c; Benedek 38cla; bloodua 202bc; bluejayphoto 68cl, 129br; Artur Bogacki 170tl; Boogich 64bl; Stephen Bridger 31bl; Andrew Briggs 15bl; Lilly Carreras 30c; Cavan Images 78tl; chrisdorney 83bc; Benjamin DAVID-TESTANIERE 61br; davidbirri 116cla; Christian Decout 57br; deimagine 120c; dennisvdw 87br; DieterMeyrl 113tl; Balate Dorin 180c; EKH-Pictures 93br; Elena Estellés 82cr; ewg3D 163tl; f8grapher 196cl; Farbregas_Hareluya 74cl; fokkebok 52cla; Ricardo Fonseca 78tl; font83 153tr; Fotomax 103br; FotoStraka 125; Gatsi 193c, 194tl; gbh007 157tl; GettyTim82 201tr; Gestur Gislason 229br; Gosiek-B 210br; Joe Gough 39tr; Heiko119 134tc; Henk Hulshof 94tc; ivotheeditors 151c; Jacek_Sopotnicki 79tr; jacquesvandinteren 195bl; janssenkruseproductions 88bc; Julius Jansson 158bl; jenifoto 39cl, 153cl; JoseIgnacioSoto 73bl; Karissaa 221; Kharichkina 5c, 98tl; Tatiana Krakowiak 55c; kruwt 95br; Fani Kurti 143c, 145tc; KvdB50 42tl; legna69 135bl; MAKROFOTO 221cra; Marco Margna 158tl; margouillatphotos 67br, 73bc; MarioGuti 65tl; mathess 155br; michalzak 162tr; mikolajn 208tr, 212tl; MNStudio 36bl, 156cl; Uwe Moser 171bl; Mumemories 230clb; mycan 205br; Naeblys 205tc; Aleksandar Nakic 222c; NatureNow 130cl; Susanne Neumann 21br; nicolamargaret 44bc; Nikada 126c; oksanaphoto 200tl; Eloi Omella 72br; omersukrugoksu 118c; Ozbalci 204tl; Nick Pandevonium 231br; Sean Pavone 121tc, 121bc; peeterv 213crb; Vera Petrunina 198c; pidjoe 47bc; 144cl; Ziga Plahutar 170bl; Poike 174br; powerofforever 231cra; Anna Pustynnikova 80bc; Rixipix 231tr; Rocky89 172c; RolfSt 52br; rusm 131br; ruza74 165br; R Scapinello 228bl; SeanPavonePhoto 71c; seraficus 149tl; Anastasiia Shavshyna 117cra; silverjohn 176br; skynesher 229tl; Oleh Slobodeniuk 9cra, 115c, 219c; Starcevic 182clb; starpik 181br; Stevanzz 144tl; steved_np3 28cl; StockByM 60cl; StockPhotoAstur 66c; Lisa Strachan 224tr; Stramyk 204br; tenra 4crb, 159tr; Markus Thoenen 114br; tihomir todorov 186cl; tomprout 144br; Tonygers 156br; Alan Tow 229cr; travellinglight 91br; Ultima_Gaina 203c; unclepodger 127bl; Flavio Vallenari 10-11c; Jaromir Vanek 230cl; Aleh Varanishcha 155bl; 200tr; vovashevchuk 212clb; VYCHEGZHANINA 211c; waterotter 231bl; Wirestock 50tl, 132bc, 157bl, 158bc, 217tr; jan van der Wolf 90c; Yakobchuk Olena 9crb; Zastavkin 225br.

Hia Franko: Suzan Gabrijan 171br.

Hvammsvik Hot Springs: Saga Sig / Hvammsvík Hot Springs & Nature Resort 228tl.

Jopie Huisman Museum: 95tl.

La Tagliata Positano: La Tagliato Positano 152tl.

Marisa Cuomo Winery: 152tc.

Murphy's Ice Cream: 38tc.

The Nordic Watercolour Museum: Per Pixel Petersson 217cr.

Projectico / Panko Concept / Kuopion Saana: 221br.

Shutterstock.com: 1476480833 72tl, 131cr; Andrew Angelov 190br; atomov 186tc; Bada1 184br; BBA Photography 28tc; Lukas Bischoff Photograph 186tl; CK-TravelPhotos 204cl; Claudio Giovanni Colombo 142br; DeymosHR 69br; Davor Dikic 173br; DinkeyDoodle 189br; Dziewul 183bl; EQRoy 223br; Marisa Estivill 74tl; Sergii Figurnyi 130tl, 187br; Nina Firsova 209br; Fotokon 187tr; Gherzak 141bl; gregorioa 63c; Robert Harding 24tr; iwciagr 183cra; Jana Janina 191bc; JeniFoto 43br; marcin jucha 171tr; krcil 226br; Julia Kuznetsova 54bc; LE-gals Photography 86cl; makasana photo 82br; Maryshot 187cl; Muster1305 157tr; MNStudio 36tl, 201br; Nahlik 18bl; Raquel Pedrosa 68tr; Sarantis Pouliezos 201cr; Jelena Safronova 213tc; saiko3p 134tr; Jaroslav Sekeres 16bl; Paul Shark 200cl; streetflash 79tl; Thea.Photo 94bl; tokar 46tl; trabantos 218br, 220cl; Merel Tuk 91br; Twin Design 87cr; Toni Lucena Viudez 14c; Irina Wilhauk 174cl; Maren Winter 102tc; zedspider 194br.

westsweden.com: Madeleine Landley 217br; Lukas Warzecha / Westsweden.com 216bl.

Cover images: *Front*: J Bjørnar Strømsholm; *Back*: AWL Images: Marco Bottigelli (tr); AWL Images: ClickAlps (bl); AWL Images: Jeremy Flint (cl); Getty Images: Manuel Breva Colmeiro (tl)

Contributors Sarah Baxter, Lisa Cunningham, Guy De Launey, Emma Gregg, Francheska Melendez, Shafi Musaddique, Chiara Rimella, Daniel Stables, Hester Underhill, Charles Usher
Project Editor Molly Price
Senior Editor Keith Drew
Senior Designer Adrienne Pitts
Designer Katie Cavanagh
US Senior Editor Jennette ElNaggar
Proofreader Kathryn Glendenning
Indexer Hilary Bird

Picture Researcher Laura Richardson
Publishing Assistant Simona Velikova
Cartographic Editor James Macdonald
Jacket Designer Gemma Doyle
Senior Production Editor Tony Phipps
Image retoucher Michelle Briers
Senior Production Controller Samantha Cross
Managing Art Editor Gemma Doyle
Editorial Director Hollie Teague
Art Director Maxine Pedliham
Publishing Director Georgina Dee

First American Edition, 2025
Published in the United States by DK Publishing,
a division of Penguin Random House LLC
1745 Broadway, 20th Floor, New York, NY 10019

Copyright © 2025 Dorling Kindersley Limited
25 26 27 28 29 10 9 8 7 6 5 4 3 2 1
001-349238-Apr/2025

All rights reserved.
Without limiting the rights under the copyright reserved above, no part of this publication may be reproduced, stored in or introduced into a retrieval system, or transmitted, in any form, or by any means (electronic, mechanical, photocopying, recording, or otherwise), without the prior written permission of the copyright owner. Published in Great Britain by Dorling Kindersley Limited

A catalog record for this book is available from the Library of Congress.
ISBN 978-0-5939-6855-0

Printed and bound in China

www.dk.com

DK books are available at special discounts when purchased in bulk for sales promotions, premiums, fund-raising, or education use.
For details, contact: DK Publishing Special Markets, 1745 Broadway, 20th Floor, New York, NY 10019
SpecialSales@dk.com

The publishers cannot accept responsibility for any consequences arising from the use of this book, nor for any material on third-party websites, and cannot guarantee that any website address in this book will be a suitable source of travel information.

The rate at which the world is changing is constantly keeping the DK team on our toes. While we've worked hard to ensure this book is accurate and up-to-date, things can change in an instant. Road conditions can worsen, gas stations can close, and weather can impact access to view points. Road closures often occur in winter months, so it's important to check ahead before embarking on your road trip. The publisher cannot accept responsibility for any consequences arising from the use of this book. If you notice we've got something wrong, we want to hear about it. Please get in touch at travelguides@dk.com

This book was made with Forest Stewardship Council™ certified paper—one small step in DK's commitment to a sustainable future.
Learn more at www.dk.com/uk/information/sustainability